Minorities
❧ in American ❧
Higher Education

Recent Trends,
Current Prospects,
and Recommendations

Alexander W. Astin

Helen S. Astin
Kenneth C. Green
Laura Kent
Patricia McNamara
Melanie Reeves Williams

Minorities ❧ in American ❧ Higher Education

 Jossey-Bass Publishers

San Francisco • Washington • London • 1982

MINORITIES IN AMERICAN HIGHER EDUCATION
Recent Trends, Current Prospects, and Recommendations
  by Alexander W. Astin

Copyright © 1982 by: Jossey-Bass Inc., Publishers
433 California Street
San Francisco, California 94104

&

Jossey-Bass Limited
28 Banner Street
London EC1Y 8QE

Library of Congress Cataloging in Publication Data

Astin, Alexander W.
    Minorities in American higher education.

    Bibliography: p. 237
    Includes index.
    1. Minorities—Education (Higher)—United States.
I. Title.
LC3731.A83   371.97'0973   81-48663
ISBN 0-87589-523-9   AACR2

Manufactured in the United States of America

The paper in this book meets the guidelines for permanence
and durability of the Committee on Production Guidelines
for Book Longevity of the Council on Library Resources.

JACKET DESIGN BY WILLI BAUM

FIRST EDITION
Code 8215

*The Jossey-Bass
Series in Higher Education*

❧ Preface ❧

This book is addressed to both practitioners and policy makers in higher education—to those college administrators, faculty, legislators, planners, and other public and private officials whose actions and policies shape the relationship between higher education and disadvantaged minorities in American society.

My impression is that today many educators and policy makers are inclined to take a pessimistic, almost fatalistic view of higher education's immediate future. Education, so the argument goes, is quite low on the list of government priorities, enrollments are expected to decline, public support is diminishing, and inflation is expected to continue. This gloomy assessment has prompted many educators to feel that there is little more that institutions can be expected to do to meet the special needs of minorities.

But the fact is that there is *much* the higher education system can do to further the cause of minorities in higher education, regardless of fiscal constraints. Nearly all private institutions and most public systems retain a great deal of autonomy in nonfiscal matters that have enormous significance for minorities: admissions procedures, the content of academic programs, methods of instruction, procedures of grading and testing, hiring of faculty and staff, and the awarding of credits and degrees. Many of the recommendations presented in the book focus on such matters, and if these recommendations were implemented by a significant proportion of institutions, they could do as much or more to facilitate the educational progress of minorities as the development of costly special programs for minorities.

The work reported here was performed at the Higher Education Research Institute (HERI) between January 1979 and December 1981 under a grant from the Ford Foundation. The foundation has, in the past fifteen years, invested a substantial amount of its resources to improve educational opportunities for Blacks, Chicanos, Puerto Ricans, and American Indians. In 1978 it was interested in evaluating minority progress during these years and in charting a course to guide future public and private efforts to facilitate the educational development of these four groups.

In preliminary discussions between the Ford Foundation and HERI staffs, it was decided that the research effort should be guided by a national commission, of which O. Meredith Wilson was appointed chairman. In addition to Wilson and myself, the commission included seven members chosen jointly by the chairman and the Ford and HERI staffs. We agreed that the commission should be small, that it should include knowledge-able members of the concerned minorities, and that there should be one or more members of the commission who could provide critical guidance in the conceptualization and design of the investigation and who were practiced in the assembling and evaluation of data.

The members of the commission are:

O. Meredith Wilson, historian and educational administrator; president emeritus of the University of Oregon and of the University of Minnesota; president and director emeritus of the Center for Advanced Study in the Behavioral Sciences.

Alexander W. Astin, president, Higher Education Research Institute; professor of higher education, Graduate School of Education, University of California, Los Angeles.

Frank Bonilla, professor of sociology and political science and director of the Centro de Estudios Puertorriqueños at the City University of New York.

Cecilia Preciado Burciaga, assistant provost for faculty affairs and director of summer session at Stanford University; formerly a research analyst with the U.S. Commission on Civil Rights in Washington, D.C.; member of various boards concerned with Chicanos, women, and higher education.

Yvonne Brathwaite Burke, partner in the law firm of Kutak, Rock and Huie and regent of the University of California; former member of U.S. Congress, California State Legislature, and Los Angeles Board of Supervisors; formerly a member of the board of trustees of the University of Southern California.

Albert H. Hastorf, professor of psychology and the Benjamin Scott Crocker Professor of Human Biology at Stanford University; currently serving as the vice-president and provost of Stanford University.

Calvin B. T. Lee, vice-president of educational planning, Prudential Insurance Company of America; former chancellor of the University of Maryland Baltimore County; former acting president, executive vice-president, and dean at Boston University; assistant director of Title III, Developing Institutions Program, U.S. Bureau of Higher Education; chairman of the board of the Community College of Baltimore.

Alfonso A. Ortiz, professor of anthropology at the University of New Mexico; president, Association on American Indian Affairs; chairman, National Advisory Council, Center for the History of American Indians, the Newberry Library.

Stephen J. Wright, consultant in higher education; former president of United Negro College Fund; former president of Fisk University and vice-president of the College Board; former dean of faculty of Hampton Institute; former president of Bluefield State College.

The full commission, together with the HERI staff, met on eight occasions for a total of eighteen working days. Commissioners frequently expressed strong dissatisfaction with the data or with the staff's interpretations of results, and their many helpful and creative suggestions improved the project substantially. Most important, however, was the commission's determination to achieve unanimous endorsement of the recommendations contained in Chapter Ten. These are, literally, the full commission's recommendations, developed in our April 10–12, 1981, meeting and revised at the July 19–21, 1981, meeting. Additional revisions were completed during the next few months and final commission endorsement was made in October 1981.

While this report emphasizes the recent and current educational status of Blacks, Chicanos, Puerto Ricans, and American Indians as reflected in large bodies of empirical data, it does not portray each group from an historical or cultural perspective. Readers who are interested in such perspectives are urged to read the separate HERI reports on Blacks (by Melanie Reeves Williams), Chicanos (by Helen S. Astin and Cecilia Preciado Burciaga), Puerto Ricans (by Laura Kent), and American Indians (by Patricia P. McNamara).* Another excellent source of cultural, historical, and political information on each group is the Spring 1981 issue of *Daedalus*.

In Chapter One we set forth the purpose of the study, the study design, and the value premises that guided the commission's work. In the next three chapters we examine patterns of enrollment and attrition. Our data show the progressive underrepresentation of each minority group at successively higher levels of educational attainment (Chapter Two), the severe underrepresentation of minorities in certain fields (Chapter Three), and the major changes in enrollment in undergraduate, graduate, and professional schools during recent years (Chapter Four).

In Chapter Five we report on factors that facilitate or inhibit minority progress in higher education. Much of the data used in this chapter was collected in commission-sponsored surveys of students, faculty, and administrators. In Chapter Six

---

*These reports can be obtained at cost from the Higher Education Research Institute, 320 Moore Hall, UCLA Campus, Los Angeles, CA 90024.

we discuss the programs that the federal government has implemented to promote minority groups' participation in higher education, and we describe the relationship between these federal and state programs.

Discussions of controversial issues relating to the higher education of minorities are presented in Chapters Seven and Eight. In Chapter Seven we present extensive data that challenge those who believe that equal access and equal opportunity now characterize American higher education. Specifically, our data show that minority college students are far more often to be found in community colleges than in the more prestigious public universities. In Chapter Eight we analyze how meritocratic values in higher education affect college admissions, testing, and grading procedures, and we suggest that the use of a value-added approach to admissions and grading will not only remove some of the major barriers to minority access and progress but will also strengthen the general pedagogical effectiveness of institutions.

In Chapter Nine we summarize the major empirical findings of the study, and in Chapter Ten we present the commission's recommendations. While most readers will want to examine the entire list of recommendations set forth in Chapter Ten, they should note that some of the recommendations are of special relevance to certain audiences. College and university faculty and administrators, for example, are encouraged to study the set of recommendations concerning the value-added approach to testing and grading, as well as the recommendations regarding minority faculty and administrators. Similarly, policy makers at the state and federal levels are particularly encouraged to consider the recommendations regarding precollegiate education, community colleges, financial aid, and the myth of equal access.

Many persons share the credit for what the commission accomplished. Wilson was a remarkable chairman: he was forthright, forceful, diplomatic, witty, flexible, and always task-oriented. And each of my other fellow commissioners played key roles. Frank Bonilla was the most persistent and articulate critic of our data and methods, and his work substantially enhanced the quality of our report. He also made many significant contributions to the value premises and final recommendations. Cecilia Burciaga never permitted us to forget the special problems confronting Chicanos and alerted us frequently to data and literature concerning Hispanics in higher education. Yvonne Brathwaite Burke brought a legal and political perspective that was extremely valuable, particularly as we examined affirmative action programs and governmental policy. Albert Hastorf contributed many insightful suggestions and was particularly helpful in our attempts to improve the quality of our data and methods. Calvin B. T. Lee added the unique perspective of a lawyer, former university administrator, scholar, and corporation executive; he was also instrumental in helping us develop the over-all plan for the study. Alfonso Ortiz kept us alert to the many languages and cultural differences and similarities among American Indians, and he did not let us forget that certain meanings simply cannot be captured by quantitative data. And finally, there is simply no way to adequately to express my gratitude to Stephen Wright. His intelligence, wit, honesty, and sensitivity rescued the commission on many occasions. I was already a Wright fan before this project started, and I suspect that his fan club now includes most of the other commissioners and HERI staff as well.

A major inspiration for some of the ideas expressed in this report was Gunnar Myrdal's monumental study of Blacks in the United States, *An American Dilemma* (1944). For sheer honesty, insight, and scholarly thoroughness, this work has no peer. Readers who want to compare the current situation with that of forty years ago should read Myrdal's work.

The idea for this study was in large part the brainchild of Fred Crossland of the Ford Foundation. Crossland's work—in particular, *Minority Access to College* (1971)—in many respects provided a model for Chapters Two through Four. Crossland attended all our commission meetings and regularly provided much-needed encouragement to me and my colleagues on the HERI staff. Although he saw his role in the commission meetings as one of an interested observer and succeeded admirably in his determination not to interfere, he became a genuine and constructive participant in our deliberations.

Much of the credit for the findings reported here must be shared with my colleagues at HERI. Important contributions to the conceptualization and execution of the overall project were made by Helen S. Astin, Ernesto Ballesteros, Kenneth C. Green, Patricia P. McNamara, Rita A. Scherrei, Lewis C. Solmon, Russell Stockard, and Melanie Reeves Williams. Many of these colleagues also contributed directly to the content of this book. Kenneth Green, for example, was largely responsible for drafting the chapter on governmental programs (Chapter Six). Patricia McNamara produced much of the material for Appendix A and, together with Rita Scherrei, was instrumental in checking and updating the data in Chapters Two through Four. Melanie Williams and Ernesto Ballesteros, together with Gerald T. Richardson and Christhart Kappner, shared the complex task of data analysis. Helen Astin also served as an expert consultant and sounding board throughout the course of the project. Laura Kent's editing greatly improved the readability of the manuscript. Margo R. King aided in manuscript preparation and was responsible for the logistics of commission meetings and communications between the project staff and the commissioners.

A number of outside persons and agencies also rendered valuable assistance in our work. Janice Petrovich prepared a special report, "Puerto Rican College Student Population in the United States." Dean Chavers offered many useful suggestions in our work on American Indians. Unpublished data and other materials pertaining to our work were kindly provided by Robert Crain, James McPartland, and Gail Thomas of the Center for Social Organization of the School, at Johns Hopkins University; and by Carol J. Smith and Linda J. Lambert of the National Advisory Committee on Black Higher Education and Black Colleges and Universities. The College Entrance Examination Board kindly gave us permission to use national data from its Scholastic Aptitude Test.

Finally, I want to express my appreciation to the Ford Foundation for its support of this project.

Los Angeles, California   Alexander W. Astin
March 1982

✦ Contents ✦

Preface ix

The Author xix

1. Studying the Higher Education of Minorities 1

2. The Educational Pipeline for Minorities 25

3. Minorities in Various Fields of Study 52

4. Recent Developments in the Educational Pipeline 77

5. Factors Affecting Minority Educational Progress 89

6. Government Programs 113

xvii

7.   Equal Access and Equal Opportunity   129

8.   Standardized Testing and the Meritocracy   154

9.   Summary of Findings   170

10.   Recommendations on the Higher Education
      of Minorities   187

      Appendix A: Assessment of the Quality of Data   213

      Appendix B: Description of Dependent or   231
                  Outcome Variables Used
                  in Regression Analyses

      References   237

      Index   251

❧ The Author ❧

ALEXANDER W. ASTIN is professor of higher education at the University of California, Los Angeles (UCLA); president of the Higher Education Research Institute; and director of the Cooperative Institutional Research Program. Previously, he was director of research for the American Council on Education (1965–1973) and the National Merit Scholarship Corporation (1960–1964). His work has appeared in more than one hundred articles and thirteen books, including *Four Critical Years* (Jossey-Bass, 1977), *Preventing Students from Dropping Out* (Jossey-Bass, 1975), *The Power of Protest* (Jossey-Bass, 1975), and *Maximizing Leadership Effectiveness* (Jossey-Bass, 1980). Astin has received awards for outstanding research from the American Personnel and Guidance Association (1965), the National Association of Student Personnel Administrators (1976), and the American College Personnel Association (1978). He has also been a fellow at the Center for Advanced Study in the Behavioral Sciences at Stanford, California (1967–1968).

Astin received his doctor's and master's degrees in psychology from the University of Maryland and his bachelor's degree in music from Gettysburg College.

Minorities
✼ in American ✼
Higher Education

Recent Trends,
Current Prospects,
and Recommendations

❧ 1 ❧

Studying
the Higher Education
of Minorities

Some versions of American history portray the United States in its early days as a land of opportunity, where success was within reach of anyone who worked hard enough and where personal achievement was limited only by an individual's ambition, drive, ingenuity, and entrepreneurial skills. But contemporary American society is characterized by a highly technological and credential-oriented occupational structure in which higher education plays a central role. Indeed, higher education serves as the principal gatekeeper for entry into the most prestigious and lucrative careers: law, medicine, science, engineering, politics, public service, and teaching. Even in business and finance, most executive positions now go to college graduates and, in some cases, only to graduates of a few elite institutions.

Currently, America's racial and ethnic minorities are grossly underrepresented in higher education and in almost all occupational fields that require a college education. Despite the nation's efforts to remedy its record of racial discrimination prior

1

to the advent of the civil rights movement in the 1950s, today minority groups continue to be underrepresented in the system as a whole and especially in those advanced fields that prepare students for positions of leadership and status in American society.

These facts prompted the Commission on the Higher Education of Minorities to undertake four major tasks:

1. To document, as extensively and as accurately as available data permit, the current representation of Blacks, Chicanos, Puerto Ricans, and American Indians in higher education, by degree level and by field;
2. To assess the educational progress of these four minority groups during the past ten or fifteen years, by degree level and by field;
3. To identify factors in the social and educational environment that facilitate or hinder the educational development of minority students; and
4. To formulate recommendations for increasing the numbers of minority students who enter and complete programs at both the undergraduate and graduate levels and to disseminate these recommendations to practitioners, policy makers, and the general public.

Value Premises

Because the National Commission appointed to oversee this project was neither neutral nor disinterested in its view toward the higher education of minorities in the United States, a brief statement of the value premises shared by all Commissioners as they guided the work of the Commission staff is in order. By making these value premises explicit and public, the Commission hoped to provide a basis for understanding the way in which this inquiry has been structured, the significance of the findings and interpretations, and the validity of the recommended actions (reported in the final chapter). The value premises can be stated as follows:

> Education is a value and a right for all Americans. However, education is unequally distributed in U.S. society,

with Blacks, Chicanos, Puerto Ricans, and American Indians the major groups with longstanding unmet claims on U.S. education.* These claims concern not only the amount of schooling they receive but also its quality, scope, and content. Further, the commissioners believe that redressing inequality in higher education is not only an essential component of any significant effort to guarantee to these groups full participation in U.S. society but also a goal worth pursuing in its own right. The attainment of full participation in higher education for these groups may in the short run require that financial and other resources be allocated in a manner governed more by considerations of the magnitude of existing inequality than by considerations of the proportions that these groups represent in the total U.S. population. Finally, the commissioners believe that U.S. society as a whole has practical and moral interests in the achievement of this goal.

None of these premises, it should be stressed, assumes that any of the four groups should give up their cultural distinctiveness, languages, or values in the process of gaining full access to higher education and full social and economic participation in U.S. life.

Context of the Study

When this project was initiated in late 1978, concern for the plight of disadvantaged minorities—which had its genesis with the civil rights movement in the 1950s and which had been strong in the 1960s and early 1970s—was on the wane. The national attention was being absorbed instead by such issues as inflation, unemployment, the energy crisis, and the defense budget. In addition, other socially and economically disadvantaged groups—including the elderly, women workers, and the

---

*There are, of course, numerous other groups with similar unmet claims. The four groups that concern this commission are distinguished by their size, the gravity of their educational disadvantage, and the original experience of forced incorporation into U.S. society.

handicapped—began asserting their claims to equitable treatment, financial resources, and compensatory services.

More recent political developments have not been reassuring. During the Reagan administration's first year in office the U.S. Congress approved major cuts in the federal budget that will sharply affect education and minority-oriented programs. And as this report was being completed in the fall of 1981, the administration was recommending even further cuts of a similar nature.

This shift in mood has been as apparent in higher education as in other sectors of American society. During the 1960s and early 1970s, partly as a result of racial protests on the campus and in the community, many colleges and universities accepted changes—open admissions, recruitment of minorities, establishment of ethnic studies programs—that acknowledged the unmet claims of minorities in the U.S. and the inequitable treatment they had received from the educational system. However, concern over rising costs, along with the fear that projected declines in the college-age population during the 1980s and 1990s would severely erode institutional revenues, led to cost-consciousness and calls for retrenchment. These newer programs, many of which had been initiated on an experimental basis or supported by special outside funding from foundations or the federal government, were especially vulnerable to funding reductions or to elimination. Adding to the budgetary anxiety was apparent public skepticism about the value of higher education and, in particular, its relative costs and benefits.

A number of observers have noted what they believe to be growing public resistance to minority-oriented programs and concerns (Gill, 1980; Jones, 1977; Lehner, 1980; National Advisory Committee on Black Higher Education and Black Colleges and Universities, 1979a). Moreover, a recent report of the National Forum on Learning in the American Future (Glover and Gross, 1979) makes it clear that even the higher education establishment has begun to subordinate minority issues to other concerns. Respondents to the National Forum's survey—including 1,556 policy and decision makers, educators, and scholars—were asked to indicate the relative importance of a number of issues both as present and as future goals. Although minority issues were generally given high priority as present goals, they were rated very low among future goals. Among such activities were promoting affirmative action for minority advancement, recruiting and training minority-group members for managerial and professional positions, providing compensatory educational opportunities to the disadvantaged, and enabling bilingual minorities to study their own culture and language.

The U.S. Supreme Court's rulings in the *DeFunis* and *Bakke* cases reflect a growing public view that higher education institutions have "gone too far" in their attempts to accommodate the special needs of minorities (O'Neil, 1975; Tollett, 1978). Similar attitude changes are evidenced by increased resistance to court-ordered busing as a means of ending racial segregation in the public schools. Finally, many politicians and members of the general public have begun to question the value of postsecondary education. Let us here briefly review their argument.

The Overeducated American

During the 1950s and 1960s, it was common practice for policy makers and educators to extol the virtues of a college education and to assert that a college education benefits the individual as well as society. This view undoubtedly gave some impetus to the massive expansion of higher education in the U.S. that began with the end of World War II. During the 1960s many institutions introduced more flexible admissions policies designed to expand higher educational opportunities for minorities and actively recruited minority students.

During the 1970s, the optimisim and euphoria that characterized the two previous decades all but disappeared from public discussion about higher education. Spurred by the threat of inflation and of what appeared to be growing public disenchantment with the costs of government (including public higher education), many policy makers and educators began to question the further expansion of higher education. This new pessimism was expressed in such assertions as:

- A College degree is much less valuable than it used to be.
- The country suffers from an "oversupply" of college-trained people.

- Job opportunities for college graduates are increasingly limited.
- Even those graduates who manage to find jobs will be "underemployed" and forced to work at menial jobs that are not commensurate with their talent and training.

These views were first given voice by Ivar Berg in his controversial book *Education and Jobs: The Great Training Robbery* (1971). Berg's basic argument is that many people who expect to trade in a college education for the "good life" will suffer disappointment because they will have to take jobs that are beneath their level of training. Even more support for this gloomy prediction was offered by the Harvard economist Richard Freeman, whose book *The Overeducated American* (1976) helped to popularize the concept of "overeducation." Similar arguments have been made by O'Toole (1977).

This concept has particular relevance to the purposes of this study, since the commission's value premises explicitly advocate increasing the numbers of Blacks, Chicanos, Puerto Ricans, and American Indians who enter and successfully complete undergraduate and graduate training. Clearly, this goal will be extremely difficult to implement if policy makers and the public at large accept the notion that Americans are already "overeducated." Thus it is valuable to examine the validity of the concept of the "overeducated American." If it proves to be invalid, then it is a dangerous fiction, one that can easily become a self-fulfilling prophecy unless challenged by our educational and governmental leaders.

The notion of the "overeducated American" is especially appealing to those politicians who, for whatever reason, oppose the expansion of higher education because the notion's advocates have attempted to buttress their argument with a good deal of economic evidence that seems, on the surface, to be scientifically valid. Stripped to its essentials, the argument runs as follows: Twenty years ago, college graduates earned much more than did people without college degrees, but this differential has narrowed to the point that a college degree no longer represents the sound economic investment that it once did. Thus, if one views the costs of attending college (including forgone earnings) as an "investment" that produces later "returns" in the form of higher earnings than would be obtained without the degree, then the "value" of a college education has diminished during recent years. Freeman and others have amassed a considerable body of data in support of this argument.

Shortcomings of the Argument. Nonetheless, the reasoning behind this argument has serious shortcomings. First, making more money is not the only reason, or even the most important reason, that people go to college. Among new freshmen entering college in fall 1980, "to be able to make more money" ranked only fifth (endorsed by 59 percent) among "very important" reasons for deciding to go to college. Students were more likely to say they decided to go to college "to learn more about things that interest me" (80 percent), "to be able to get a better job" (78 percent), "to gain a general education and appreciation of ideas" (73 percent), and "to meet new and interesting people" (65 percent). Making more money was ranked fourth in importance among students attending predominantly black colleges (Astin, King, and Richardson, 1980).

But even if it were true that people go to college primarily to ensure higher future income, the evidence generally used to support the argument that a college education will not enable them to do so is based on some highly questionable assumptions. Briefly, economists who argue that Americans have become over-educated present data showing that the so-called rate of return on a college education has fallen from roughly 14 percent to less than 10 percent during the past twenty years. In other words, if one looks at college as an economic investment, it turns out to be a poorer investment today than it was ten or fifteen years ago.

What assumptions must one make in order to accept this argument? First, it is necessary to assume that people who decide *not* to go to college will instead work at a full-time job during the time they would have been in college and, more important, that they will maintain the same standard of living they would have followed had they attended college. We are also asked to assume that they will take the money that they would otherwise have spent on a college education, put it in a savings account, and leave it there while the interest compounds.

It takes little more than a moment's pause to realize that

these assumptions are unrealistic. For example, it seems unlikely that a young high school graduate with a full-time job will live as frugally as a college student. Considering the extreme ease with which most Americans incur debt, it is not unreasonable to assume that the typical young family in the U.S. follows what might be termed the "American law of family economics": One somehow manages to spend everything one makes, and a little more. But perhaps the most unrealistic assumption of all is that the money for attending college will be available to invest if the person opts not to go to college. The bulk of most students' expenses are paid from two sources: parents and governmental aid. It is extremely unlikely that parents would make the same resources available to those of their children who opted not to attend college, and even less likely that governmental agencies would provide the same grants and loans to young people who do not attend college. In short, these economic analyses are based on such unrealistic assumptions about human behavior that it is difficult to take seriously the arguments about the "declining rate of return" on an investment in a college education.

But perhaps the most serious shortcoming of the "over-educated American" argument is the use of lifetime earnings as the principal measure of the value of college attendance. As we pointed out earlier, and as is clear from fifteen years of continuing surveys of college students, the desire for increased earnings is by no means the only, or even the most important, reason for attending college. Other evidence also suggests that, even if having a degree conferred *no* economic benefit, a great many people would still attend college. Many students, for example, are pursuing careers that pay modestly but require a college education (school teaching, nursing, and so forth). Others attend college to develop certain skills or talents; still others simply enjoy the learning process itself.

A large body of research (Astin, 1977a; Bowen, 1977; Chickering, 1974; Feldman and Newcomb, 1969; Pace, 1979) shows that students benefit from attending college in other than simply monetary respects. They develop a more positive self-image, a greater sense of intellectual and interpersonal competency, and more tolerant views and attitudes toward others.

These studies also show that college plays a major role in the development of an informed public. Those who argue that Americans are overeducated are, in effect, asking us to discount all these other benefits. Indeed, if one views higher education in terms of the many personal benefits it confers on the student, one can make a strong case that Americans, and in particular America's disadvantaged minorities, are undereducated, and that if more citizens took advantage of the opportunities for learning and personal development offered by a college education, the quality of life in general would improve substantially.

Unemployment and Underemployment. To reject the idea that Americans are overeducated is not to deny that some college graduates are having problems finding a good job. Today close to half of the young adults in the U.S. attend college, compared with fewer than a third just twenty years ago. Because so many people today are college graduates, a bachelor's degree no longer *guarantees* a good job. But does this mean that fewer people should be getting college degrees? What if the same kind of logic had been applied to the high school diploma twenty-five years ago? When the number of persons graduating from high school reached more than 75 percent of the age group, policy makers could have argued that a high school diploma no longer offered the job opportunities that it had in the 1920s and 1930s. While such a statement would have been literally true, would society have benefited if the number of people finishing high school had been deliberately reduced?

Perhaps the most persuasive evidence about the importance of education today is contained in the unemployment statistics: The less education one has, the greater are one's chances of being unemployed. Although we have all heard anecdotes about holders of doctoral degrees who are cabdrivers and elevator operators, the fact is that people with doctorates have a lower unemployment rate (less than 1 percent) than almost any other group (Maxfield, 1980). Even among people with only a bachelor's degree, the unemployment rate is only half as great as it is among people with no college degree (Dearman and Plisko, 1981, p. 234). Thus, although a college graduate's prospects for getting a good job may not be as good as they used to be, the prospects for a person without a college degree are just that much worse. Graduating from college may no longer be a sufficient condition for getting a good job, but it certainly appears to be a necessary one.

Even if one rejects the myth of the overeducated American, the potential problem of underemployment for college graduates remains. While it is true that college graduates generally have a competitive advantage over job seekers without college degrees, many graduates are forced to settle for jobs that seem beneath their level of training and education. Ochsner and Solmon (1979) recently examined how college graduates utilize their training on the job. They report that more than half of recent college graduates change their careers *after* they leave college. While college graduates are more likely to be dissatisfied with their first job than with subsequent jobs, this dissatisfaction tends to dissipate with time. Ochsner and Solmon suggest several possible reasons for early dissatisfaction. Some new college graduates, for example, are willing to settle for jobs that may not be very rewarding, but which have long-range career potential. The researchers also argue that even menial or low-level jobs can be made more challenging and interesting if employers make an effort to find ways to use the special talents and skills of the college graduate on the job. Ochsner and Solmon also point out that, to a certain extent, jobs are what one makes them: Many college graduates who possess skills not required in formal job descriptions can find ways to use these skills on the job and thus expand opportunities for promotion and advancement.

Relevance for Minorities. Does the overeducation argument have any special relevance for minorities? Recent research (Astin, 1977a) suggests that minority college graduates may actually have a competitive advantage over white graduates in certain job fields. Among students who take jobs in business immediately after completing the baccalaureate degree, the starting annual salaries for Blacks were found to average about $1,300 more than the starting salaries for Whites with similar background characteristics (for example, type of college attended, grade-point average). Similarly, among graduates who took positions as elementary or secondary school teachers immediately after college, the average starting salary for Blacks was approximately $1,000 a year more than that for Whites with similar backgrounds. It seems clear that these findings reflect a combination of the strong affirmative action pressures that have been exerted recently on employers and of the substantial underrepresentation of Blacks among college graduates. This combination of strong demand and short supply has no doubt served to increase the salaries that recent black college graduates can command in certain fields. More important, however, is the fact that the over-education argument appears to be even less relevant in the case of minorities than it is for the general population.

It is ironic, then, that the myth of the overeducated American probably poses its greatest threat to minorities. Acceptance of the myth provides budget-conscious politicians with an easy victim—education—when costs must be cut. Acceptance of the myth enables politicians to argue that public support for higher education should be reduced. But if reduced public funding lessens the number of people who can avail themselves of higher education opportunities, enrollment declines will be most severe among poor students and students with borderline levels of academic preparation. Since all four minority groups that are the subject of this study—Blacks, Chicanos, Puerto Ricans, and American Indians—include disproportionate numbers of poor people and people with relatively poor academic preparation, it is almost a foregone conclusion that any public policy that encourages a reduction in college enrollments will have its greatest negative impact on these groups.

Design of the Study

The study was originally designed to concentrate on two areas: (1) a description of the current and recent situation of the four minority groups with respect to their rates of educational access and attainment, and (2) an analysis of the factors that influence the access and attainment of these minority groups. During the course of the study, the commission overseeing the project added a third major area of activity: an analysis of controversial issues relating to the higher education of minorities. The specific questions addressed under each of these three major categories of research activity are the following:

Educational Access and Attainment

- To what extent are Blacks, Chicanos, Puerto Ricans, and American Indians represented at various levels of education? At what points do they tend to terminate their formal education?
- What is the representation of each of these four minority groups by field of study and type of institution?
- How has the representation of each minority group changed since the mid 1960s?

Factors Influencing Educational Development

- How are the educational access and attainment of minority students influenced by their family background, socioeconomic status, and personal characteristics?
- What features or characteristics of educational institutions and programs (for example, type of high school, type of higher education institution, student peer groups, faculty attitudes, special institutional programs) are most critical in affecting the progress of minority students?
- How is the progress of minority students affected by the type of financial aid they receive during undergraduate and graduate training?
- Which governmental programs seem to be the most and least effective in facilitating minority progress in higher education?

Controversial Issues

- To what extent are minorities afforded equal access to higher education? Is equality of access more a myth than a reality?
- How valid is the current popular stereotype of the overeducated American? What implications for minority progress in higher education does acceptance of this stereotype have?
- In what way does standardized testing, as currently used,

impede the educational development of minorities? How can standardized testing be employed to contribute to educational development?

• How do the meritocratic aspects of the U.S. higher education system affect minority progress?

Research into questions of the first two categories—educational access and attainment and factors influencing educational development—was conducted by a series of analyses of empirical data. While considerable use was made of existing data sources, substantial amounts of new data were also collected. Examination of the third major category was accomplished by a series of essays drawing upon the existing literature and, in some instances, upon relevant empirical data (see Chapters Seven and Eight).

Three types of empirical data were collected. Information about the minority *talent pool* consisted of measures of the number and personal characteristics of persons from each minority group who are available to be served by the higher educational system. Data concerning *programs* encompassed the types of institutions and programs to which minorities are exposed. Financial and other types of special intervention techniques are also included in this category. Measures of *outcomes* reflected the extent to which minorities enter and successfully complete higher education programs at various levels.

From these data sets, the commission was able to examine three phenomena:

The distribution of minority talent among programs: the numbers and types of minorities who enroll in various types of institutions and who undertake particular programs of study at those institutions. Also included here are financial aid (amount and type) and other special programs received by minorities.

The effects of programs on educational outcomes: the extent to which particular programs are successful in increasing minority access to higher education and in facilitating minority progress through the attainment of undergraduate and graduate degrees.

The relationship between the minority talent pool and outcomes: at any level in higher education minority access or attainment necessarily depends on the number of students who have not dropped out at a lower level and on their motivation, family background, and academic preparation.

These data were used, in turn, as the basis of two different types of study. The descriptive studies simply describe the characteristics of the minority talent pool, the programs they undertook, and the resultant outcomes at various levels of higher education. The analytical studies concern the relationships among the three types of descriptive information and, in particular, the *effects* of programs on outcomes.

The Role of Evaluation

Since some of the individual studies conducted in connection with this project might be described as evaluation research, our position with respect to evaluation should be clarified.

All too often, evaluation studies of special programs for disadvantaged minorities are resisted by the supporters of such programs. Their resistance is, however, understandable for at least two reasons. First, budget-conscious policy makers tend to regard evaluations as a tool for identifying weak or ineffective programs that can subsequently be eliminated to conserve costs. Second, the persons responsible for operating such programs are, almost by definition, committed to believing in the value and effectiveness of such programs. In these circumstances, evaluation research will, at best, only confirm what is already "known" and, at worst, produce information that leads to the dismantling of the program.

The commission and the staff for this project believe that such views distort the real purpose of evaluation research, which is to produce information that will strengthen or enhance the effectiveness of minority-oriented programs. The results of well-designed evaluative research can be used to answer such questions as the following: Which elements of the program seem most effective and so might be expanded or elaborated? Which elements of the program seem least effective and so should be changed or eliminated? What types of students benefit most from the program? What are the unplanned or unforeseen outcomes of the program? How do the outcomes of the program compare with those of traditional or standard programs?

Even if evaluation research demonstrates that a given program is totally ineffective, it does not follow that the objectives of the program should be abandoned. Indeed, we believe that continued efforts should be made to carry out the original purposes of ineffective programs, either by making major revisions in the programs or by replacing the original programs with new ones.

Data Collection

To assure as complete a study as possible, data from a variety of sources were utilized: the Current Population Surveys (CPS) and the decennial census of the U.S. Bureau of the Census, surveys of minority enrollments conducted by the Office for Civil Rights and the National Center for Education Statistics, annual surveys of entering freshmen conducted jointly by the University of California, Los Angeles and the American Council on Education, the National Longitudinal Study (NLS) of high school graduates of 1972 conducted by the National Center for Education Statistics (NCES), annual surveys of new doctoral recipients conducted by the National Academy of Sciences–National Research Council, surveys of scientific manpower conducted by the National Science Foundation, and special analyses of national testing data from the College Entrance Examination Board–Educational Testing Service and the American College Testing Program. Many of the statistics were already computed and published in tabular form. In other instances, it was necessary to obtain raw data from the original source and conduct extensive reanalyses at the Higher Education Research Institute (HERI). (For a full discussion of the advantages and limitations of these various data sets, see Appendix A.)

Descriptive data analyses are reported primarily in Chapter Two ("The Educational Pipeline for Minorities"), Chapter Three ("Minorities in Various Fields of Study"), and Chapter Four ("Recent Developments"). In addition, extensive analyses of information on the types of institutions attended by minorities are reported in Chapter Seven ("Equal Access and Equal Opportunity").

Student Data. The basic design of our analysis of factors influencing student development was similar to designs followed in several earlier studies (Astin, 1975; 1977a). Students are studied longitudinally from the point of initial contact with an educational program (typically, at initial entry to college as freshmen) until some subsequent point. Changes in the students over this period are then compared with such environmental factors as type of college attended, financial aid, and so forth. Data are also collected regarding the students' background at the time of initial entry to the program: socioeconomic background (parental education, parental income, parental occupation, and so forth), high school activities and achievements, values and attitudes, and plans and aspirations. By using such background information to control statistically initial differences among students, one can estimate the effects of the educational programs.

Two major sources of longitudinal data were used to study the development of minority students. The first, which followed minority students during the first two undergraduate years, involved a national sample of freshmen who entered college in the fall of 1975 and who were followed up two years later in the fall of 1977. These data were originally collected for a national study of the impact of student financial aid on retention during the first two undergraduate years (Astin and Cross, 1979). For a fuller discussion of the freshman survey, the follow-up survey, and response rates by racial and ethnic groups, see Chapter Five and Appendix A.

The second major source of longitudinal data involved a national sample of students entering college as freshmen in fall 1971 and followed up nine years later, in winter 1980. This follow-up was conducted specifically for the current project; for a complete discussion and analysis of this effort, see Appendix A.

Additional student information was obtained from a national sample of minorities who received graduate fellowships for doctoral study from the Ford Foundation between 1969 and 1976. The questionnaire was constructed in two stages. During the first stage, HERI staff members interviewed former Ford

Fellows to identify critical areas that should be covered by the questionnaire. A preliminary questionnaire was pretested with former fellows, and the final questionnaire was mailed out to all current and former fellows in fall 1980. With one follow-up mailing to nonrespondents, the total number of respondents numbered 630, or 71.7 percent of the original group of fellowship recipients.

The final student data collection activity consisted of a "natural experiment" to estimate the impact of the fellowship award itself. For this purpose the same follow-up questionnaire sent to the 1971 freshmen was also sent to all Ford Fellows who began their undergraduate studies in 1971. In addition, a control group of applicants for the Ford graduate awards who did not receive fellowships was selected from among those who also began college in 1971. The fellowship recipients and the control group numbered approximately 200 each. The principal purpose of this special survey was to compare the degree completion rates and career progress of the two groups.

Faculty Data. Two major sources of data on college and university faculty were developed as part of the current project. First, all faculty and administrators ($N = 31,000$) at a sample of ninety-eight colleges and universities were selected for a major questionnaire survey. These institutions represented a stratified subsample of the 487 institutions participating in the 1971 survey of entering freshmen that provided the basis for the nine-year longitudinal follow-up of students described above. This faculty survey was designed to replicate, on a smaller scale, the national surveys of the nation's college faculty conducted in 1969 by the Carnegie Commission on Higher Education and the American Council on Education (ACE) and repeated in 1972–1973 by ACE. By comparing the 1980 survey findings with those of the earlier surveys, we hoped to answer such questions as the following: Have the characteristics, attitudes, and behaviors of educators changed over time? Do educators at institutions with significant minority enrollments have different attitudes toward minority issues than educators at institutions that do not have significant minority enrollments?

The second faculty survey, which was integrated into our

research design midway through the project at the commission's suggestion, was intended to tap the experiences and perceptions of minority educators. It was felt that those minority-group members who—despite cultural, educational, social, financial, and psychological barriers—managed to pursue successful academic careers as faculty and administrators would have special insights into the barriers that hinder and the conditions that facilitate the educational achievement of students from their racial or ethnic group. We believed that their experience as students themselves and as teachers working with minority students was a valuable information resource. Lists of minority faculty and staff members were developed through a variety of techniques, including contacts with minority organizations and with minority friends and colleagues around the country. Our goal was to identify approximately 150 minority faculty members from each of the four minority groups. Approximately 600 faculty and staff members became participants in our series of surveys. First, we sent each subject an open-ended survey that posed thirteen questions about educational barriers and facilitators and about what higher education could do to better serve minority students. Responses were compiled and categorized to produce a second questionnaire with summaries of the responses to each of the original thirteen questions. Respondents were asked to review these various response options and to indicate, in order of priority, which three they perceived as most important or significant.

Institutional Data. A variety of sources were consulted to secure data about the environments of the various colleges and universities attended by the minority students and staffed by the faculty who participated in our surveys. A major source of such information was the Higher Education General Information Survey (HEGIS), conducted annually by the National Center for Education Statistics. This survey yields information on a wide range of institutional characteristics including enrollments, educational expenditures, library resources, physical plant, curriculum, institutional type, and control. Data on the institution's "selectivity" (average level of academic preparation of the entering student, as measured by college admissions tests), available from HERI's master institutional files on American higher educational institutions (Astin and Henson, 1977), were also included.

Information about the academic environments of the institutions were obtained by aggregating responses obtained from our faculty surveys. These aggregated measures make it possible to estimate for each institution overall faculty attitudes toward minority issues.

Finally, each of the 487 institutions participating in the 1971 freshman survey was asked to send us any documents describing minority-oriented programs or summarizing the results of evaluations of such programs. This attempt at data collection proved to be of limited value, since only about fifty institutions responded to this request, and in general the documents they sent did not include much evaluative information.

Other Data Collection Activities. During the course of the commission's work, we learned that practically no data were available concerning the flow of Puerto Rican students between the island and the mainland. Accordingly, Dr. Janice Petrovich, whose special area is socioeconomic development and higher education in Latin America and the Caribbean, was commissioned to write a special report on Puerto Ricans who come from the island to the mainland for their college education. Using 1979–80 data on high school students who had taken the Scholastic Aptitude Test, provided by the College Entrance Examination Board, she compared island residents with mainland residents on socioeconomic characteristics, degree aspirations, and other relevant traits. The report also discusses the social-class stratification of the island's educational system, in which children from affluent families tend to go to private secondary institutions and thus to gain entrance either to mainland postsecondary institutions or to the University of Puerto Rico.

National Commission

When the project was in its initial design stages, during fall 1978, the Higher Education Research Institute and the Ford Foundation jointly selected a National Commission to serve as an advisory board and a policy arm for the project. The major function of the Commission was to advise the HERI staff concerning proposed and completed projects and to assist in the interpretation and dissemination of findings to policy makers, practitioners, and the general public. The commission was structured to include both men and women, nonminorities and minorities (including at least one member of each of the four minority groups studied), and representatives of various sectors of academic and public life.

Nine commssion meetings were held throughout the project. These meetings proved to be extremely productive, since they gave commissioners and staff a chance to get to know each other and to discuss and debate the various issues being studied. Subcommittees comprising both commission and staff members were formed to consider specific issues such as federal programs, the quality of the data used in the project, and minority women. A major outcome of the commission's involvement in the project was the decision to produce five reports: an overall summary report of the entire study (the present volume) and four separate reports on each of the minority groups that would discuss in more detail the history and special problems of each group.

The dates and places of each meeting were as follows: February 25–26, 1979, Los Angeles; June 1–2, 1979, Los Angeles; October 5–6, 1979, Los Angeles; January 12–13, 1980, San Antonio (Tex.); March 21–22, 1980, New York; November 7–8, 1980, Los Angeles; April 10–12, 1981, Ramona, (Calif.); and July 19–21, 1981, Los Angeles.

The San Antonio and New York City meetings were designed to focus on the special problems of Chicanos and Puerto Ricans, respectively. At these meetings the commissioners had an opportunity to meet with several local people who were involved with special programs focused on these two groups. The April 10–12, 1981, meeting was designed to review draft sections of the five reports. The final commission meeting, held on July 19–21, was devoted to developing final draft reports of the major findings and recommendations from the project.

Limitations of the Study

The principal limitations of the study can be discussed under three general headings: the selection of minority groups, the limits of college education as a remedy for the problems of minorities, and the limitations of the various data sources upon which the study relied.

Selection of Minority Groups. The decision to limit the study to Blacks, Chicanos, Puerto Ricans, and American Indians was a difficult one. A number of other racial and ethnic subgroups in the United States—Cubans, Samoans, Filipinos, and other Asians, to name just a few—are educationally and economically disadvantaged and have been subjected to prejudice and discrimination of various sorts over the years. The Ford Foundation's decision about which groups to include and which to exclude was made primarily on the basis of size, disadvantagement, and available data. Thus, the four groups that were finally selected are the largest and the most educationally and economically disadvantaged. While Asians represent a slightly larger group than either Puerto Ricans or American Indians, they are by no means a homogeneous group, and the histories of the different subgroups (Chinese, Japanese, Koreans, and so forth) differ considerably. More important for this particular study, however, is that the subgroups that make up the majority of Asians residing in the United States (Chinese and Japanese) do not appear to be educationally disadvantaged; indeed, evidence suggests that their educational attainment may even be higher than that of white Americans (U.S. Commission on Civil Rights, 1978).

Limits of Higher Education. Higher education was selected as the focus of this study because the Ford Foundation and the persons associated with the project believe that higher education represents an important means for improving the social and economic condition of Blacks, Puerto Ricans, American Indians, and Chicanos in the U.S. (Bundy, 1977). One major problem confronting all these groups is powerlessness, and higher education is clearly one of the main routes whereby individuals can attain positions of economic and political power. Further, the quality of life in general can be improved through higher education, which provides more options in terms of employment and geographical mobility. Finally, higher education can expand leisure options by exposing the individual to a wide range of experiences in the arts, music, literature, history, science, and technology (Bowen, 1977; Pace, 1979).

But higher education is by no means a cure-all for the problems of disadvantaged minorities in the U.S. It seems likely that the vestiges of racial prejudice will persist in the minds of many Americans for years to come, no matter how many minority students complete higher education programs. Perhaps more significant is the fact that many of the educational problems confronting these groups occur *prior* to higher education, at the elementary and secondary levels. Indeed, the results of this study dramatize the need for a much more intensive national effort to upgrade the quality of elementary and secondary education for minorities in the U.S. While it is true that higher education can play some role in this process, through the selection and training of administrators and teachers in the lower schools, most of the problems of precollegiate minority education are probably beyond the direct control of higher education. While the commission does not believe that this reality relieves the higher education system of the responsibility of doing the best job possible with those minority students who do enter academic institutions, it also recognizes that curing the problems of precollegiate education for minorities rests heavily on federal, state, and local governments.

Limitations of the Data. It would be an understatement to say that most of the data sources utilized in this project suffered from serious limitations. These various technical problems, which have been noted by other investigators (Abramowitz, 1976; Brown and Stent, 1977; Chavers, 1979; Olivas, 1979), and which are discussed in considerable detail in Appendix A, are only briefly mentioned here.

One serious problem concerns sample size. Since most of the sources drawn upon in the commission's work (particularly for longitudinal data) rely on sample surveys, the absolute number of persons surveyed among the smaller minority groups (American Indians and Puerto Ricans, in particular) was often so small as to raise serious questions about the reliability of the results. This problem of small sample size affected the findings from almost every data source: the Current Population Surveys of the Bureau of the Census, the Cooperative Institutional Research Program of UCLA and ACE, and the National Longitudinal Study of the National Center for Education Statistics.

A related problem, the representativeness of various samples, is especially acute in the case of the smaller minority groups, where sampling errors have more serious consequences than is the case with Blacks. The data sources particularly affected by this problem include the Cooperative Institutional Research Program (which samples institutions) and the Current Population Surveys of the U.S. Bureau of the Census (which samples households).

Still another limitation concerns the relatively low response rates from mailed surveys. In the case of the nine-year follow-up of the 1971 entering freshmen, this problem was severe enough to necessitate a series of intense follow-up procedures. Fortunately, these procedures were reasonably successful, thereby greatly increasing the confidence that one can place in the persistence rates estimated from these data (see Appendix A for details). Although response rates to the faculty surveys were substantially higher, and returns from the survey of former Ford graduate fellows higher still, one must exercise some caution in the interpretation of findings based on any of these questionnaire surveys.

A final limitation of the data used in this project concerns racial definition. Studies by the HERI staff show that self-definitions such as those used in the Cooperative Institutional Research Program are highly reliable for Blacks, Chicanos, and Puerto Ricans. Many other data sources, however, rely on other means to identify race or ethnicity. The enrollment surveys of the National Center for Education Statistics permit reporting institutions to use any means that they choose to identify various racial or ethnic categories of students. The most serious problem in definition occurs with American Indians. Self-definitions (with no qualifications beyond "American Indian") are extremely unreliable, and unfortunately produce systematic rather than random errors. Thus, nearly *every* source of data pertaining to American Indians greatly exaggerates the representation of this group at all educational levels. (See Appendix A for a fuller discussion of this problem.)

❧ 2 ❧

The Educational Pipeline
for Minorities

Much of the technical effort in this project was directed at gathering and synthesizing the best available data on the progress of disadvantaged minorities through the nation's higher educational system. If one views the educational system as a kind of pipeline leading ultimately to positions of leadership and influence in our society, it is possible to identify five major "leakage" points at which disproportionately large numbers of minority-group members drop out of the pipeline: completion of high school, entry to college, completion of college, entry to graduate or professional school, and completion of graduate or professional school. The loss of minorities at these five transition points accounts for their substantial under-representation in high-level employment (Arce, 1976; Brown and Stent, 1977; de los Santos, 1980; Olivas, 1978; Institute for the Study of Educational Policy, 1976).

The data on how many minority-group members drop out of the educational system at each of the five transition points

25

are, with few exceptions, less than complete. Indeed, for certain minority groups and certain transition points, reliable information is almost completely lacking. Nonetheless, by piecing together data from several different sources, one can construct a reasonably accurate picture of the progress of Blacks, American Indians, Chicanos, and Puerto Ricans in higher education.

High School Graduation

Virtually the only recent data showing the proportions of various groups that complete high school come from the Current Population Surveys (CPS) conducted annually by the U.S. Bureau of the Census. From these surveys, one can determine two important facts about the individuals surveyed: whether or not they completed high school, and whether or not they are currently attending school. The major limitations of these data are that they do not permit reliable analyses of results for American Indians and that the sample sizes for Chicanos and Puerto Ricans tend to be very small. To remedy this latter problem the HERI staff asked the Bureau of the Census to provide copies of the CPS data tapes covering five consecutive surveys, 1974 through 1978. (1974 was the first year in which Chicanos and Puerto Ricans were separately identified, rather than being counted together in the category "Spanish origin".)

Rates were first calculated separately for each of the five surveys. An inspection of these rates for Whites and Blacks (for whom the sample sizes for any given year were adequate) did not reveal any significant trends during the five-year span. Results from the five surveys were then combined, yielding more acceptable sample sizes for Chicanos and Puerto Ricans.

Table 1 shows the actual dropout rates for the CPS sample population. A dropout is defined as a person who had not completed high school and who was not enrolled as a student at the time of the October survey. As the data show, the proportion of dropouts at each age level increases steadily until age nineteen or twenty, after which the proportions stabilize. The reason for the steady increase is clear: Most dropouts leave during the last years of high school. That dropout rates do not change appreci-

Table 1. Percentage of High School Dropouts, by Age and Racial or Ethnic Group
(Weighted Five-Year Averages, 1974–1978)

| Group | Age | | | | | | | | | | | | Ages 20–25 Combined | |
	14	15	16	17	18	19	20	21	22	23	24	25	(N)	Mean Percentage
Whites	1	2	6	10	13	16	18	17	18	18	18	18	(58,873)	17.8
Blacks	1	2	6	12	20	27	27	30	31	32	29	28	(6,560)	29.4
Chicanos	2	6	16	23	31	41	43	45	50	51	56	53	(2,508)	49.7
Puerto Ricans	2	4	12	19	36	42	52	49	54	62	41	56	(548)	52.5

Notes. A dropout was defined as any person who, at the time of the survey, was not a high school graduate and was not enrolled in school.
Data on American Indians are not provided by the Current Population Surveys.

Source. Current Population Survey Public Use Tapes for October Surveys, 1974–1978, obtained from the Bureau of the Census, U.S. Department of Commerce.

ably beyond age twenty (at least among Whites and Blacks) suggests that high school dropout rates have remained fairly constant during recent years.

In veiw of the stability of dropout rates from age twenty on, we computed a mean for those aged twenty to twenty-five to provide an estimate of dropout rates for the four groups. These means (shown in the last column of Table 1) underscore a critical issue for minorities: High school dropout rates for Blacks are substantially higher than those for Whites, and dropout rates for both Chicanos and Puerto Ricans are substantially higher than those for Blacks. In fact, half of the Chicanos and Puerto Ricans in the sample did not finish high school, compared with fewer than 20 percent of the Whites and about 30 percent of the Blacks.

How reliable are these estimates? It seems safe to assume that the figures for Whites are very accurate, given the large sample sizes for this group in the CPS surveys; this assumption is supported by the lack of variation (less than 1 percentage point) in the group's dropout rates between ages twenty and twenty-five. Similarly, even though the sample sizes for Blacks are much smaller than those for Whites, their dropout rates vary little between ages twenty and twenty-five (from 27 percent to 32 percent). The dropout rates for Chicanos show somewhat wider variability (from 43 percent to 56 percent), probably because of the smaller sample sizes. Even so, the lowest estimate for Chicanos (43 percent) is still 11 percentage points higher than the highest estimates for Blacks (32 percent) and 25 percentage points higher than the highest estimates for Whites (18 percent).

Since the estimates for Puerto Ricans are based on the smallest samples, it is not surprising that their dropout rates show the greatest variability between ages twenty and twenty-five (from 41 percent to 62 percent). Despite this variation, the lowest estimate for Puerto Ricans is still substantially greater than the highest estimate for Blacks and more than twice as high as the highest estimate for Whites.

As Table 1 indicates, the different groups also vary in *when* they drop out of high school. Rates for Whites and Blacks are identical through age sixteen and only slightly higher for Blacks at age seventeen. At ages eighteen and nineteen, dropout rates for Blacks increase sharply over those for Whites. The pattern for Chicanos and Puerto Ricans is somewhat different: As early as ages fourteen and fifteen, their dropout rates are higher than those of Whites and Blacks, and these rates accelerate greatly at ages sixteen and seventeen. Their dropout rates, like those of Blacks, continue to increase through ages eighteen and nineteen.

Allowing for the fact that respondents were necessarily somewhat older at the time of the survey than at the time they actually dropped out, it seems clear that significant numbers of Hispanics leave high school as early as the ninth grade and that attrition continues throughout the high school years. Blacks and Whites, in contrast, do not begin to drop out in large numbers until the tenth grade. These findings suggest that efforts to combat attrition among Puerto Ricans and Chicanos should begin during the junior high school years and continue throughout the high school years, while efforts to combat attrition among Whites and Blacks would probably be more fruitful if they focused on the early high school years.

Among Chicanos, the proportion of dropouts increases steadily between ages nineteen and twenty-four. (The figure for age twenty-five is slightly lower than that for age twenty-four though higher than for earlier age levels.) Does the lower proportion of dropouts at earlier age levels constitute evidence that the high school dropout rates of Chicanos have been declining? To test this possibility, we computed the average proportion of dropouts among twenty- and twenty-one-year-olds for the two most recent surveys (1977 and 1978) and for the earliest available surveys (1974 and 1975). The results not only failed to confirm a trend toward declining dropout rates but produced evidence in support of the opposite interpretation: The average proportion of dropouts among Chicanos aged twenty and twenty-one was 44.1 percent in 1977–78, compared with 38.7 percent in 1974–75. Including the nineteen-year-olds in the computation changes the figures very little: 43.9 percent versus 39.0 percent. If the eighteen-year-olds are included, the discrepancy becomes even greater: 41.4 percent versus 35.8 percent. In short, high school dropout rates among Chicanos have not decreased and may have actually increased, at least during the 1970s.

Why, then, should the cumulative data in Table 1 show an increasingly high proportion of dropouts at each age level? Perhaps sampling errors are to blame. Another possibility is that recent immigrants from Mexico—who would be more likely than native-born persons never to have attended or completed high school—are more concentrated among older than among younger Chicanos. Such speculation could, of course, be tested empirically if better data on Chicanos in the U.S. were available.

How do these figures agree with published reports from the U.S. Bureau of the Census? To explore this issue we combined results from the seven most recent March Current Population Surveys (1973–1979) and show the results in Table 2. The completion rates tend to be slightly higher than those obtained from our own analyses of October CPS tapes (Table 1), although the differences are only a matter of a few percentage points. Dropout rates for Whites average around 15 percent (as compared to 17.8 percent in Table 1). For Blacks they average around 28 percent (as compared to 29.4 percent in Table 1). The rates for Hispanics in Table 2 are somewhat more discrepant when compared to the separate rates for Chicanos and Puerto Ricans shown in Table 1. Could this larger discrepancy be attributable to the fact that those Hispanics who are neither Chicanos nor

Table 2. Percentage of Different Age Cohorts Who Have
Completed High School

	Year of Survey						
Group	1973	1974	1975	1976	1977	1978	1979
Ages 20–21[a]							
Whites	85	85	84	86	85	85	86
Blacks	72	72	71	73	75	73	75
Hispanics	NA	56[b]	59	59	61	61	62
Ages 25–29							
Whites	82	83	85	86	87	86	87
Blacks	64	68	71	74	75	77	75
Hispanics	NA	52[c]	52	58	58	57	57

[a]From 1976 on data include ages 20–24.
[b]Separate figure for Chicanos is 53 percent.
[c]Separate figure for Chicanos is 47 percent.
Source. Current Population Survey Public Use Tapes for October Surveys, 1974–1978, obtained from the Bureau of the Census, U.S. Department of Commerce.

Puerto Ricans have considerably higher levels of high school completion?

An opportunity to test this possibility was provided in a census report based on a 1974 survey, the results of which are shown in Table 3. Note that our hypothesis about the other Hispanics is correct: among persons aged twenty to twenty-four, the high school graduation rate is 50 percent higher among other Hispanics than among Chicanos (Puerto Rican rates for this group are not available because of small sample sizes). Similarly, college entry rates were fully twice as high among other Hispanics as among Chicanos. For persons twenty-five years or older, high school graduation rates are nearly twice as high among other Hispanics as among either Chicanos or Puerto Ricans. Among this same age cohort, college entry and college completion rates are more than twice as great among other Hispanics as among either Chicanos or Puerto Ricans. In short, the data in Table 3 dramatize the fact that educational attainment figures based on an aggregated Hispanic category are likely to be substantially higher than the separate rates for either Chicanos or Puerto Ricans.

As mentioned earlier, data from the CPS surveys do not permit reliable analyses of dropout rates among American Indians, so other sources must be used. A study conducted by the Office for Civil Rights in 1976 estimated the high school

Table 3. Percentage of Different Hispanic Groups Who Graduate from High School, Attend College, and Complete College (1974)

Group	20–24 Years Old		25 Years or Older		
	Completed High School	Entered College	Completed High School	Entered College	Completed College
Male					
Chicanos	53	17	31	12	5
Puerto Ricans	NA	NA	31	13	6
Other Hispanics	76	39	57	28	12
Female					
Chicanos	51	16	28	6	2
Puerto Ricans	NA	NA	29	9	3
Other Hispanics	74	30	51	19	9

Source. Current Population Survey Public Use Tapes for October surveys, 1974–1978, obtained from the Bureau of the Census, U.S. Department of Commerce.

dropout rate among American Indians to be 36 percent (U.S. Commission on Civil Rights, 1978). This survey's estimates of high school dropout rates average about 10 percent lower than those shown in Table 1. For example, the estimated rate for Puerto Ricans is 36 percent; for Chicanos, 39 percent. The rates for Blacks and Whites are 26 and 14 percent, respectively. These rates are not only lower than those shown in Tables 1 and 2 but also lower than those obtained from several single-year analyses using census data from 1975 (U.S. Bureau of the Census, 1975) and 1978 (U.S. Bureau of the Census, 1978). Thus, it seems reasonable to conclude that the high school dropout rate for American Indians is probably higher than the estimated 36 percent, possibly as high as 50 percent.

In summary, our data illustrate four important facts concerning high school attrition:

1. Minorities drop out of high school at a rate that is substantially higher than the dropout rate for Whites.
2. Blacks drop out of high school at a rate (27–29 percent) that is about two-thirds higher than the rate for Whites (15–18 percent). Most of this attrition occurs at the high school level and is spread fairly evenly across all three years.
3. Approximately half of the Hispanic students—Chicanos and Puerto Ricans—never finish high school; their high school dropout rates are about two-thirds higher than the dropout rate for Blacks and *three times* higher than the rates for Whites. This attrition appears to begin during the junior high school years and to continue through the high school years.
4. Although the data for estimating high school dropout rates for American Indians are meager, it appears that they are more likely than Blacks to leave high school before graduation.

College Entry

How many minority students who graduate from high school enter college immediately? To explore this question, we aggregated data from five October Current Population Surveys

(1974 through 1978) to produce larger sample sizes (see Table 4). We considered only high school graduates, a constraint that reduced the sample sizes; but, with the possible exception of Puerto Ricans, the groups were large enough to permit computation of reasonably reliable estimates.

Instead of looking at different age groups, we looked at the number of years since high school graduation: from none (for those who graduated from high school in June and enrolled in college for the fall term) to four years after completion of high school. Table 4 shows the proportions of the high school graduates in each minority group who were enrolled as full-time college students at the time of the October survey. In evaluating these data, the reader should bear in mind that estimates of college enrollments obtained by the Bureau of the Census are probably somewhat inflated. Because a household informant does not always have up-to-date information on the enrollment status of other household members, he or she may tend to err by

Table 4. Percentage of High School Graduates Enrolled as Full-Time College Students, by Racial or Ethnic Group (Weighted Five-Year Averages, 1974–1978)

Number of Years Since High School Graduation[a]	Group			
	Whites	Blacks	Chicanos	Puerto Ricans
None	45 (9,477)	41 (1,143)	38 (282)	54 (50)
One	37 (8,492)	35 (1,025)	26 (270)	41 (44)
Two	33 (10,287)	32 (1,223)	24 (314)	37 (63)
Three	31 (9,577)	27 (1,160)	17 (256)	30 (57)
Four	18 (9,653)	19 (1,118)	12 (247)	25 (53)
Overall Mean	32.8 (47,486)	30.8 (5,669)	23.4 (1,369)	37.4 (267)

Note. In each cell, the number of high school graduates included in the five consecutive October surveys of the Current Population Surveys is shown in parentheses.
[a]Since high school graduation usually takes place in June and the surveys are conducted in October, each year since graduation represents sixteen months.

indicating that a household member is enrolled as a college student when that person is in fact not enrolled. Similarly, household informants may confuse trade or vocational schools with degree-granting colleges and universities.

As would be expected, the proportion of high school graduates enrolled in college declines with years since graduation. Since some high school graduates delay entry to college for a year or so, these declining figures overestimate the actual retention rates of those who enter college immediately after completing high school. As is perhaps surprising, Table 4 indicates that Puerto Rican high school graduates are somewhat more likely to enter college immediately out of high school than are the graduates from the other three groups. Since Puerto Ricans maintain their top position each year beyond high school graduation, this initially high figure of 54 percent does not seem to be attributable to a sampling error or to some other artifact. One possible explanation is that a very high proportion of Puerto Ricans live in New York City, where the City University of New York operated an open-admissions program during the first few years of these surveys.

The other groups follow the pattern observed with high school graduation: Whites are most likely to enter college immediately after high school, Chicanos are least likely, and Blacks fall in between. This relative ordering is maintained until at least four years after high school graduation.

To compare our locally computed estimates of college entry rates with published figures from the Bureau of the Census, we combined data from the last seven March CPS surveys (Table 5). For Whites in their early twenties the rates show virutally no change during the past seven years, with an average rate of college attendance of 41 percent. Among Blacks and Hispanics, however, there appears to be some modest increase since the first two or three years of the surveys, although the rates have dropped slightly since 1977.

The last column of Table 5 represents an estimated college entry rate for high school graduates. We adjusted the average college entry rate for the seven-year survey by the differential high school dropout rates. For Whites we used a rate of 17 percent; for Blacks, 28 percent. Since separate data were not

Table 5. Percentage of Different Age Cohorts Who Have Attended College

Group	Year of Survey							Overall College Entry Rates[d]
	1973	1974	1975	1976	1977	1978	1979	
Age 20–21[a]								
Whites	41	41	39	42	41	40	41	47
Blacks	25	29	26	26	32	30	29	39
Hispanics	NA	19[b]	21	22	25	26	23	38
Age 25–29								
Whites	38	42	43	46	47	48	48	
Blacks	22	24	28	28	31	35	31	
Hispanics	NA	20[c]	21	21	24	25	25	

[a]From 1976 on data include ages 20–24.
[b]Separate figure for Chicanos is 17 percent.
[c]Separate figure for Chicanos is 18 percent.
[d]Mean rate adjusted for high school dropout rates (that is, rates show percentage of high school graduates who attend college).

available for Chicanos and Puerto Ricans, we used a Hispanic high school dropout rate of 40 percent. The results for Blacks and Whites compare favorably with the locally computed college entry rates: For Whites the rate in Table 5 is 47 percent (compared to 45 percent in Table 4; for Blacks the corresponding rates are 39 and 41 percent). While the estimate for Hispanics of 38 percent agrees exactly with the Chicano rate shown in Table 4, one would have expected that the rate shown in Table 5 would be higher, since it includes both Puerto Ricans (who appear to have a higher college entry rate than Chicanos) and other Hispanics (who tend to have higher educational attainment levels than either Chicanos or Puerto Ricans; see Table 3). Perhaps these figures reflect the recent increase in college attendance rates among Hispanics. Thus, if one takes only the last four years for Hispanics shown in Table 5, the adjusted college entry rate for high school graduates is 40 percent.

To what extent are these estimates of college entry rates consistent with other sources? Perhaps the best alternative source of information on this subject is the National Longitudinal Study (NLS) conducted by the National Center for Education Statistics. For Whites, the figures are exactly the same as in Table 4: 45 percent of the high school graduates of 1972 entered college in the fall of 1972. (An additional 5 percent had entered by the fall of 1973.) Other NLS rates were 37 percent for Blacks (4 percentage points lower than the figures computed by HERI and only 2 points lower than the census figures shown in Table 5), and 37 percent for Hispanics (as compared with the census figure of 38 percent in Table 5 and the HERI rates of 38 percent for Chicanos and 54 percent for Puerto Ricans shown in Table 4). Since Chicanos make up about 60 percent of the Hispanic category, and since they outnumber Puerto Ricans by about four to one, it is to be expected that the NLS estimate for Hispanics would come closer to the HERI figure for Chicanos than to the figure for Puerto Ricans. The reason that NLS estimates are slightly lower than HERI estimates for the three minority groups is not clear. One possible explanation is that minority household informants are more likely than white household informants to overreport enrollment patterns or possibly to confuse technical or vocational school enrollment with college enrollment.

The only data we could find that show the college attendance rate for American Indians come from the NLS. The main problem with these data is, of course, the small sample size ($N = 214$). Thus, the NLS estimate that 27.4 percent of American Indian high school graduates enter college immediately out of high school must be viewed with some caution.

The underrepresentation of American Indians among college students is best indicated by the 1970 census figures (U.S. Bureau of the Census, 1973). Whereas American Indians accounted for 0.436 percent of the college-age population in the U.S., they accounted for only 0.165 percent of college students in 1970. According to Crossland (1971), American Indians were the most underrepresented minority in American higher education at that time, being only half as likely as the next-most-underrepresented group, Chicanos, to attend college.

Another way to estimate college attendance rates is to look at the ethnic composition of the entering freshman class in higher education. Three different sources of data are available to generate such estimates: the National Longitudinal Study (NLS), the Office of Civil Rights (OCR) estimates of racial enrollments, and the annual survey of entering freshman conducted by the

Cooperative Institutional Research Program (CIRP). Table 6 shows four estimates based on these alternative data sources. Basically, we looked at alternative estimates for two entering freshman classes: 1972 and 1976. Because the CIRP survey is based only on a 15 percent sample of the entering freshman class, three-year averages based on these surveys are used to provide more reliable estimates. Thus, for the 1972 freshman class, the average CIRP estimates for 1971, 1972, and 1973 were used. Several differences in the sampling procedures should be noted. While the NLS looks at high school graduates who go directly to college, the CIRP surveys all first-time, full-time entering freshmen (approximately 97.5 percent of whom graduated in the same year as the survey). A more important difference, however, involves the OCR survey, which includes both full- and part-time freshmen. The last column in Table 6 shows the ethnic composition of the college-age population in 1975 to provide a basis for interpreting the figures obtained from the other surveys.

Table 6 shows clearly that the CIRP tends to generate lower estimates of minority enrollments than the other surveys. (American Indians represent an exception to this general rule.) Thus, Black and Chicano enrollments as estimated by the NLS tend to be about 50 percent higher than those estimated from the CIRP. A similar discrepancy occurs in the 1976 estimates: OCR figures run nearly 50 percent higher for Blacks and more than 100 percent higher for Chicanos. One reason for the higher Chicano and Puerto Rican rates in the 1976 OCR survey is certainly attributable to the fact that this survey used an aggregate Hispanic category. We have thus taken 60 percent of the aggregate category to represent Chicanos and 15 percent to represent Puerto Ricans. According to the data reported in Table 3, the figures in Table 6 are most certainly overestimates of the true numbers of Chicano and Puerto Rican freshmen.

Another problem with the OCR data is that they include part-time as well as full-time students. This fact will also tend to inflate the figures for Chicanos and Puerto Ricans, since Hispanics in higher education have a higher rate of part-time enrollment (47.4 percent) than either Whites (41.1 percent) or Blacks (38.0 percent) (Dearman and Plisko, 1980).

Table 6. Alternative Estimates of Minority Representation Among College Freshmen (Percentage of Entering Class)

Group	Cooperative Institutional Research Program (Mean 1971–72–73)	National Longitudinal Study (1972)	Cooperative Institutional Research Program (Mean 1975–76–77)	Office of Civil Rights (1976)	U.S. Population: 18–22-Year-Olds in 1975
Whites	89.1	81.0	86.5	78.6	86.0
Blacks	7.6	11.5	8.7	12.0	12.1
Chicanos	1.3	2.1	1.5	3.2	3.5
Puerto Ricans	.4	.5	.7	.8	.8
American Indians	1.0	.6	.9	.9	NA

It is also possible to argue that the CIRP estimates are spuriously low because of low participation by minorities in the completion of the annual freshmen questionnaire survey. Under these circumstances, which estimates are to be believed? If one compares the four estimates with the figures for the entire U.S. population (last column of Table 6), the CIRP estimates seem more plausible. Thus, both the NLS and OCR estimates would suggest that Black freshmen enrollments are at parity with Black representation among college-age members of the U.S. population. However, if Blacks have a higher dropout rate from high school than Whites do (Tables 1 and 2), and if black high school graduates are less likely to attend college than white high school graduates (Tables 4 and 5), how is it possible that black representation among entering college freshmen is proportional to their representation in the college-age population? Clearly, this argument suggests that the NLS and OCR estimates are spuriously high; the problem comes in determining whether the CIRP estimates are correct or whether the true figures fall somewhere in between CIRP and the other surveys. If one applies the high school completion and college entry rates discussed earlier to the population figures shown in the last column of Table 6, it is possible to estimate what the ethnic composition of the entering freshman class ought to be. By these calculations, the figures for black enrollments fall in between the CIRP and other estimates (10.0), as does the estimate for Chicanos (1.8 percent). The estimated figure for Puerto Ricans comes quite close to the 1972 estimate (.45 percent), but considerably lower than the other estimates, including the 1976 CIRP estimate.

In passing it should be noted that the figures for Ameican Indians in all four surveys are almost certainly inflated, perhaps by as much as 100 percent over the true figure, given the fact that only half of those who are self-identified as "American Indians" are usually considered American Indians by any conventional definition (see Chavers, 1979; McNamara, 1979, 1982).

In summary, among high school graduates, the minority group whose members are least likely to go directly to college seem to be American Indians (only about 27 percent of whom enroll in college immediately after high school); followed by

Chicanos (38–40 percent), Blacks (39–41 percent), Whites (45–47 percent), and Puerto Ricans (about 50 percent). Again, the reader is reminded that estimates for Chicanos, Puerto Ricans, and Blacks may be slightly inflated.

Completion of College

One of the best sources of data on college completion rates comes from the National Longitudinal Study. Table 7 shows the 1976 status of those 1972 high school graduates who entered college. Clearly, Whites are much more likely to complete a bachelor's degree in four years than are the members of the three minority groups. Once again, Hispanics and American Indians have the lowest rates, with Blacks in between. As a matter of fact, the degree completion rates of Whites are more than twice as great as those of either Hispanics or American Indians. In all likelihood, this difference is attributable in part to the high concentration of both Hispanics and American Indians in community colleges. Although three fourths of community college entrants indicate, as freshmen, that they intend to get at least a bachelor's degree (Astin, King, and Richardson, 1980), the chances of their actually transferring to a senior institution and

Table 7. Persistence of College Entrants from the High School Class
of 1972, by Racial or Ethnic Group

	Group			
Status in 1976	Whites (N = 7,643)	Blacks (N = 1,081)	Hispanics (N = 326)	American Indians (N = 58)
Percentage who:				
Completed bachelor's degree	34	24	13	16
Completed two or more years of college	38	40	44	47
Completed less than two years of college	28	36	43	38

Source. National Center for Education Statistics (1973).

completing the baccalaureate are slim. Even after taking into account their generally poorer academic preparation, one finds that community college students are substantially less likely than four-year college students to receive a baccalaureate (see Astin, 1975, and Chapter Five of this volume).

The NLS data reported in Table 7 have one limitation: Only four years had elapsed between high school graduation in 1972 and the time of the follow-up in 1976. Other research has shown that many students take longer than four years to complete the baccalaureate. Therefore, if it were possible to follow these students for another five to ten years, we would surely find that larger proportions had completed college, especially among those who had completed two or more years of college at the time of the follow-up survey. Even among those who had completed less than two years of college, there are doubtless some who eventually attain the baccalaureate.

Another way to estimate college completion rates is by means of published data from the Current Population Surveys. Table 8 shows the percentages of persons aged twenty-five to twenty-nine who have completed four or more years of college. We selected this particular age group because it allows at least seven (and up to eleven) years after graduation from high school to complete college. Note that while the percentages show slight increases in the first three years of the survey, they remain relatively stable during the four most recent surveys. Even as late

Table 8. Percentage of Persons Aged Twenty-five to Twenty-nine Who Have
Completed Four or More Years of College
(Current Population Surveys, 1973–1979)

			Year of Survey					Estimated College Completion Rate Among College Entrants
Group	1973	1974	1975	1976	1977	1978	1979[a]	
Whites	20	22	23	25	25	25	24	59.0
Blacks	8	8	11	13	13	12	12	42.0
Hispanics	NA	6[b]	9	7	7	10	7	31.3

[a]1979 figures are expressed as a percentage of all students who entered college (from Table 5).

[b]Exact rate is 6.0, compared to a rate of 5.7 for Chicanos.

as 1979, we find the college completion rate twice as high among Whites as among Blacks, and more than three times as high among Whites as among Hispanics.

The last column of Table 8 estimates college persistence rates by combining data from Table 5 and the 1979 figures from Table 8. Thus, it appears that college completion rates are about a third higher among white than among black college entrants, and nearly twice as high among Whites as among Hispanics. (Similar results for Hispanics are reported by Pasqueira, 1973–1974; Leon, 1975; and Guerra, 1970.)

Is it possible to use these various sources of data to compute college completion estimates for American Indians? If one compares the data in Tables 7 and 8, it seems reasonable to conclude that approximately half of those students in Table 7 who had completed two or more years of college at the time of the follow-up do eventually finish the bachelor's degree. In other words, when those who have completed the degree are combined with half of those who had no degree but who had completed two or more years of college, the college completion rates come fairly close to those shown in the last column of Table 8. Applying this rule of thumb to the figures in Table 7, we derive an estimate of college completion for American Indians of 39 percent, which is slightly lower than the rate for Blacks but higher than that for Hispanics.

Our final estimate of college completion rates comes from the HERI nine-year longitudinal follow-up of a national sample of students who entered college as freshmen in fall 1971. (The procedures used in this follow-up are reported in Appendix A.) We compared these nine-year (1971–1980) results with the results obtained from the CPS and NLS data. Considering that the two methods used very different data sources, they produce remarkably similar estimates (Table 9). Blacks and Whites show the highest completion rates, while American Indians and Hispanics show the lowest rates. The fact that persistence rates for Blacks and Hispanics are estimated to be higher in the HERI data than in the NLS–CPS data may mean that we underestimated the number of non-degree holders from the 1976 NLS follow-up who eventually completed their degrees.

Table 9. Two Estimates of Percentage of College Entrants
Who Complete College

| | Data Source | |
| | National Longitudinal Study and Current Population | Commission (HERI) Follow-up of 1971 Freshmen |
Group	Surveys	(Conducted in 1980)
Whites	59.0	55.6
Blacks	42.0	50.9
Chicanos	31.3	39.7
Puerto Ricans	31.3	41.8
American Indians	39.0	38.6

Why are the college completion rates so much lower for Hispanics and American Indians than for Blacks and Whites? Again, it appears that the high concentration of American Indians and Hispanics in community colleges during the early undergraduate years contributes significantly to these higher attrition rates. (These issues are discussed in more detail in Chapters Four, Five, and Seven.)

Graduate and Professional Enrollments

By far the best available source of data for estimating rates of graduate school attendance among baccalaureate recipients is the U.S. Office of Civil Rights 1976 Fall Enrollment Survey. By comparing the number of first-year graduate or professional students with the number of baccalaureate degrees awarded during the preceding academic year (1975–76), we computed rates of graduate school attendance for each minority group. The results of these analyses are shown in Table 10.

Perhaps most striking about the data in Table 10 is the similarity in the graduate school attendance rates. The two highest rates are for Blacks and American Indians, and even the lowest rates (for the two Hispanic groups) are not substantially different from the rate for Whites. These results suggest strongly that the transition from undergraduate to graduate school is not a major point of attrition for minorities.

Table 10. Comparison of Bachelor's Degree Recipients and First-Year
Graduate Students

Group	Bachelor's Degrees Received in 1975–76		First-Year Graduate Enrollments in Fall 1976		Ratio of First-Year Graduate Enrollments to Bachelor's Degrees Received
	N	%	N	%	
Whites	811,772	87.6	547,108	84.3	.60
Blacks	59,187	6.4	41,483	6.4	.70
Chicanos[a]	15,732	1.7	9,052	1.4	.58
Puerto Ricans[b]	3,933	.4	2,263	.3	.58
American Indians	3,498	.4	2,478	.4	.71
Total	927,085	100.0	649,125	100.0	.70

[a]Percentages for Chicanos are based on their representing 60 percent of all Hispanic students.

[b]Percentages for Puerto Ricans are based on their representing 15 percent of all Hispanic students.

Source. U.S. Department of Health, Education and Welfare (1978b).

An alternative way to compute graduate school attendance rates is to use the CPS data on the proportion of a given age cohort who have completed four or more years of college and the proportion who have completed five or more years of college. The latter are shown in Table 11, together with graduate school attendance rates, calculated by dividing the percentages in Table 11 by those in Table 8 for the 1979 survey (last column in Table 11). Note that, once again, the graduate school attendance rates for minorities are not substantially different from those for Whites and, in the case of Blacks, slightly higher.

Why the rates in Table 11 are roughly twice as large as those in Table 10 is not entirely clear. One possibility is that the "four years of college completed" does not in all cases represent bachelor's degrees. A second possibility is that the rates shown in Table 10 are substantially inflated by the large number of part-time graduate students; the OCR data do not distinguish first-year graduate enrollments for full-time and part-time students. It could also be argued that the first-year graduate enrollments are inflated by students who delayed entry to graduate school, but this factor is presumably counterbalanced by the many bachelor's degree recipients from 1975–1976 who delayed entry to graduate school.

Table 11. Percentage of Persons Aged Twenty-five to Twenty-nine Who Have
Attended Graduate or Professional School

Group	Year of Survey							Estimated Rate of Graduate School Entry Among College Graduates[a]
	1973	1974	1975	1976	1977	1978	1979	
Whites	7.0	7.4	8.1	8.2	8.6	8.3	8.1	33.8
Blacks	1.5	2.4	2.3	4.2	3.9	3.5	4.3	35.8
Hispanics	NA	1.6[b]	3.0	2.8	2.8	3.6	2.3	32.9

[a]1979 figures are expressed as a percentage of all students who completed four or more years of college (from Table 8).

[b]Figure for Chicanos considered separately is 1.5 percent.

Source. Current Population Survey Public Use Tapes for October surveys, 1974–1978, obtained from the Bureau of the Census, U.S. Department of Commerce.

In summary, these data suggest that the transition from undergraduate to graduate school does not represent as serious an obstacle for the educational development of minorities as do the earlier transition points in higher education.

Attainment of Graduate and Professional Degrees

Table 12 compares the racial composition of first-year graduate enrollments in Fall 1976 with that of graduate degree recipients in 1978-79. Note that, for master's degree recipients, the percentage of Blacks is actually slightly higher than the percentage among first-year graduate students. In all likelihood, this reflects the high concentration of Blacks in education, a field where a master's degree is much more likely than in many other graduate fields (see Chapter Three). The lowest black representation occurs among recipients of the doctor's degree (3.6 percent). The other three minority groups obtained master's degrees roughly in proportion to their representation among first-year graduate enrollments. Their rate of attainment of doctor's degrees, however, like that for Blacks, is substantially lower than their representation among first-year graduate students. Indeed, the representation of Chicanos and Puerto Ricans among doctor's degree recipients is only half that observed among first-year graduate enrollments. (Even these are likely to be overestimates

Table 12. Attainment of Graduate Degrees

Group	Fall 1976 First-Year Graduate Enrollments		1978–1979 Master's		1978–1979 Doctor's		Estimated Rate of Graduate Degree Attainment[d]
	N	%	N	%	N	%	
Whites	547,108	84.3	249,051	88.8	26,128	90.9	50.3
Blacks	41,483	6.4	19,393	6.9	1,267	4.4	49.8
Chicanos[a]	9,052	1.4	3,326	1.2	263	.9	39.6
Puerto Ricans[b]	2,263	.3	832	.3	66	.2	39.6
American Indians	2,478	.4	999	.4	104	.4	44.5
Total[c]	649,125	100.0	280,482	100.0	28,774	100.0	

[a] Percentages for Chicanos are based on their representing 60 percent of all Hispanic graduate students.
[b] Percentages for Puerto Ricans are based on their representing 15 percent of all Hispanic graduate students.
[c] Includes other Hispanics, Asians and nonresident aliens.
[d] The sum of graduate degrees obtained divided by first-year graduate enrollments.
Sources. U.S. Department of Health, Education and Welfare (1978b); Dearman and Plisko (1981).

for the Hispanic groups, since we have assumed that the Chicanos and Puerto Ricans account for the same proportion of Hispanics at the doctor's level as at the first-year graduate level. Evidence reported in Chapter Three suggests that this assumption is probably not justifiable.)

In interpreting the data in Table 12, one must remember that limitations in available data required us to understate the time lag between initial entry to graduate school (Fall 1976) and actual attainment of the doctorate (1978–79). Since the number of minority students in higher education has been growing in recent years, this bias likely led us to underestimate the actual rates of attainment of the doctorate among minorities. However, many persons obtain both a master's and doctor's degree, and they would have been counted twice. With these qualifications in mind, we estimated the rates of graduate degree attainment by dividing the total number of graduate degrees earned by the first-year graduate enrollments. The results of these computations are shown in the last column of Table 12: Whites have the highest rate of attainment of graduate degrees (50.3 percent) followed by Blacks (49.8) and American Indians (44.5). By far the lowest estimated rates of graduate degree attainment occur among Hispanics (39.6 percent).

These data show clearly that the dropout rates among minorities in graduate school are substantially higher than those for white students. In particular, Hispanics and American Indians appear to have substantially higher rates of attrition from graduate and professional school than either Whites or Blacks.

Estimating rates of attainment of advanced professional degrees proved to be a very complex task. Although unpublished data on professional degrees earned by race were, like the graduate degree data, available from the 1978–79 National Center for Education Statistics' *Earned Degrees* survey, no comparable data were available on first-year professional enrollments from the 1976 OCR survey. First-year enrollment data were available, however, from professional associations in the two largest fields: medicine and law.

For medical degrees, we first compared the most recent U.S. Department of Education's data on earned degrees (1978–

79 graduates) with data on first-year medical enrollments from four years earlier (1975–76) published by the Association of American Medical Colleges. These ratios were plausible for three groups—Whites (98 percent), Blacks (74 percent), and American Indians (63 percent), but were impossibly high for Chicanos (124 percent) and improbable for Puerto Ricans (97 percent) when we used our rule of thumb to disaggregate the Hispanic category. A similar problem occurred when we compared 1978–79 data on earned degrees in law with the American Bar Association's data on first-year law enrollments for 1976–77 (we assumed a three-year lag to be appropriate in the case of legal education). Again, results were plausible for three groups—Whites (89 percent), American Indians (91 percent), and Blacks (71 percent)—but not for Chicanos (100 percent) or Puerto Ricans (114 percent).

In the case of medicine, we then consulted the American Medical Association's annual reports on *Medical Education in the United States*, which give medical degrees awarded by race. To minimize the effect of minor yearly fluctuations, we compared degrees awarded during six academic years (1974–75 through 1979–80) with first-year enrollments from 1971–72 through 1976–77. We also made adjustments for the fact that some individuals, minorities in particular, take longer than four years to complete their medical degrees.*

To determine completion rates for law students, we spoke with the Office of the Consultant on Legal Education to the American Bar Association. We were able to determine only that the overall rate of degree completion for minorities was 77.4 percent, compared to 84.4 percent for all students. We consequently decided to use the 77.4 percent rate for each of the four minority groups.

These degree completion rates for law and medicine served as a basis for estimating degree completion rates in the other advanced professional fields. Since data on professional degree completion rates were not available for dentistry and

---

* Information for making these adjustments was obtained in telephone conversations with officials of the Association of American Medical Colleges.

veterinary medicine, we used the rates obtained for medicine (which accounts for about 75 percent of the total minority enrollment in these three fields). Since law and medicine account for about 48 and 41 percent, respectively, of minority enrollments in *all* advanced professional fields, we used the mean completion rate of these two fields as the rate for the remaining 11 percent of minority professional enrollments.

By multiplying the appropriate completion rate by the actual minority enrollment in each professional field as reported in fall 1976 by the National Center for Education Statistics, we estimated overall rates of advanced professional and graduate degree attainment for each minority group. We then obtained an overall estimate of graduate and professional degree attainment through a weighted combination of these professional rates with the graduate rates shown in Table 12. These final rates are shown in Table 13.

The data in Table 13 once again document the fact that members of all four minority groups have higher dropout rates in both graduate and professional schools. The fact that Hispanics have the highest overall dropout rates is primarily attributable to their relatively poor retention in graduate (rather than professional) schools. While all four minority groups have their lowest dropout rates in the field of medicine, the *differences* between white and minority dropout rates are greater in medicine than in any other field.

Summary

By combining the findings reported in Tables 2 through 13, one can map the persistence and attrition patterns for each minority group starting with high school and finishing with the completion of graduate and professional school. These results are summarized in Table 14. These figures represent our best attempts to reconcile conflicting data sources and, in particular, to reflect the most recently available data about each group. In interpreting these data, one should keep in mind the following three considerations: rates for Whites and Blacks are clearly the most accurate; rates for Chicanos and Puerto Ricans are probably

Table 13. Estimates of Graduate and Advanced Professional Degree Completion Rates

Group	Field					Total of All Graduate and Advanced Professional Fields
	Medicine	Law	Other Advanced Professional Fields	All Advanced Professional Fields	Graduate Degrees	
Whites	99.3	85.1	92.2	91.1	50.3	58.7
Blacks	83.1	77.4	80.3	80.0	49.8	54.5
Chicanos	88.3	77.4	82.9	82.4	39.6	48.8
Puerto Ricans	73.3	77.4	75.4	75.5	39.6	46.9
American Indians	81.7	77.4	80.0	79.1	44.5	52.1

Sources. Journal of the American Medical Association, annual reports on medical education in the United States 1971–1980; U.S. Department of Health, Education and Welfare (1978b); Dearman and Plisko, 1981; Association of American Medical Colleges (1979); American Bar Association (1978).

Table 14. Persistence in Higher Education by Racial or Ethnic Group

| | | | Percentage Who: | | |
Group	Complete High School	Enter College	Complete College	Enter Graduate or Professional School	Complete Graduate or Professional School
Whites	83	38	23	14	8
Blacks	72	29	12	8	4
Chicanos	55	22	7	4	2
Puerto Ricans	55	25	7	4	2
American Indians	55	17	6	4	2

on the high side, particularly at the graduate level; and rates for American Indians reflect the largest amount of guess work.

An examination of the data in Table 14 suggests the following conclusions:

- All minority groups are increasingly underrepresented at each higher transition point in the higher educational system.
- Chicanos, Puerto Ricans, and American Indians are the most underrepresented of the four minority groups. The single most important factor in this underrepresentation is their extremely high rate of attrition from secondary school. The second most important factor is their greater-than-average attrition rate from undergraduate colleges.
- Blacks fall about midway between Whites and the other minority groups in terms of their likelihood of completing graduate or professional degrees. Their underrepresentation appears to be attributable to greater-than-average losses at all transition points except entry to graduate or professional school.
- With the exception of transition from undergraduate to graduate school, all four minority groups suffer disproportionately high losses at all transition points in higher education.

✣ 3 ✣

Minorities
in Various Fields
of Study

As the preceding chapter makes clear, Blacks, Chicanos, Puerto Ricans, and American Indians are all underrepresented in postsecondary education, and the degree of underrepresentation becomes more severe at each higher level, owing to the loss of minority-group members at several critical "leakage" points in the educational pipeline. In this chapter we examine the representation of different minority groups in, and their preferences for, specific academic fields (especially fields associated with high-level careers) at successive degree levels.

Which Are the Critical Fields?

Because we are interested primarily in careers requiring at least a baccalaureate, the broad occupational categories used by the U.S. Bureau of the Census are inappropriate for our purposes. At the same time, given the hundreds of major fields of study and occupational titles, we needed to limit the number of categories so that our results would be interpretable and, just as important, so that the tabulations for each minority group would be reliable. With these considerations in mind, we defined ten categories of major fields. Each was selected either because it represents a career that is usually associated with a position of affluence, status, and power in American society or because it is chosen by a large proportion of students or because it fulfills both these criteria. Our ten categories together account for about 90 percent of the baccalaureate degrees awarded in the United States in 1978–79 (Dearman and Plisko, 1981).

Allied health, which accounted for approximately 7 percent of all baccalaureates earned in 1978–79, comprises the following specific majors: for freshmen, health technology (medical, dental, laboratory), nursing, pharmacy, and therapy (occupational, physical, speech); for degree recipients, all fields classified as health professions by the National Center for Education Statistics (NCES).

Arts and humanities, which accounted for approximately 13 percent of all baccalaureates awarded in 1978–79, comprises the following specific majors: for freshmen, English, fine arts, journalism (writing), language (modern), language (other), music, philosophy, speech and drama, communications (radio, television, and the like), and other arts and humanities; for degree recipients, all fields listed by NCES under the aggregate headings of area studies, communications, fine and applied arts, foreign languages, and letters.

Education, which is associated with teaching and administrative positions in the public schools, accounted for 14 percent of the baccalaureates, 39 percent of the master's degrees, and 25 percent of the doctorates granted in the U.S. in 1978–79. It comprises the following specific majors: for freshmen, education and physical education and recreation; for degree recipients, all fields classified as education by NCES.

Physical sciences and mathematics accounted for 4 percent of the baccalaureates and 11 percent of the doctorates awarded in the U.S. in 1978–79. Graduate degrees in the physical sciences and mathematics usually lead to well-paying and highly respected positions in education, government, and industry. This category comprises the following specific majors: for freshmen, chemistry, earth science, mathematics, physics, statistics, and other physical sciences; for degree recipients, all fields listed by NCES under the headings mathematics and physical sciences.

Social sciences is the most popular category among undergraduates. Accounting for 21 percent of the baccalaureates and 20 percent of the doctorates awarded in the U.S., it comprises the following specific majors: for freshmen, anthropology, economics, history, political science (government, international relations), psychology, social work, sociology, and other social sciences; for degree-recipients, all fields listed by NCES under the aggregate headings of psychology, public affairs and services, and social sciences.

Biological sciences accounted for approximately 5 percent of all baccalaureates and 11 percent of all doctorates awarded in 1978–79. Holders of a doctorate in the biological sciences can generally get well-paying and prestigious positions in the public and the private sector. The category comprises the following specific majors: for freshmen, biology (general), biochemistry, biophysics, botany, zoology, other biological sciences; for degree recipients, all fields classified by NCES as biological sciences.

Business accounted for about 19 percent of all baccalaureates awarded in 1978–79, making it one of the most popular undergraduate fields. A major in business constitutes an entry to positions of leadership in American business and industry. The category comprises the following specific majors: for freshmen, accounting, business administration, and other business fields; for degree recipients and graduate enrollments, all fields classified by NCES as business and management.

Engineering, like business, provides an entry to leadership positions in business and industry. Accounting for 6.4 percent of all baccalaureates and 5.7 percent of all doctorates in 1978–79, it comprises the following specific majors: for freshmen, aeronautical, civil, chemical, electrical, industrial, mechanical, and other engineering fields; for degree recipients and graduate enrollments, all majors listed under engineering by NCES.

Law is not offered as an undergraduate major, yet it constitutes an important professional field that produces substantial proportions of graduates who have come to play an increasingly influential role in American society not only as attorneys but also as legislators, politicians, and judges.

Medicine, dentistry, and veterinary medicine are prestigious and highly paid professions. Of the first professional degrees awarded in this category in 1978–79, 65 percent were in medicine, 28 percent in dentistry, and 7 percent in veterinary medicine.

Data Sources

The information in this chapter was derived from several sources. Data on the major fields and career plans of entering college freshmen came from the Cooperative Institutional Research Program (CIRP), which annually surveys approximately 300,000 freshmen at a representative national sample of some 500 to 600 higher education institutions of all types. Data on baccalaureates, master's degrees, and doctorates awarded came from two publications of the U.S. Department of Health, Education, and Welfare—*Data on Earned Degrees Conferred from Institutions of Higher Education by Race, Ethnicity and Sex, Academic Year 1975–1976* and *Racial, Ethnic and Sex Enrollment Data from Institutions of Higher Education: Fall 1976* (1978a)—as well as from unpublished preliminary tabulations provided by the National Center for Education Statistics (NCES) on degrees earned in 1978–79. Data on the major field and career plans of high school students came from questionnaires administered by the American College Testing Program and the College Entrance Examination Board–Educational Testing Service—two organizations that conduct major college admissions tests.

Three caveats are in order. First, the NCES collects and reports data for the general category Hispanic rather than separately for Chicanos, Puerto Ricans, and other Hispanic groups. Therefore, we have made the simplifying assumption that 60 percent of the degrees and graduate enrollments in this category are accounted for by Chicanos, 15 percent by Puerto Ricans, and the remaining 25 percent by members of other Hispanic groups who are U.S. residents. (Note that degrees earned by nonresident aliens are excluded from the calculations.)

The second cautionary note concerns American Indians: Since the CIRP data and probably most of the NCES data rely on self-reports regarding race and ethnicity, it seems reasonable to conclude that the figures for American Indians are inflated, perhaps by as much as 100 percent. For a more detailed discussion of these problems, see the commission's report on American Indians (McNamara, 1982).

The final caution concerns the estimates of major field choices for entering freshmen. The only direct source of data is the CIRP annual freshman survey. While this sample survey is based on a complex institutional stratification design that includes separate cells for predominantly black colleges, the design does not otherwise control specifically for sampling errors in racial and ethnic enrollments. Estimates of such enrollments obtained from CIRP freshmen surveys have typically been smaller than the Bureau of the Census's estimates, although there is reason to believe that census estimates may be inflated.

Accordingly, the following procedures were used to obtain freshman estimates by field: The overall ethnic enrollments among 1971 entering freshmen were estimated to be as follows: Blacks, 9.3 percent; Chicanos, 2.2 percent; Puerto Ricans, 0.63 percent; and American Indians, 0.24 percent. These estimates were obtained by applying the percentages for college entry (Table 14) to the following percentages for the general population of persons aged eighteen to twenty-four: Blacks, 11.5 percent; Chicanos, 3.6 percent; Puerto Ricans, 0.9 percent; and American Indians, 0.5 percent. The resulting freshman enrollment percentages were allocated among the various major fields in proportion to the weighted percentages within each minority group choosing each field in the 1971 CIRP survey. For example, if Chicanos are assumed to account for 2.2 percent of all entering freshmen, and if 10 percent of the Chicanos in the CIRP choose a given field, then the percentage of entering freshmen accounted for by Chicanos choosing that field could be estimated as 0.10×2.2, or 0.22. In effect, this procedure assumes that the weighted freshman major field choices of Chicanos who participate in the CIRP are representative of the choices of all Chicano freshmen.

Minority Representation by Field

Table 15 shows the distribution of various racial or ethnic groups in each of the ten categories of major fields from the point of initial entry into postsecondary education (when, as freshmen, they indicated their probable major and career choice on the CIRP questionnaire) through baccalaureate completion and to the attainment of graduate degrees. Note that by comparing the CIRP data for the entering freshmen of 1971 with the figures for baccalaureate recipients, we can simulate a longitudinal study. In other words, if the percentage for a particular racial or ethnic group drops between 1971 and 1975–76, the implication is that members of that group have left the particular major field category during their undergraduate years. Conversely, any increase in percentage suggests that the field has experienced a net gain in members of a particular racial or ethnic group; such an increase further implies, of course, that these students have "defected" from some other major field (that is, they have changed from a probable major in, for instance, biological sciences to an actual major in, for instance, an allied health field). Similarly, the data for master's degrees and doctorates are from the 1978–79 academic year, permitting one to infer changes over time. Let us review each of the ten fields.

Table 15 shows that the allied health fields experienced a substantial loss of Blacks from initial entry (when Blacks constituted 10.8 percent of all freshmen naming a probable major in an allied health field) to baccalaureate completion (when Blacks constituted 5.1 percent of bachelor's degree recipients in such fields), and a somewhat smaller loss between the baccalaureate and the doctorate. (It should be pointed out, however, that very few doctorates are awarded in these fields.) The figures for Chicanos and Puerto Ricans, however, indicate smaller losses during the undergraduate years, and the results for American Indians show a gain. These latter patterns are repeated in many

Table 15. Distribution of Various Majors by Racial or Ethnic Groups

	Entering Freshmen, Fall 1971	Baccalaureate Recipients, 1975–76	Master's Recipients, 1978–79	Doctorate Recipients, 1978–79
Allied health		(N=53,498)	(N=12,022)	(N=496)
Whites	84.5	90.6	89.5	93.8
Blacks	10.8	5.1	5.3	3.1
Chicanos	2.1	1.4	1.4	0.3
Puerto Ricans	0.4	0.3	0.3	—
American Indians	0.2	0.3	0.4	0.3
Arts and humanities		(N=132,262)	(N=22,252)	(N=3,334)
Whites	88.6	90.8	91.9	92.5
Blacks	7.8	4.6	3.6	3.5
Chicanos	1.2	1.9	1.6	1.5
Puerto Ricans	0.5	0.5	0.4	0.4
American Indians	0.1	0.3	0.2	0.2
Education		(N=155,768)	(N=109,041)	(N=7,234)
Whites	83.8	87.0	86.2	87.5
Blacks	10.5	9.1	9.9	8.6
Chicanos	3.0	1.7	1.5	1.1
Puerto Ricans	0.7	0.4	0.4	0.3
American Indians	0.3	0.5	0.4	0.6
Physical Sciences and Mathematics		(N=36,407)	(N=7,284)	(N=3,185)
Whites	90.4	92.0	92.3	92.2
Blacks	6.1	4.0	2.2	1.9
Chicanos	0.7	1.2	0.8	0.6
Puerto Ricans	0.2	0.3	0.2	0.6
American Indians	0.1	0.3	0.5	0.3
Social Sciences		(N=207,738)	(N=38,809)	(N=5,854)
Whites	81.0	86.7	86.6	91.4
Blacks	13.9	8.4	8.4	4.7
Chicanos	2.1	2.0	1.8	1.1
Puerto Ricans	1.0	0.5	0.5	0.3
American Indians	0.2	0.4	0.4	0.5

Table 15. Continued

	Entering Freshmen, Fall 1971	Baccalaureate Recipients, 1975–76	Graduate Enrollments, Fall 1976	Master's Recipients, 1978–79	Doctorate Recipients, 1978–79
Biological Sciences		(N=53,797)	(N=39,520)	(N=6,415)	(N=3,205)
Whites	89.3	90.4	92.6	91.4	93.3
Blacks	6.9	4.3	2.8	3.4	1.5
Chicanos	0.8	1.7	0.9	1.1	0.6
Puerto Ricans	0.7	0.4	0.2	0.3	0.2
American Indians	0.3	0.3	0.3	0.2	0.2
Business		(N=141,040)	(N=137,735)	(N=45,976)	(N=700)
Whites	82.4	88.8	91.3	90.7	94.6
Blacks	12.9	6.7	4.4	4.7	2.6
Chicanos	2.2	1.7	1.0	1.0	0.4
Puerto Ricans	0.4	0.4	0.2	0.2	0.1
American Indians	0.3	0.3	0.3	0.3	0.4
Engineering		(N=42,688)	(N=44,514)	(N=11,417)	(N=1,635)
Whites	87.9	91.3	90.4	88.3	85.8
Blacks	6.0	3.2	1.9	2.2	1.5
Chicanos	2.5	1.7	1.1	1.1	0.8
Puerto Ricans	0.7	0.4	0.3	0.3	0.2
American Indians	0.4	0.4	0.2	0.2	0.1

	Entering Freshmen, 1971	Professional Enrollments, Fall 1976	Professional Degree Recipients, 1975–76
Law		(N=116,066)	(N=35,254)
Whites	83.7	91.0	91.8
Blacks	10.2	4.6	4.3
Chicanos	2.0	1.7	1.5
Puerto Ricans	0.8	0.4	0.4
American Indians	0.3	0.4	0.3
Medicine, dentistry, and veterinary medicine		(N=83,601)	(N=21,978)
Whites	88.1	89.2	89.8
Blacks	6.7	5.3	4.5
Chicanos	1.0	1.7	1.7
Puerto Ricans	0.7	0.4	0.4
American Indians	0.3	0.5	0.3

Notes. Percentages in each cell do not total 100 because the categories Asians, other Hispanics, and other have been omitted. Percentages for Chicanos and Puerto Ricans are based on their representing 60 percent and 15 percent, respectively, of all Hispanic degree recipients.

Sources. Cooperative Institutional Research Program data tapes for 1971 freshmen; U.S. Department of Health, Education and Welfare (1978a, 1978b).

of the subsequent tables, suggesting that results for the three smaller minority groups should be interpreted cautiously, with the following points in mind:

- Since Chicanos, Puerto Ricans, and American Indians each account for a relatively small fraction of the total student population at any point, the figures are subject to much more error than are the figures for Blacks and Whites.
- There is reason to believe that our estimates of the numbers of Puerto Ricans and Chicanos, based on NCES data, are somewhat inflated, especially at the postgraduate levels. (See Chapter One and Appendix A on limitations of the data.)
- There is reason to believe that NCES figures on American Indians may be highly inflated, primarily because of the methods used by reporting institutions to identify members of this group. (Again, see Chapter One and Appendix A.)

The findings for arts and humanities majors also show a substantial drop for Blacks between college entry (7.8 percent), baccalaureate completion (4.6 percent), and doctorate completion (3.5 percent). The proportions of Chicanos and Puerto Ricans remain fairly stable at the various degree levels (reflecting in part the inclusion of foreign language majors in this category), while American Indians again show increases from initial college entry.

The pattern of results for the field of education differs considerably from the pattern for previous fields in that the proportion of Blacks shows only a small drop from college entry (10.5 percent) to baccalaureate (9.1 percent), and then shows an *increase* at the master's level (9.9 percent). There is then only a small drop-off at the doctorate level (to 8.6 percent). Clearly, education is a popular choice among Blacks at all degree levels; in fact, their representation among advanced-degree recipients is not too much lower than their representation in the population at large (11.5 percent). Both Hispanics and American Indians either maintain their representation or show increases between the baccalaureate and the graduate degrees.

In the physical science and mathematics fields, Blacks are, relative to their representation among entering freshmen, underrepresented among freshmen planning to major in physical sciences or mathematics by about 40 percent. Similarly, there are only half as many Blacks among doctorate recipients (1.9 percent) as among baccalaureate recipients (4.0 percent) in these fields. Although Hispanics are not significantly underrepresented among baccalaureate recipients, their proportion among doctorate recipients decreases from the baccalaureate level (by half among Chicanos and by one third among Puerto Ricans).

The social sciences is a category especially popular among Blacks, who constitute 13.9 percent of the freshmen planning to major in the social sciences. This overrepresentation disappears at the baccalaureate and master's degree levels and drops still more at the doctorate level. There is a similar decline between college entry and the doctorate level for Hispanics. American Indians, by contrast, show substantial increases at each higher point in the social science field.

Our data on the distribution of biological science majors includes figures for graduate *enrollments* in fall 1976. (NCES reports these data only for selected major fields.) By comparing these graduate enrollment figures with the figures for baccalaureate recipients, one can get some sense of the attrition that occurs at the critical transition point between college and graduate school. Since graduate enrollments include both those students who aspire to a doctorate and those who aspire only to a master's degree, it is not surprising that the figure for graduate enrollments is larger than the figures for either of these graduate degrees. That it is four times larger than the combined total of master's degree and doctorate recipients results from two factors: the average length of time spent by graduate students to obtain graduate degrees and attrition from graduate school.

Blacks show consistent drops in representation among biological science majors from college entry (6.9 percent) to baccalaureate completion (4.3 percent), master's completion (3.4 percent), and doctorate completion (1.5 percent). A similar pattern of loss between the baccalaureate and the graduate degrees occurs for Chicanos and Puerto Ricans.

Among business majors, the representation of Blacks drops sharply between college entry (12.9 percent) and baccalaureate completion (6.7 percent), decreases further among graduate school enrollments (4.4 percent), and drops still further at the doctorate level (2.6 percent). (It should be pointed out that, as is the case with allied health fields, relatively few doctorates are awarded in business.) The representation of Hispanics among business majors also declines at each successive level. The proportion of American Indians actually increases slightly between the baccalaureate (0.3 percent) and the doctorate (0.4 percent), although of the 700 doctorates in business awarded in 1978–79, only three went to people identifying themselves as American Indians.

In the engineering fields all minority groups are drastically underrepresented. For instance, Blacks constitute 9.3 percent of the entering freshman class but only 6.0 percent of the freshmen naming engineering as their probable major field. Between the baccalaureate and the master's degree, this underrepresentation increases by about one third (from 3.2 percent to 2.2 percent), and proportionately there are fewer than half as many blacks among doctorate recipients (1.2 percent) as among baccalaureate recipients. A similar decline in representation from college entry to the doctor's degree is found among Hispanics and American Indians.

The racial and ethnic composition of the group of freshmen who name prelaw as their probable major field is roughly the same as the racial composition of the entire entering freshman class. The proportions of Blacks and Puerto Ricans enrolling in law school show a decline of about 50 percent; for Chicanos and American Indians, the proportions among law school enrollments are about the same as their proportions among freshmen planning to major in a prelaw curriculum, but (as pointed out earlier) these figures should be accepted with caution. Perhaps most interesting is that the racial composition of the class receiving law degrees in 1978–79 is very similar to the racial composition of law school enrollments in the fall of 1976, suggesting that minority students are only slightly more likely than white students to drop out of law schools. This conclusion is consistent with data reported in Chapter 2 (Table 13), which show minority attrition rates from law school to be 22.6 percent, compared to 14.9 percent for Whites.

Although the proportion of Blacks among freshmen planning to major in premedical curricula (6.7 percent) is slightly higher than their proportion among medical school enrollments (5.3 percent), the drop is not as great as might be expected, given the extreme selectivity of medical schools. Hispanics and American Indians are even better represented among professional enrollments than among freshmen choosing a premedical major. These results suggest that recent efforts of medical schools to recruit minority students have, to some degree, been successful. The proportion of Blacks receiving a medical degree decreases by about 15 percent from their professional enrollments; the proportion of American Indians decreases by 40 percent; but Hispanics are as well represented among medical degree recipients as among professional enrollments. Thus, attrition from medical, dental, and veterinary schools seems to be higher for Blacks and American Indians than for Whites and Hispanics. This assumption is consistent with data reported in Chapter 2 (Table 13), with the exception that Puerto Ricans were also found to have higher attrition rates than Whites or Chicanos.

In summary, these results indicate that the degree of minority underrepresentation differs substantially by field. Thus, Blacks are severely underrepresented in the biological sciences, the physical sciences and mathematics, and engineering and somewhat underrepresented in the arts and humanities and medicine. Relatively few black freshmen plan to major in these fields or in arts and humanities or premedicine. Underrepresentation of Blacks becomes severe at the doctoral level in nearly all fields, and particularly in mathematics, natural sciences, and engineering. In contrast, Blacks are fairly well represented in education (especially at the doctorate level) and the social sciences, and a reasonably large proportion receive degrees in law and in the medical professions.

Although the data must be treated cautiously because of the relatively small numbers involved, Chicanos seem to be most underrepresented, at the freshman level, in arts and humanities,

Table 16. Percentage of Each Racial or Ethnic Group Enrolled
in Various Majors

	Entering Freshmen, Fall 1971	Baccalaureate Recipients, 1975–76	Master's Recipients, 1978–79	Doctorate Recipients, 1978–79
Allied health				
Whites	9.6	6.0	5.4	2.3
Blacks	11.2	4.6	4.1	1.6
Chicanos	9.2	4.8	5.2	0.9
Puerto Ricans	6.2	4.8	5.2	0.9
American Indians	9.6	4.7	5.9	1.9
Arts and humanities				
Whites	13.6	14.8	8.2	11.8
Blacks	11.5	10.3	4.1	9.1
Chicanos	12.1	16.3	8.9	17.9
Puerto Ricans	11.0	16.3	8.9	17.9
American Indians	7.6	12.1	5.4	6.7
Education				
Whites	9.9	16.7	37.7	24.2
Blacks	11.2	24.0	55.8	49.3
Chicanos	13.7	17.0	43.3	30.0
Puerto Ricans	10.3	17.0	43.3	30.0
American Indians	11.3	21.2	45.1	41.3
Physical Sciences and Mathematics				
Whites	5.1	4.1	2.7	11.2
Blacks	3.3	2.4	0.8	4.8
Chicanos	1.7	2.7	1.6	6.8
Puerto Ricans	2.0	2.7	1.6	6.8
American Indians	2.3	3.3	3.7	7.7
Social Sciences				
Whites	13.3	22.2	13.5	20.5
Blacks	19.9	29.6	16.8	21.6
Chicanos	12.8	26.5	18.1	23.0
Puerto Ricans	20.1	26.5	18.1	23.0
American Indians	12.3	25.3	14.6	28.8

biological sciences, premedicine, and physical sciences. Puerto Rican freshmen are most underrepresented in allied health fields, business, and physical sciences. In contrast, Hispanics are fairly well represented among those receiving doctorates in arts and humanities, education, and the social sciences and among those receiving degrees in law or the medical professions. Although data on American Indians are even less reliable than those for Hispanics, the evidence indicates that, relative to their

Table 16. Continued

	Entering Freshmen, Fall 1971	Baccalaureate Recipients, 1975–76	Graduate Enrollments, Fall 1976	Master's Recipients, 1978–79	Doctorate Recipients, 1978–79
Biological Sciences					
Whites	3.5	6.0	4.0	2.4	11.4
Blacks	2.6	3.9	1.7	1.1	3.7
Chicanos	1.3	5.7	2.5	1.8	7.5
Puerto Ricans	4.2	5.7	2.5	1.8	7.5
American Indians	4.5	4.1	3.0	1.6	5.8
Business					
Whites	11.5	15.4	13.9	16.7	2.5
Blacks	15.6	16.1	9.3	11.1	1.4
Chicanos	11.5	15.2	9.2	11.6	1.1
Puerto Ricans	7.0	15.2	9.2	11.6	1.1
American Indians	11.0	12.2	9.4	13.5	2.9
Engineering					
Whites	7.1	4.8	4.4	4.0	5.4
Blacks	4.6	2.3	1.3	1.3	2.0
Chicanos	8.0	4.7	3.3	3.3	4.9
Puerto Ricans	8.1	4.7	3.3	3.3	4.9
American Indians	11.0	4.3	2.7	2.4	1.9

Sources. Cooperative Institutional Research Program data tapes for 1971 freshmen; U.S. Department of Health, Education and Welfare (1978a, 1978b).

representation among baccalaureate recipients, American Indians are substantially underrepresented in arts and humanities, biological sciences, and engineering.

Major Field Preferences of Minorities

Table 15 focuses on the distribution of various racial and ethnic groups in each of ten categories of major fields at various levels. Note that a given minority group may be underrepresented in a particular field at a particular transition point either because the total number of that group surviving to that particular point is small or because the predilection of that particular minority group for a particular field is weak or for both these reasons. (The percentage of different minority groups who reach various points in the higher educational system was documented in Chapter Two.) We now examine a second aspect of underrepresentation by field: the predilection of a given minority group to choose some fields and to avoid others. Table 16 shows the proportions of students from each racial or ethnic group in each of eight categories of major fields at different points. (Since law and medicine attract students from a wide variety of undergraduate majors, results for these two fields are not reported.)

Table 16 shows that the allied health fields are especially popular among Black freshmen, with more than one in ten saying they plan to major in an allied health field. By baccalaureate completion, the proportion of Blacks drops to 4.6 percent, and only 1.6 percent of Black doctorate recipients get a degree in allied health. Similar declines occur for the other ethnic groups in this field. One factor contributing to the decline at each higher level may be that some allied health programs are shorter than the traditional four-year college program, with a certificate or an associate degree being appropriate and sufficient for an entry-level position.

Regarding the arts and humanities, both Blacks and American Indians are less likely than are other racial or ethnic groups to plan to major in or to receive degrees in these fields. Thus, their underrepresentation among doctorate recipients in arts and humanities is in part a function of the low popularity of these fields among these two minorities. That relatively large proportions of Hispanics get bachelor's and advanced degrees in arts and humanities is probably attributable to the inclusion of foreign languages in this major field category.

As a freshman choice, education is more popular among minorities (especially Chicanos) than among Whites, and its popularity relative to other fields increases through the baccalaureate and up to the master's degree for all racial or ethnic groups. Among degree recipients at all levels, however, education is more popular among Blacks and American Indians than among other groups. Indeed, close to half (49.3 percent) of the doctorates earned by Blacks are in the field of education. Education is also more popular as a graduate field among Hispanics and American Indians than among Whites, though not to the same extent as is true for Blacks. These findings make it clear that the severe underrepresentation of minorities in most doctoral fields is exacerbated by their concentration in education.

All four of the minority groups under consideration manifest an aversion to the physical sciences and mathematics, and this tendency continues through all degree levels, being especially severe among Blacks. Proportionally, fewer than half as many Blacks as Whites get master's or doctoral degrees in these fields.

Both Blacks and Puerto Ricans show a strong predilection for the social sciences as entering freshmen. Blacks are somewhat more inclined than are other minorities to get the baccalaureate in these fields, but this tendency becomes less marked by the doctorate level. American Indians, in contrast, though less likely as freshmen than any other racial or ethnic group to name the social sciences as their probable major, are more likely than any other to receive a doctorate in a social science.

Majors in the biological sciences are relatively unpopular among Blacks all at levels, particularly at the graduate level. Thus, the proportion of Whites receiving doctorates in these fields is almost three times as great (11.4 percent) as the proportion of Blacks (3.7 percent). Hispanics are about as inclined as Whites to get baccalaureates in biological sciences, but the popularity of these fields among Hispanics drops off at the graduate level. American Indians also appear to avoid biological science majors, especially at the doctoral level.

As entering freshmen, Blacks seem especially attracted to business majors, whereas Puerto Ricans show the least interest in these fields. At the baccalaureate level, however, business seems an equally popular choice for all racial or ethnic groups. At the master's level (which is somewhat more meaningful than the doctoral level in this field, since the M.B.A. has become an increasingly useful degree for some entry-level positions in business), American Indians seem more inclined than do other minority groups to get degrees in business.

Among entering freshmen, American Indians are markedly more likely than other racial or ethnic groups to name engineering as their probable major, and Blacks are markedly less so. At the baccalaureate level, engineering sinks even lower in popularity among blacks, whereas the proportions of other groups who receive bachelor's degrees in engineering fields are roughly the same (4–5 percent). The popularity of engineering relative to other fields remains about the same at the graduate level for all groups except American Indians; only 1.9 percent of the American Indian doctorate recipients, compared with 4.9 percent of Hispanic doctorate recipients, receive a degree in engineering.

In summary, the following conclusions are suggested by the data in Table 16:

- As entering freshmen, Blacks show a strong preference for majors in social science, business, education, and allied health; they have little inclination to major in biological sciences, engineering, or the physical sciences and mathematics. Their preference for education persists through the baccalaureate and graduate degree levels. They are less likely than others to get baccalaureates or doctorates in arts and humanities, and they continue to avoid the biological sciences, engineering, and physical sciences and mathematics.
- As entering freshmen, Chicanos are more likely than other minorities to prefer arts and humanities and education as probable majors; their choice of arts and humanities persists through the doctorate. Relatively few Chicano freshmen name the biological or physical sciences as their probable major.
- As entering freshmen, Puerto Ricans are somewhat more likely than others to be attracted to the social sciences; they also prefer education and arts and humanities as probable majors. Relatively few name probable majors in allied health, business, biological sciences, or physical sciences.
- Although the data must be regarded as no more than suggestive, American Indians appear to prefer education and social sciences and to avoid arts and humanities, biological science, and physical science and mathematics. Although as freshmen they seem attracted to engineering fields, their tendency to get baccalaureates in this field is no higher than average, and they are less likely than others to get a doctorate in engineering.
- Taken together, these findings suggest that virtually all four of the minority groups under consideration avoid the biological sciences, engineering, and the physical sciences and mathematics.

Considering the substantial underrepresentation of minorities with graduate degrees in arts and humanities, natural sciences, and engineering, it is not surprising that they are also underrepresented among employed scientists and engineers and among employed college teachers. For instance, a recent report from the National Research Council (Maxfield, 1980) indicates that only 1.1 percent of doctoral scientists and engineers are Black, 0.8 percent are Hispanic, and 0.3 percent are American Indians. Similarly, the American Council on Education (1973) reports the following analysis of teaching faculty in 1973: Whites, 94.8 percent; Blacks, 2.9 percent; American Indians, 0.8 percent; Chicanos, 0.3 percent; Puerto Ricans, 0.3 percent.

The Role of Academic Preparation

Of the many possible explanations for the tendency of minorities to choose some fields and to avoid others, one explanation that merits attention concerns the level of preparation required by different fields: Could it be that minority-group members, because they often have poor academic preparation, opt for major fields of study that are relatively undemanding?

To examine this hypothesis we analyzed data on a large national sample of students who, in their senior year of high school in 1974–75, took college admissions tests (the SAT or the ACT) and, at the same time, completed a questionnaire on which they indicated their probable major field of study in college. The analyses reported in this section are intended to answer three questions: (1) Do students planning to major in different fields of study in college differ significantly in their level of academic preparation, as measured by scores on college admissions tests? (2) If so, are these patterns of differences the same for minority students as for white students? (3) Do minority students in secondary school tend to prefer those major fields that attract students with relatively poor preparation and to avoid those fields that attract students who are relatively well prepared?

The first five columns of Table 17 show the number of high school seniors, by racial or ethnic group, naming each of eight categories of fields as their probable college major. The

Table 17. College Admission Test Scores of High School Seniors, by Racial or Ethnic Group and Anticipated Major in College

	Number of Students					Mean Composite SAT (Rank)				
	Whites	Blacks	Chicanos	Puerto Ricans	American Indians	Whites	Blacks	Chicanos	Puerto Ricans	American Indians
Physical sciences and mathematics	6,670	365	61	37	22	1,142 (1)	845 (2)	1,016 (2)	915 (2)	979 (1)
Engineering	11,160	706	95	73	36	1,109 (2)	848 (1)	1,018 (1)	918 (1)	969 (2)
Biological sciences	11,150	888	123	70	41	1,066 (3)	807 (3)	921 (3)	897 (3)	855 (3)
Social sciences	14,630	1,967	201	107	48	1,029 (4)	735 (4)	866 (4)	796 (7)	839 (5)
Allied health fields	13,440	1,499	142	84	56	958 (5)	710 (6)	846 (5)	800 (6)	868 (4)
Business	16,370	2,016	159	66	68	950 (6)	695 (7)	807 (7)	814 (5)	798 (7)
Arts and humanities	14,770	1,369	115	58	47	930 (7)	732 (5)	845 (6)	831 (4)	808 (6)
Education	10,220	1,488	123	54	59	884 (8)	632 (8)	751 (8)	738 (8)	755 (8)
Total	98,410	10,298	1,019	549	377					

Note. ACT composite scores have been converted to SAT equivalents following Astin, Christian, and Henson (1977).
Sources. Astin, Christian, and Henson (1975); unpublished data provided by the College Entrance Examination Board–Educational Testing Service and the American College Testing Program.

second five columns show the mean SAT composite (verbal plus mathematical) scores of each of the five racial or ethnic groups choosing each of the eight field categories. (Medicine and law are not included, since they draw students from a variety of undergraduate majors.) The eight field categories are ranked from 1 to 8 for each racial or ethnic group, according to the mean SAT scores of Whites naming these fields. Note that these mean differences are not trivial: Whites in the first-ranked field (physical sciences and mathematics) have mean scores more than 250 points higher than those of Whites in the lowest-ranked field (education). Since the standard deviation of the SAT composite score is approximately 125 points, the mean scores in the highest and lowest fields are *more than two* standard deviations apart. (This means that only about 2 percent of the education majors score as well as the *average* student in physical science or mathematics.) Differences between the highest-ranked and the lowest-ranked fields are almost as large for each of the four minority groups.

More important, the ranking of the eight categories of majors is almost the same for the five racial or ethnic groups: The engineering category and the physical sciences and mathematics category rank either first or second, the biological sciences category ranks third, and education ranks at the bottom for all five groups.

To explore whether minority preferences for various majors observed during the undergraduate and graduate years are already present during the high school years, we calculated the proportion of each of the five groups expressing, as high school seniors, a preference for each of the eight categories of majors (Table 18). The last four columns of Table 18 show the relative degree of over- or underrepresentation for each of the four minority groups. Except for Puerto Ricans, minority high school seniors manifest a preference for education and a tendency to avoid engineering and the physical sciences and mathematics.

Moreover, if we look at the distribution of each racial or ethnic group (as indicated in Table 18 and the first five columns of Table 17) among major field choices, we find confirmation of the patterns reported in Tables 15 and 16. Those fields with the

Table 18. Major Field Preferences During the Senior Year in High School, by Racial or Ethnic Group

Proposed College Major Field	Rank in Composite SAT Among Whites	Percentage Preferring Field					Percentage Overrepresentation (+) or Underrepresentation (−) Relative to Whites Among			
		Whites	Blacks	Chicanos	Puerto Ricans	American Indians	Blacks	Chicanos	Puerto Ricans	American Indians
Physical sciences and mathematics	1	6.8	3.5	6.0	6.7	5.8	−49	−12	−3	−15
Engineering	2	11.3	6.9	9.3	13.3	9.5	−39	−18	+18	−16
Biological sciences	3	11.1	8.6	12.1	12.8	10.9	−24	+7	+13	−4
Social sciences	4	14.9	19.1	19.7	19.5	12.7	+28	+32	+31	−15
Allied health fields	5	13.7	14.6	13.9	15.3	14.9	+7	+1	+12	+9
Business	6	16.6	19.6	15.6	12.0	18.0	+18	−6	−28	+8
Arts and humanities	7	15.0	13.3	11.3	10.6	12.5	−11	−25	−29	−17
Education	8	10.4	14.4	12.0	9.8	15.6	+38	+15	−6	+50

highest SAT scores (physical sciences and mathematics, engineering) are the same ones in which minorities are most severely underrepresented, whereas the field with the lowest SAT score (education) is the one in which minorities are least likely to be underrepresented.

Perhaps the major exceptions to these patterns of academic preparation occur in the case of the social sciences and the arts and humanities. Although social sciences rank fourth among the eight fields in mean SAT composite scores, three of the four minority groups show substantial *over*representation in terms of their preference for social sciences. However, all four minority groups tend to avoid arts and humanities, even though this field category ranks next to the bottom in terms of the mean SAT composite scores of Whites. Given that the social sciences may represent a means for dealing with many of the social problems that confront minorities, this strong predilection of minority high school seniors toward the social sciences is perhaps understandable, but their reasons for avoiding the arts and humanities are not immediately apparent.

These results seem to warrant the following conclusions:

- High school students who are planning on different major fields in college differ substantially in their levels of academic preparation, as reflected in college admission test scores. Specifically, students with the highest scores, regardless of race or ethnicity, tend to prefer majors in the natural sciences, engineering, and mathematics. Students with the lowest test scores, in contrast, are strongly oriented toward education and, to a lesser extent, business and the arts and humanities.
- With the possible exception of Puerto Ricans, minority students during their senior year in high school already show a strong preference for an education major and a tendency to avoid majors in the physical sciences and mathematics and in engineering.
- The relative overrepresentation of minorities in education and their underrepresentation in the natural sciences, engineering, and mathematics during the undergraduate and graduate years appear in part to be attributable to their

relatively poor academic preparation at the secondary school level.

Summary

Our analyses show clearly that minority underrepresentation at various levels of postsecondary education is not uniform across fields. Perhaps the best way to summarize the findings shown in Tables 15 and 16 is to indicate those points in the higher education system at which there is a relative loss of minority representation in particular fields. Table 19 summarizes these results in terms of the percentage gain or loss in the relative representation of each minority group relative to their representation in the college-age population. For example, Blacks account for 5.1 percent of the baccalaureate recipients in allied health fields (Table 15), as compared to 11.5 percent of the college-age population. This underrepresentation of all bachelor's recipients in allied health is thus 56 percent $(100 - 100 \ [5.1/11.5])$. In almost all categories in Table 19 minorities are underrepresented. Moreover, the extent of underrepresentation is substantial in almost all fields. For example, if underrepresentation is 50 percent, the percentage of minority students in a given field would have to *double* in order to yield proportionate representation; underrepresentation of 75 percent means that the percentage would have to *triple* to yield proportionate representation. As would be expected, the percentage of underrepresentation tends to get larger at each higher level of attainment; no doubt such trends reflect the relatively high dropout rates of minority undergraduates and graduate students. The only exceptions to this trend occur in the case of American Indians, although it must be remembered that the figures for bachelor's and doctor's recipients among American Indians are probably exaggerated.

The results in Table 19 and in previous tables warrant the following conclusions:

- Among entering college freshmen, minorities are substantially underrepresented in all fields of study except the social sciences, education, and allied health (Blacks only) and business (Blacks only).

Table 19. Minority Overrepresentation (+) or Underrepresentation (−) at Three Transition Points, by Field of Study

	Blacks			Hispanics			American Indians		
Field	Entering Freshmen	Baccalaureate Recipients	Doctorate Recipients	Entering Freshmen	Baccalaureate Recipients	Doctorate Recipients	Entering Freshmen	Baccalaureate Recipients	Doctorate Recipients
Allied health	− 6	−56	−73	−42[a] −55[b]	−61	−92	−52	−40	−40
Arts and humanities	−32	−60	−70	−46[a] −43[b]	−47	−58	−74	−40	−60
Biological sciences	−40	−63	−87	−77[a] −17[b]	−53	−83	−37	−40	−60
Business	+12	−42	−77	−39[a] −57[b]	−53	−89	−44	−60	−40
Education	− 9	−21	−25	−16[a] −27[b]	−53	−69	−45	00	+20
Engineering	−48	−72	−87	−31[a] −20[b]	−53	−77	−25	−20	−80
Law	−11		−63[c]	−44[a] −11[b]		−58[c]	−40[c]		−40[c]
Medicine and dentistry	−11		−61[c]	−72[a] −22[b]		−53[c]	−40[c]		−40[c]
Physical sciences and mathematics	−47	−65	−83	−80[a] −73[b]	−67	−73	−78	−40	−40
Social sciences	+21	−27	−59	−14[a] + 6[b]	−44	−69	−56	−20	00
All students	−19	−43	−64	−39[a] −30[b]	−52	−76	−52	−24	−40

Note. Over- and underrepresentation are determined by comparing each percentage from Table 15 with the percentage of minorities in the college-age population.
[a] Chicanos.
[b] Puerto Ricans.
[c] Denotes the first professional degree.

- Underrepresentation increases at each higher level of education such that all minorities are substantially underrepresented in almost all fields at both the bachelor's and doctor's levels. (The only possible exceptions to this generalization are education and the social sciences, where Blacks seem to be only slightly underrepresented and where American Indians do not appear to be underrepresented.)
- Underrepresentation is most severe at all levels in engineering, biological sciences, and physical sciences and mathematics. To achieve proportionate representation in these fields at the doctorate level, the number of minorities receiving doctorates would have to increase by between 300 and 600 percent.
- Among minorities receiving doctorates and advanced professional degrees in fields other than education, underrepresentation is least severe in the social sciences, law, and medicine. Proportionate representation in these fields would be achieved if the number of minority degree recipients doubled.
- Minority underrepresentation in general, and in particular in the natural sciences, engineering, and mathematics, appears to originate in part in the relatively low levels of academic preparation among all minority groups at the precollegiate level.

4

Recent Developments in the Educational Pipeline

At the turn of the century, only a handful of Blacks were enrolled in higher education institutions; by 1910, the number was still under 1,000 (Crossland, 1971). During the next forty years, however, the number of Blacks attending the nation's colleges and universities increased more than a hundredfold: By 1950, approximately 100,000 Blacks were enrolled in higher education. Crossland attributes these dramatic changes to the decline in illiteracy among Blacks, which fell from 81 percent in 1870 to 16 percent by 1930. The continuing growth of black and other minority enrollments since 1950 is probably accounted for in large part by the Supreme Court's rejection of the "separate but equal" doctrine in the 1954 *Brown* decision and by the civil rights movement of the late 1950s and 1960s.

As Chapters Two and Three indicate, however, minority underrepresentation increases at each higher level of postsecondary education and is especially severe in the sciences and engineering (see also Brown and Stent, 1977; Olivas, 1979). Nonetheless, the last two decades have witnessed dramatic increases in the number of minority students at all levels of higher education and in virtually all fields (Blake, 1980; Carter and Segura, 1979; Mingle, 1978; Preer, 1981; Smartt, 1980). In this chapter we document these trends. We focus on trends since 1960 for two reasons: First, most of the major social programs intended to increase minority enrollments were instituted after 1960; and, second, data on minority enrollments prior to 1960 are sparse. We first discuss trends in minority representation at different levels of higher education and then we discuss trends in minority representation by field.

Trends by Educational Level

In this section, we look at recent trends in high school completion, college entry, college completion, and doctorate attainment. Since data on American Indians and Hispanic groups were generally not collected or reported before the early 1970s, statistics for the 1960s are necessarily limited to Blacks and Whites.

High School Completion. Table 20 shows trends between 1970 and 1977 in the high school dropout rates of Whites and Blacks. While Whites became increasingly likely to drop out of high school, the pattern for Blacks is strikingly different: Dropout rates decreased substantially, to the point that among sixteen- and seventeen-year-olds in 1977, the rate for Blacks was lower than the rate for Whites. Among eighteen- and nineteen-year-olds, however, the dropout rate for Blacks was still substantially higher in 1977 than that for Whites (by 6 percentage points), even though the gap narrowed considerably since 1970 (when it was 17 percentage points).

College Entry. Table 21 shows trends since 1960 in the rate of college entry among the traditional college-age population. For the total population, these rates rose between 1960 and 1970 and then declined slightly. But just as the high school dropout rates among Blacks have decreased in recent years, so their college enrollment rates have risen sharply: Between 1960 and

Table 20. Trends in High School Dropout Rates, 1970–1977

	Percentage of High School Dropouts Among					
	Whites			Blacks		
Age	1970	1977	Percentage of Change	1970	1977	Percentage of Change
16 and 17	7.3	8.8	+20	12.8	7.6	−41
18 and 19	14.1	15.9	+13	31.2	21.9	−30
20 and 21	14.6	14.5	− 1	29.6	24.5	−17

Note. Dropouts are those persons not enrolled in school who are not high school graduates.

Source. U.S. Bureau of the Census, *1970 Census of the Population,* PC(1)-D1; *Current Population Reports,* Series P-20.

1970, the proportion of eighteen- to twenty-four-year-old Blacks attending college more than doubled; between 1960 and 1977, it tripled. Among Hispanics in this age group, in contrast, the proportion enrolling in college dropped slightly between 1970 and 1977.

How have these trends affected the racial and ethnic composition of entering freshman classes? To explore this question, we examined data from fifteen consecutive years of the Cooperative Institutional Research Program (CIRP), which annually surveys first-time, full-time freshmen. Since the CIRP survey is based on a stratified sampling of institutions, and since the composition of the institutional sample changes slightly from year to year, institutional sampling errors represent a source of

Table 21. Trends in College Enrollment Rates
of Eighteen- to Twenty-four-Year-Olds, 1960–1977

Group	Percentage of Group Enrolled in			Percentage of Change	
	1960	1970	1977	1960–1977	1970–1977
Blacks	7.0	15.5	21.1	+201	+36
Hispanics	NA	18.9	17.0	NA	−10
Total Population	21.9	26.9	26.1	+ 19	− 3

Source. U.S. Bureau of the Census, *1970 Census of the Population,* PC(1)-D1; *Current Population Reports,* Series P-20, Nos. 110, 222, and 321; Series P-23, No. 80.

possible random variation from year to year. To obtain a more consistent picture of trends over the fifteen years, we computed a three-year moving average for each enrollment group. The figure for the 1974 freshman class, for example, is an average of the figures for the 1973, 1974, and 1975 entering classes. (Since the first five years of the survey did not include separate figures for Chicanos and Puerto Ricans, data for these two groups are available only from 1971 on.)

The representation of Blacks among entering college freshmen increased substantially between 1966 and 1976, from 5.0 percent to 8.7 percent, a 74 percent increase (see Table 22). Sedlacek and Pelham (1976) report similar trends during the early 1970s in their analysis of black enrollments at 110 large universities. Since 1976, however, the figures have remained fairly stable. A similar pattern emerges for Chicanos: A small but fairly steady increase from 1971 to 1976, and increased represen-

Table 22. Trends in First-Time, Full-Time Freshmen Enrollments, 1966–1980 (Three-Year Moving Averages)

| | Percentage of Freshman Class | | | |
Year	Blacks	Chicanos	Puerto Ricans	American Indians
1966	5.0			.6
1967	5.0			.7
1968	5.4			.6
1969	5.9			.5
1970[a]	6.2			.6
1971	7.5	1.1	.2	1.0
1972	7.6	1.3	.4	1.0
1973	8.0	1.4	.5	1.0
1974	8.1	1.5	.6	.9
1975	8.3	1.6	.6	.9
1976	8.7	1.6	.7	.9
1977	8.4	1.4	.8	.8
1978	8.7	1.2	.9	.9
1979	8.8	1.4	.9	.9
1980	9.2	1.7	.9	.9

Note. Figures for the first year (1966) and last year (1980) are based on only one year; all others are based on three years.

[a]Because of errors in the original 1970 weights, the 1970 figures represent an average of 1969 and 1971.

Source. Cooperative Institutional Research Program (1966–1980).

tation with some up-and-down variation from 1976 through 1980. For Puerto Ricans, the steady increase continued to 1977; then the figure levels off at 0.9 percent. The proportion of American Indians among entering freshmen increased between 1966 and 1971 but has changed very little during the past ten years. (The figures for American Indians are probably inflated; see Chapter One and Appendix A.)

Considering the expansion in college enrollments between the mid 1960s and the mid 1970s, the increase in the representation of all four minorities during the same period is all the more remarkable: Minorities have come to account for a larger proportion of an expanding population. Nevertheless, it should be added that virtually no further progress has been made during the past five or six years.

College Completion. As Table 23 indicates, college completion rates for the total population aged twenty-five to twenty-nine (the average member of which would have been out of college for six or seven years) have increased dramatically during the last four decades, reflecting the tremendous expansion of American higher education, especially during the 1950s and 1960s. The increase was even more marked for Blacks than for the total age group, at least up until 1975. Thus, in 1960, the college completion rate of Blacks was only half that of the total population; in 1978, it was two thirds of that for the total age group.

In 1976 the National Center for Education Statistics (NCES) began collecting data on the race and ethnicity of degree recipients. By comparing the results of the 1976 and the 1979 surveys, one gets some sense of recent short-term trends in minority representation among baccalaureate holders. As Table

Table 23. Trends in College Completion Rates Among
Twenty-five–to–Twenty-nine–Year-Olds, 1940–1978

| | | | Year | | | | Percentage of Change | |
| | | | | | | | 1960– | 1970– |
Group	1940	1950	1960	1970	1975	1978	1978	1978
Total population	5.8	7.7	11.1	16.4	22.0	23.3	+110	+42
Blacks	1.6	2.8	5.4	10.0	15.2	15.3	+183	+53

24 indicates, the proportion of Hispanics in this group increased by a modest 15 percent during the three-year interval, the proportion of Blacks by only 4 percent, and the proportion of American Indians decreased slightly (by 3 percent). These trends are consistent with those reported for entering freshmen in Table 22: Assuming a period of four to six years between college entry and baccalaureate completion, we would expect the growth rate in baccalaureates awarded to be larger for Chicanos and Puerto Ricans than for Blacks. Similarly, we would expect little or no change (and perhaps even a slight decline) for American Indians.

Just as the *trends* shown in Tables 22 and 24 are reasonably consistent, so are the *absolute proportions*, except in the case of Chicanos. Thus, the proportions of Blacks, Puerto Ricans, and American Indians are higher among entering freshmen than among degree recipients five or six years later, as one would expect, given the relatively high dropout rates of these minority groups (see Chapter Two). But the proportion of Chicanos among baccalaureate recipients seems to be somewhat *higher* than their proportion among entering freshmen. Since Chicanos are, however, more likely than students in general to drop out of undergraduate programs, one or both of these estimates (Tables 22 and 24) must be in error. One possible explanation is that the CIRP sample underrepresents institutions enrolling relatively high proportions of Chicanos. The other possibility is that the estimates based on NCES data are inflated, either because

Table 24. Trends in Baccalaureates Awarded, 1975–76 to 1978–79

			Percentage of Baccalaureates Awarded		
Year Awarded	N	Black	Chicanos[a]	Puerto Ricans[b]	American Indians
1975–76	927,085	6.38	1.70	.43	.38
1978–79	911,637	6.61	1.96	.49	.37
Percentage of change		+4	+15	+15	−3

[a]Percentages for Chicanos are based on their representing 60 percent of all Hispanic baccalaureate recipients.

[b]Percentages for Puerto Ricans are based on their representing 15 percent of all Hispanic baccalaureate recipients.

Source. 1975–76 data obtained from the U.S. Department of Health, Education, and Welfare (1978a); 1978–79 data obtained from unpublished material.

Chicanos represent less than 60 percent of all Hispanic degree recipients or because the reporting institutions exaggerate the numbers of Hispanics among degree recipients. Whatever the explanation, it seems clear that the representation of Hispanics among baccalaureate recipients is increasing, while the representation of Blacks and American Indians has stabilized.

Doctorate Attainment. The best available data on the race and ethnicity of doctorate recipients comes from the annual surveys of new doctorate recipients conducted by the National Academy of Sciences–National Research Council. As Table 25 shows, the representation of all four minority groups increased between 1973 and 1977, but there have been only slight changes since 1977; indeed, the proportions of Blacks and American Indians have declined from the 1977 levels.

Trends by Field

Perhaps the best data on changing minority representation in higher education are those on law and medical school enrollments. Table 26 shows trends over the last twelve years in first-year medical school enrollments. All four minority groups made dramatic gains between 1968–69 and 1974–75. The proportion of Blacks increased more than two and a half times, the proportion of Chicanos increased sevenfold, and the proportions of Puerto Ricans and American Indians increased fivefold during

Table 25. Trends in Doctorates Awarded, 1973–1979

Group	Percentage of Doctorates Awarded						
	1973	1974	1975	1976	1977	1978	1979
Blacks	2.58	3.15	3.66	3.99	4.26	4.08	4.14
Chicanos	.60	.73	.89	1.03	.97[a]	1.11[a]	1.08[a]
Puerto Ricans	.16	.22	.23	.25	.24[b]	.28[b]	.27[b]
American Indians	.48	.48	.53	.54	.85	.69	.65

[a] Percentages for Chicanos are based on their representing 60 percent of all Hispanic doctoral degree recipients.

[b] Percentages for Puerto Ricans are based on their representing 15 percent of all Hispanic doctoral degree recipients.

Source. National Academy of Sciences–National Research Council.

Table 26. Trends in First-Year Medical School Enrollments, 1968–1980

Year	Total First-Year Enrollment	Percentage of Total First-Year Enrollment			
		Blacks	Chicanos	Puerto Ricans	American Indians
1968–69	9,863	2.7	.2	<.1	<.1
1969–70	10,401	4.3	.4	..1	.1
1970–71	11.348	6.2	.6	.2	.1
1971–72	12,361	7.2	1.0	.3	.2
1972–73	13,726	6.4	1.1	.3	.2
1973–74	14,185	6.6	1.2	.4	.3
1974–75	14,963	6.5	1.4	.5	.4
1975–76	15,351	5.9	1.4	.4	.5
1976–77	15,667	6.0	1.5	.3	.5
1977–78	16,134	6.0	1.3	1.4[a]	.3
1978–79	16,620	5.8	1.5	1.6[a]	.3
1979–80	17,014	5.7	1.5	1.9[a]	.3
1980–81	17,186	6.5	1.5	.5	.4

[a]Enrollment counts combined mainland and island Puerto Ricans.
Source. Association of American Medical Colleges (1979).

this period. Considering that the size of the first-year medical school class grew by more than 50 percent during this same period, these increases in the representation of minorities are all the more remarkable and may in part be attributable to the vigorous efforts to recruit minorities made at all levels of post-secondary education during the late 1960s and early 1970s. Nevertheless, it is important to note that the proportions have leveled off (and, in the case of Blacks, have even declined) since 1974–75.

As Table 27 indicates, the pattern with respect to minority enrollments in law schools is much the same as for medical schools: The proportions increased substantially for all minority groups during the early 1970s but have tended to stabilize since that time. For instance, the peak year for Blacks was 1976–77; since then, their proportions among total law school enrollments have dropped slightly. It should be pointed out that gains in minority representation in law schools were not as dramatic as gains in medical schools and that the proportions for each minority group were smaller among total law school enrollments than among first-year medical school enrollments.

Table 27. Trends in Total Law School Enrollments, 1970–1980

		Percentage of Total Enrollment			
Year	Total Enrollment	Black	Chicanos	Puerto Ricans	American Indians
1969–70	68,386	3.1	.6	.1	<.1
1971–72	82,499	3.9	.9	.1	.1
1972–73	94.486	4.3	1.0	.1	.1
1973–74	101,707	4.5	1.2	.2	.2
1974–75	110,713	4.5	1.2	.2	.2
1975–76	116,991	4.4	1.1	.3	.2
1976–77	117,451	4.7	1.2	.3	.2
1977–78	118,557	4.5	1.2	.3	.3
1978–79	121,606	4.3	1.2	.4	.3
1979–80	122,801	4.3	1.3	.4	.3
1980–81	125,397	4.4	1.3	.4	.3

Source. American Bar Association (1978).

Data on recent trends in the representation of Blacks and American Indians among employed doctorate-level scientists and engineers come from National Science Foundation surveys conducted in 1973, 1977, and 1979. As the first row of Table 28 indicates, the proportion of Blacks in the total group increased by 19 percent over the six-year period, though even in 1979, Blacks constituted less than 1 percent of this group. The proportion of American Indians increased by 61 percent over the same period.

The remainder of Table 28 shows six-year trends in Black and American Indian representation among scientists and engineers employed by colleges and universities. Though the increase for Blacks was only 4 percent between 1973 and 1977, and though there was no change between 1977 and 1979, Blacks are somewhat better represented among scientists and engineers in academe than among all employed scientists and engineers. The same is true for American Indians, whose proportion increased by 50 percent between 1977 and 1979.

More interesting than these overall figures are trends for specific fields within academe. Between 1973 and 1979, the proportions of Blacks in psychology and the social sciences (fields in which they were fairly well represented in 1973) in-

Table 28. Trends in Representation of Blacks and American Indians Among Employed Doctorate-Level Scientists and Engineers, 1973–1979

| | Percentage | | | | | | Percentage of Change 1973–1979 | |
| | Blacks | | | American Indians | | | Blacks | American Indians |
	1973	1977	1979	1973	1977	1979		
All doctorate-level scientists and engineers	.94	.94	1.12	.18	.21	.29	+19	+ 61
Employed by Colleges and Universities								
Total	1.19	1.24	1.24	.24	.24	.36	+ 4	+ 50
Engineering	.58	.42	.52	.23	.19	.09	−10	− 61
Physical sciences	1.41	1.14	.86	.18	.10	.44	−39	+144
Environmental sciences	.12	.21	.06	.27	.03	.18	−50	− 33
Mathematics and computer sciences	1.09	.80	.88	.09	.14	.34	−19	+278
Life sciences	1.28	1.28	1.24	.21	.21	.32	− 3	+ 52
Psychology	1.29	2.18	1.85	.32	.43	.68	+43	+112
Social sciences	1.42	1.55	1.90	.35	.38	.32	+27	− 9

Source. National Science Foundation (1973, 1977).

creased substantially, but the proportions in other science and engineering fields within academe declined. The representation of American Indians among university psychologists, physical scientists, mathematicians and computer scientists, and life scientists increased, but their representation in other science and engineering fields dropped over the six-year period. One possible explanation for these declines in minority representations in science and engineering departments is the increasing demand for these severely underrepresented groups in business and industry.

In brief, the figures in Table 28 indicate a very mixed pattern with respect to improvement in the proportions of Blacks and American Indians working in science and engineering fields.

Summary

The data reviewed in this chapter appear to warrant the following conclusions regarding recent trends in minority representation in postsecondary education:

- Between 1970 and 1977, Blacks became substantially less likely to drop out of high school, whereas Whites, especially sixteen- and seventeen-year-olds, became increasingly likely to drop out. Nonetheless, the high school dropout rate of Blacks is still about one-third higher than that of Whites.
- Minority representation among entering college freshmen increased by 50 to 100 percent from the mid 1960s to the mid 1970s but has changed little since the mid 1970s.
- The proportion of twenty-five–to–twenty-nine–year-old Blacks who had completed four or more years of college increased by more than 150 percent between 1960 and 1975, growing from less than half to about two thirds of the proportion for the total population. Since 1976, the proportion of Hispanics among baccalaureate recipients has increased moderately, while the proportions of Blacks and American Indians have remained relatively stable.
- Between 1973 and 1977 the share of doctorates awarded to all four minority groups increased substantially. Since 1977,

however, the proportions of Blacks and American Indians among doctorate recipients have declined, while the proportion of Hispanics increased in 1978 and then dropped slightly in 1979.

- From the late 1960s through the mid 1970s, the proportions of all four minority groups among first-year medical school enrollments grew by more than 200 percent, even as the size of the first-year class was increasing by more than 50 percent. Since 1974–75, however, minorities have made virtually no gains in representation among first-year medical students.

- The proportions of minorities among total law school enrollments increased by about 68 percent between 1969–70 and 1976–77, even though the total law school population grew by about 70 percent during the same period. Since 1976–77, however, the proportion of Blacks, Hispanics, and American Indians among law students has changed very little.

- The proportions of Blacks and American Indians among employed scientists and engineers changed very little between 1973 and 1977.

In summary, these findings reveal dramatic increases in the representation of Blacks, Chicanos, Puerto Ricans, and American Indians at all levels of higher education between the mid 1960s and the mid 1970s. However, there has been little change in minority representation in higher education since the mid 1970s.

✻ 5 ✻

Factors Affecting Minority Educational Progress

In this chapter we summarize the major findings from the longitudinal analyses of the factors that influence minority students' educational development. These analyses are based primarily on two longitudinal samples, one covering the first two years of undergraduate work (1975 freshmen followed up in 1977), and the other a nine-year span covering undergraduate and graduate work (1971 freshmen followed up in 1980). Table 29 shows the various sample sizes used in these analyses. Note that, for the 1971–1980 cohort, there are two samples ("limited" and "extended"). The limited sample, which includes very small numbers for two of the groups, utilizes the long follow-up questionnaire and therefore permits an analysis of a wide range of student outcomes. The extended samples, in contrast, are utilized to study only one outcome (retention or persistence), but they involve much larger sample sizes for the smaller minority groups (Chicanos, Puerto Ricans, and American Indians).

Table 29. Sample Sizes for Longitudinal Analyses

	Group				
Sample	Blacks	Chicanos	Puerto Ricans	American Indians	Whites
1975–1977	2,779	534	178	368	
1971–1980 limited[a]	1,287[e]	315	70	81	2,065[f]
1971–1980 extended:					
All institutions[b]	2,082[e]	1,353	371	344	2,282[f]
Four-year institutions[c]	2,436[e]	827	425	405	2,617[f]
Two-year colleges[d]	513[e]	1,306	108	107	602[f]

[a]Limited to persons who returned the long form of the the 1980 mailed follow-up questionnaire.

[b]Includes 1971–1980 limited sample and those contacted by telephone follow-up.

[c]Includes only those entering four-year colleges or universities in 1971 from the 1971–1980 limited sample, from those contacted by telephone follow-up, and from those for whom 1980 follow-up data were provided by the freshman institution.

[d]Includes only those entering two-year colleges in 1971 from the 1971–1980 limited sample, from those contacted by telephone follow-up, and from those for whom 1980 follow-up data were provided by the freshman institution.

[e]Represents a 40 percent subsample.

[f]Represents a 20 percent subsample.

Analyses

As indicated in Chapter One, the analyses of factors that influence minority students' educational development were conducted in two stages. Thus, for each student outcome (for example, completion of a baccalaureate), a two-stage stepwise linear multiple regression analysis was conducted so that the students' entering characteristics were first controlled before any attempt was made to assess the influence of environmental characteristics. These statistical controls are necessary because students entering different colleges may not be comparable initially. Controlling for entering characteristics, in effect, statistically "matches" students entering different college environments.

Thirty outcome measures were used in these longitudinal analyses, including three from the two-year longitudinal panel and twenty-seven from the nine-year panel. From the two-year panel the three variables included the student's cumulative grade-point average (GPA), undergraduate persistence during the first two years, and satisfaction with the undergraduate college. Outcome measures for the limited 1971–1980 sample included undergraduate measures of GPA, satisfaction, and persistence (attainment of a baccalaureate during the nine-year interval); four measures of graduate attainment (enrollment in graduate or professional school, attainment of an advanced degree, attainment of a doctorate or advanced professional degree, and attainment or current pursuit of a doctorate or advanced professional degree); eight measures of follow-up career aspirations (businessperson, engineer, medical professional, allied health professional, schoolteacher, college teacher, scientific researcher, lawyer, and nurse); and nine measures of the students' final undergraduate major field of study (biosciences, physical sciences and mathematics, premedicine, education, allied health, arts and humanities, social sciences, engineering, and business). The final three outcome measures based on the extended 1971–1980 sample were: persistence in a two-year college, persistence in a four-year college or university, and general persistence (all institutions). With the exceptions of the measures of satisfaction and grade-point average, all outcome measures were scored as dichotomous variables. For a more complete description of each outcome measure, see Appendix B.

The results of the regression analyses for each of the thirty outcome measures are presented in the following order: results are summarized separately for four different classes of independent (entering freshman and environmental) variables—academic preparation, career and study plans, demographic characteristics, and other student characteristics. Then results are summarized separately for each category of dependent (outcome) variables.*

Academic Preparation

Generally speaking, the quality of the student's academic preparation at the time of college entry proved to have more

---

*Details on the results of each regression analysis can be obtained at cost by writing to the Higher Education Research Institute, 320 Moore Hall, UCLA Campus, Los Angeles, CA 90024.

frequent and stronger relationships to most outcome measures than any other single category of freshman or environmental variable. Let us summarize the results for five measures of academic preparation: high school grades, aptitude test scores, study habits, high school, curriculum, and perceived need for tutoring.

High School Grades. Not surprisingly, the students' high school grades prove to be by far the most important predictor of college GPA in all samples. Prediction tends to be somewhat better for American Indians and Whites (average $r = .50$) than for the three other minority groups (average $r = .35$). Furthermore, the student's average grade in high school or rank in class (both measures were used) proves to be the most consistent and substantial predictor of most measures of undergraduate per-persistence (except in the case of Puerto Rican students, for whom high school grades do not appear to be a factor in persistence). For American Indians and Whites, high school grades are also positive predictors of undergraduate satisfaction.

Aptitude Test Scores. The student's academic aptitude, as measured by standard admissions tests (Scholastic Aptitude Test and the American College Test) does *not* show substantial relationships to many outcomes. As a matter of fact, test scores contribute to the prediction of college grades for only two groups (Blacks and Chicanos), and the magnitude of the relationship is quite small in comparison to the relationship between high school grades and college grades. Test scores predict undergraduate persistence for only one group (Blacks), and once again the relationship is weak in comparison to the relationship for high school grades.

Study Habits. The students' secondary school study habits were assessed in two ways: a list of items shown in previous research (Astin, 1975) to be predictive of undergraduate persistence, and an item that asked the students to indicate their perceived degree of preparedness in study skills. Items relating to good study habits are positively related to persistence for Blacks, Chicanos, American Indians, and Whites, confirming the results of earlier research on undergraduate persistence (Astin, 1975). In addition, study habits are significantly related to undergraduate GPA for three groups (Chicanos, American Indians, and Whites). The student's perceived degree of preparation in study habits is not related to GPA or persistence, but it is positively related to satisfaction for *all* five student groups.

Secondary School Curriculum. Having been enrolled in a college preparatory curriculum (as opposed to general or vocational) is positively related to persistence for Blacks and Chicanos. Persistence among Black students is also greater for those who have taken relatively many science and foreign language courses in secondary school.

Perceived Need for Tutoring. Students were asked at the time of college entry to indicate whether or not they needed tutoring or remedial work in general or in specific subject areas. The most consistent results occur with Blacks in the area of mathematics. A perceived need on the part of the entering black students for tutoring or remedial help in mathematics is negatively related to all three academic outcomes: undergraduate grades, undergraduate persistence, and completion of a graduate degree. Other findings are generally inconsistent. Thus, a perceived need for remedial help in reading and composition is positively related to undergraduate GPA among Blacks, and positively related to persistence among American Indians. Similarly, among Blacks, a general felt need for tutoring is negatively related to GPA but positively related to persistence. Persistence among American Indians is positively related to a perceived need for help in social studies, but negatively related to a perceived help in English.

Demographic Characteristics

Results are summarized here for six categories of demographic characteristics: sex, age, parental income, parental education, parental occupation, and racial composition of the high school.

Sex. Consistent with almost all previous research on predicting college grade-point average, being a woman is positively related to undergraduate grades for all groups except Chicanos and American Indians. Being a woman is also positively related to persistence among Blacks, but negatively related among

Chicanos and Whites. Finally, Puerto Rican women were more satisfied with their undergraduate colleges than were Puerto Rican men, whereas black women were more satisfied than black men.

Age. The relatively older students show somewhat poorer rates of undergraduate persistence among three groups (Blacks, Chicanos, and Whites). This finding, which is consistent with previous research on college persistence (Astin, 1975), may reflect the fact that the student who is relatively old at the time of college entry took somewhat longer to complete secondary school. Nevertheless, for two groups (Whites and Chicanos) the older students perform relatively better academically than the younger students. Finally, older Whites were relatively more satisfied with their undergraduate experience, older Blacks relatively less satisfied.

Parental Income. Given the low incomes of most minority families and the considerable current interest in financial aid, the family income of minority students has attracted a good deal of national attention in recent years. Our results show clearly that the lower the family income, the poorer a minority student's prospects in higher education. Thus, all significant relationships between parental income and various student outcome measures are positive. Among Blacks, for example, parental income is positively related to undergraduate GPA, undergraduate persistence, and satisfaction. For Chicanos, parental income is positively related to undergraduate GPA and satisfaction. For Puerto Ricans, there is a substantial positive relationship between parental income and undergraduate persistence. (The only significant relationship for Whites is a positive association between parental income and undergraduate satisfaction.) It should be stressed that these reported relationships (as well as all others described in this section) refer to the *unique* contribution of parental income to various outcomes when all other freshman and environmental characteristics are simultaneously controlled. Thus, to the extent that financial aid policies are designed to compensate for disadvantages associated with poverty, these programs have still fallen short of their goal.

Parental Education. With one notable exception, the educational level of the students' parents shows a pattern of relationships to various student outcomes that closely parallels the pattern found for parental income. Thus, student persistence is positively associated with parental education among Blacks, Chicanos, American Indians, and Whites. Parental education is also positively related to entry to graduate school among Whites and Blacks, and positively related to satisfaction among American Indians. The single exception is that for Puerto Ricans parental education is negatively associated with persistence among students entering two-year colleges and negatively associated with entry to graduate school. The reason for this anomaly is not immediately apparent from the data, although it should be noted that parental *income* shows substantial positive relationships to persistence among Puerto Ricans.

Parental Occupation. The occupations of the students' parents generally show weak relationships, if any, to various measures of GPA, persistence, and satisfaction. The only consistent pattern occurs with the outcome measures assessing the student's career choice at the time of the follow-up. Thus, choosing a career as a medical professional (doctor, dentist, and the like) is positively associated with having a father who is also a medical professional. This relationship holds among Blacks, Chicanos, Puerto Ricans, and Whites. Since these analyses also controlled simultaneously for the student's initial (entering freshman) career choice, it seems safe to conclude that students are more likely to persist in their initial desire to become a physician or dentist if their father is also a physician or dentist.

Racial Composition of the High School. A measure of the racial composition of the student's high school shows consistent relationships to various outcome measures only among Blacks. Blacks who attended predominantly minority high schools had lower GPAs, were less satisfied, and persisted at lower rates than Blacks attending integrated secondary schools. In short, it appears that attending a segregated minority high school poses special disadvantages for Blacks who attend postsecondary institutions. Again, it should be emphasized that these relationships were obtained while controlling for all other factors that might affect these outcomes (high school grades, parental income and education, and so forth).

Career and Study Plans

Not surprisingly, the students' intended majors and probable career plans prove to be by far the strongest predictors of these same plans after two and nine years. Of the thirty-four regressions involving career or major field outcomes, the entering freshman measure of that outcome proves to be the strongest single predictor in all but three instances. These findings show clearly that the student's initial choice of a career or major is not a random event, and that it has considerable influence on the student's long-range career development. The student's initial choices of a career and a major also prove to have a number of substantial relationships to undergraduate GPA and undergraduate persistence. (These findings are discussed later in this chapter.)

Student aspirations as measured by the highest degree that they sought at the time of college entry prove to be related to undergraduate persistence and entry to graduate or professional school. In other words, the minority students' initial degree aspirations are found to be consistently related to their actual degree attainment. Again, we have evidence supporting the argument that minority students' initial plans and aspirations are important determinants of their later accomplishments.

Other Student Characteristics

The four other categories of entering student characteristics summarized here are measures of self-concept, attitudes, smoking, and need for personal counseling.

Self-Concept. The entering freshmen were asked to complete a number of self-ratings on a variety of traits (academic ability, originality, drive to achieve, and so forth). One consistent pattern of relationships involving these measures emerges: The students' self-rating on academic ability is significantly and positively related to undergraduate GPA for all groups except Chicanos.

Since these significant relationships were obtained while simultaneously controlling for all other entering and environmental factors, it appears that a minority student's *perceived* academic ability is a positive indicator of later academic achievement independent of any other measures of academic ability. This finding, it might be added, is consistent with earlier studies of the relationship between self-concept and academic achievement (Astin, 1971, 1977a).

Attitudes. The entering freshmen were asked about a number of attitudinal items relating to minority issues and student rights. Most of these questions prove to have no relationship or only trivial relationships to most outcomes. There is also a slight tendency for more liberal attitudes to be negatively associated with GPA and persistence, although there are some inconsistencies even in these relationships. In short, it appears that the attitudes and values of minority students are not important predictors of their performance in higher education.

Smoking. A question assessing the student's smoking habits was included because earlier research has shown that smokers do worse academically and persist at lower rates than nonsmokers (Astin, 1977a). These earlier results were consistently confirmed in this present analysis, although it should be stressed that the significant relationships occurred only for Blacks and Whites. Thus, being a smoker is negatively associated with undergraduate grades, undergraduate persistence, and satisfaction for both these groups. While the association between smoking and dropping out of college has been noted by other investigators (Dvorak, 1967; Pumroy, 1967), the reasons for the association are not clearly understood. Smoking may be a symptom of rebelliousness and nonconformity—traits directly associated with dropping out. Smoking may directly interfere with concentration or produce physiological stress that interferes with the ability to study or to conform to the academic and social demands of college.

Environmental Factors

The results of the longitudinal analyses are summarized separately for four general categories of environmental factors:

institutional characteristics, field of study, financial aid, and place of residence.

Institutional Characteristics. We analyzed three general institutional characteristics: type of institution (level of degree offered, source of control, race, and sex), quality as defined by several different measures, and geographical region.

Our first concern was simply to examine the persistence rates at various types of institutions. For this purpose we selected only those students who entered college in 1971 stating that they intended to obtain at least a bachelor's degree. Persisters were defined as those who had a bachelor's degree nine years later, at the time of the follow-up in 1980. Using a complex procedure to compensate for those students who could not be located at the time of the follow-up (see Appendix A), we estimated persistence rates separately for each racial or ethnic group (Table 30). For all categories of students, the proportions who completed their bachelor's degrees within nine years are much higher—two or three times higher—in universities and four-year colleges than in two-year colleges. American Indians and Chicanos have their highest degree completion rates in the four-year colleges, while Puerto Ricans have their highest rates in the universities; Blacks show very similar rates in four-year colleges, universities, and predominantly Black colleges.

Do these extreme variations in degree completion rates simply reflect differences in the levels of academic preparation of students entering different types of institutions, or do they also

Table 30. Percentage of 1971 Freshmen Who Completed
a Baccalaureate Degree, by Ethnicity and Type of Institution

| | | Type of Institution Attended Freshman Year | | | |
| | All | | Other Four-Year | Two-Year | Black |
Group	Institutions	Universities	Colleges	Colleges	Colleges
Blacks	50.9	68.0	66.6	24.4	64.8
Chicanos	39.7	62.6	70.4	19.5	—
Puerto Ricans	41.8	70.3	60.1	27.0	—
American Indians	38.6	45.8	58.9	22.5	—
Whites	55.6	73.3	72.7	29.0	—

reflect differential institutional effects? To explore this question, the institutions were first divided into six categories based on the level of degree offered (two-year college, four-year college, university) and control (public or private). Partial correlations (after control of entering freshman characteristics) between each of these six categorical measures and student persistence in the extended (1971–1980) longitudinal sample are shown in Table 31. By far the largest number of significant partial correlations occur with two-year public colleges. In each instance, the relationship is a negative one, suggesting that minority students' chances of completing a baccalaureate program are substantially reduced by initial college attendance at a community college. In other words, the low bachelor's degree completion rates of minorities who enroll at community colleges are not simply the result of their relatively poor level of academic preparation. This result, which confirms a substantial body of earlier research (Astin, 1975, 1977a) showing a negative relationship between enrolling at a community college and completing a bachelor's degree, would appear to have special significance for minorities, who tend to be highly concentrated in community colleges. Private two-year colleges, however, do not appear to have the same untoward effect on persistence as do the public community colleges.

Among four-year institutions, the public and private colleges show contrasting effects on persistence. The public four-year colleges appear to have a negative effect on persistence for Puerto Ricans and Whites, whereas the private four-year colleges have a positive effect. (This latter result confirms earlier research on persistence; see Astin, 1975). Attendance at a private university appears to facilitate persistence for Puerto Ricans, but it inhibits persistence among American Indians. Public universities do not appear to have any differential effect on student persistence.

Regarding the other student outcomes, the six measures of college type listed in Table 31 show only scattered and inconsistent effects. Attending a private university, for example, has negative effects on undergraduate GPA for Chicanos and American Indians, negative effects on satisfaction for Chicanos and Whites, and positive effects on satisfaction for Puerto Ricans

Table 31. Undergraduate Persistence and Institutional Types
(Partial Correlations after Control of Entering Freshman Characteristics)

1971 Freshman Sample

Type of College Entered	All Students					Two-Year College Entrants					Four-Year Colleges and University Entrants				
	Blacks	Chicanos	Puerto Ricans	American Indians	Whites	Blacks	Chicanos	Puerto Ricans	American Indians	Whites	Blacks	Chicanos	Puerto Ricans	American Indians	Whites
Public															
University	.03	.05[a]	−.03	.08	−.01	—	—	—	—	—	.02	.00	−.03	−.01	−.03
Four-year college	−.01	.08[a]	−.08	.07	−.03	—	—	—	—	—	−.03	.02	−.21[a]	.08	−.04[a]
Two-year college	−.06[a]	−.20[a]	.01	−.10[a]	−.14[a]	−.14	−.05	−.18[a]	−.08	−.11[a]	—	—	—	—	—
Private															
University	−.05[a]	.04	.12[a]	−.07	−.04[a]	—	—	—	—	—	.03	−.04	.13[a]	−.18[a]	−.02
Four-year college	.04[a]	.07[a]	.03	.01	.15[a]	—	—	—	—	—	.00	.01	.13[a]	.08	.06[a]
Two-year college	.03	.04	−.02	−.04	−.03	.14[a]	.05	.18[a]	.08	.11[a]	—	—	—	—	—

[a]Significant at the .05 level of confidence.

and American Indians. Private two-year colleges have positive effects on both undergraduate GPA and satisfaction among Blacks. Among American Indians, public two-year colleges have positive effects on undergraduate grades but negative effects on entry to graduate school.

Another type of college examined in these longitudinal analyses was traditionally black institutions. Attending a predominantly black college appears to reduce the black student's chance of persisting to the baccalaureate, an effect which was observed in both two-year and four-year institutions. Attending a predominantly black institution also shows a negative effect on undergraduate satisfaction, but the effects on undergraduate grades are positive and substantial in magnitude. Thus, it would appear that black undergraduates will tend to get higher grades at a black college than at other colleges, but they will also be less satisfied and less likely to persist to the completion of a baccalaureate.

This pattern of effects contrasts with the pattern found earlier for Blacks who entered college in 1968 (Astin, 1977a). Conceivably, the relatively more favorable effects of white versus black colleges observed in the current study reflect the white college's increasing sensitivity to the special needs of black students.

To explore the possible significance of institutional quality on various student outcomes, several different measures of quality were used: average faculty salary, educational and general expenditures per student, student-faculty ratio (an inverse measure), tuition, selectivity (the average academic ability of the entering freshmen), and prestige (a combination of selectivity and large size, with substantially greater weight given to selectivity; see Astin and Lee, 1971).*

Table 32 shows the partial correlations (after control of entering student characteristics) between each quality measure

*The use of these measures as indices of quality is not to suggest that the commission endorses or otherwise supports the use of such measures in judging institutions. Rather, we chose to label these indices as measures of institutional quality simply because such measures have traditionally been associated with institutional quality in the literature on higher education (for a fuller discussion of this issue, see Astin, 1981).

Table 32. Effects of College Quality on Student Persistence
(Partial Correlations After Control of Entering Freshman Characteristics)

1971 Freshman Sample

Quality Measure	All Students					Two-Year College Entrants					Four-Year College and University Entrants				
	Blacks	Chicanos	Puerto Ricans	American Indians	Whites	Blacks	Chicanos	Puerto Ricans	American Indians	Whites	Blacks	Chicanos	Puerto Ricans	American Indians	Whites
Prestige	.05[a]	.13[a]	.12[a]	-.01	.06[a]	-.08	-.19[a]	-.25[a]	-.20[a]	-.10[a]	.09[a]	.04	.16[a]	-.11[a]	.06[a]
Selectivity	.08[a]	.15[a]	.10[a]	.01	.10[a]	.09[a]	-.20[a]	-.11	.10	.00	.09[a]	.04	.17[a]	-.07	.07[a]
Enrollment size	-.02	-.01	-.04	-.05	-.05	-.07	-.10[a]	-.25[a]	-.14	-.07	.02	.01	-.08	-.16[a]	-.02
Educational and general expenditures per student	.05[a]	.17[a]	.08	.10[a]	.02	.00	.01	-.02	.01	.03	.08[a]	.03	.11[a]	.08	.01
Tuition	.02	.15[a]	.10[a]	-.02	.09[a]	.04	.09[a]	.14	-.06	.06	.04[a]	.01	.19[a]	.01	.07[a]
Student-faculty ratio	-.07[a]	-.00[a]	-.04	-.03	-.05[a]	.00	.02	-.06	.00	-.02	-.02	-.02	-.10[a]	-.11[a]	-.03

[a]Significant at the .05 level of confidence.

and persistence in the extended 1971–1980 longitudinal sample. (Enrollment size is included simply because it is used to construct the prestige measure.) The data show a clear-cut tendency for quality to be positively related to student persistence (the negative coefficients for student-faculty ratio reflect the fact that this is an inverse measure of quality). In the sample of all students, there is at least one significant positive correlation between quality and persistence for each minority group as well as for Whites. Indeed, for Chicanos all five quality measures are positively related to persistence, whereas for Blacks and Whites, four of the five measures show significant relationships. Among four-year college and university entrants, quality measures show a similar pattern of positive effects on persistence, with the exception of the American Indian students, for whom the measures show both positive and negative relationships. A closer examination of the coefficients for American Indians suggests that they are less likely to persist in the relatively large institutions. This result may reflect an earlier finding (Astin, 1975) that students from relatively small towns are less likely to persist in large institutions than students from larger urban areas. Assuming that many of the American Indians in this sample came from relatively small towns or rural areas, we may be observing here a simple replication of that earlier finding.

A dramatically different pattern of effects of quality measures occurs, however, in the two-year college sample. Institutional prestige and enrollment size show consistently negative effects on persistence among two-year college entrants, whereas the other quality measures show mixed positive and negative effects. One obvious reason that quality shows a different pattern of relationships among two-year college students is that two-year colleges tend to score very low on most traditional quality measures and also to show less variability on such measures than the four-year colleges. That prestige and enrollment size show the strongest negative relationships to persistence may reflect the fact that the community colleges (which also have negative effects) tend to be considerably larger in size than the private two-year colleges. Institutional size within the two-year college sector, in other words, may be simply a surrogate measure for control (public or private).

Quality measures also show consistently positive effects on graduate attainment (defined here as obtaining or currently working toward a doctorate or advanced professional degree). Table 33 shows the partial correlations (after control for entering student characteristics) between six measures of quality and graduate attainment. Every quality measure shows positive effects in at least two minority groups. All six measures show significant effects among American Indians, and five of the six show significant effects among Blacks. Why should the quality of the undergraduate institution facilitate the completion of advanced graduate degrees among minorities? A number of explanations are possible. For example, the intellectual climate of the more prestigious and selective undergraduate institutions may foster the development of motivation for advanced training. Another possibility is that the more visible and prestigious undergraduate institutions may have better connections to the graduate and professional schools, thereby facilitating their students' transition from undergraduate to graduate training. Whatever the explanation, it seems clear that the prospects for completing advanced graduate and professional training among minorities are substantially enhanced if they are able to attend relatively selective and prestigious undergraduate colleges.

Table 33. Graduate Attainment and the Quality of the Undergraduate Institution (Partial Correlations After Control of Entering Freshman Characteristics)

Undergraduate Quality Measure	Group				
	Blacks	Chicanos	Puerto Ricans	American Indians	Whites
Prestige	.12	.14		.23	.05
Selectivity	.12			.24	
Average faculty salary	.10	.11		.13	
Educational and general expenditures per student	.07			.21	.05
Tuition	.13	.12		.23	
Student-faculty ratio			−.17	−.27	

Notes. Only significant (p<.05) partial correlations are reported.
    Attainment was defined as having obtained (or currently working toward) a doctorate or advanced professional degree at the time of the follow-up.

The various quality measures show only scattered relationships to the other student outcome measures. Not surprisingly quality measures tend to show negative relationships with undergraduate GPA for Blacks, American Indians, and Whites. In all likelihood, these negative effects reflect the more stringent academic standards of the more prestigious and selective institutions. Quality measures tend to be positively related to satisfaction among Blacks, Puerto Ricans, and Whites.

Regarding the location of the institution, by far the most consistent pattern of relationships involving geographical measures concern the effects of attending college in the Northeast on black students. Without exception, Blacks attending colleges in the Northeast get higher grades, are less likely to drop out, and are more likely to be satisfied with their undergraduate experience than Blacks attending institutions in the other regions. A variety of explanations for these relationships are possible. It may be, for example, that the colleges in the Northeast are more sophisticated and progressive in dealing with the special needs of Black students because of the high concentration of Blacks in that region of the country and the liberal tradition of the Northeast in the area of civil rights.

Attending colleges in the southeastern states tends to be negatively related to undergraduate grades and satisfaction among Blacks, but shows no significant relationship to persistence. Among Puerto Ricans, attending colleges in the southwestern region of the United States is associated with higher GPAs and higher persistence rates. Attending college in the Plains states is positively associated with persistence among Chicanos, but negatively associated with persistence among Puerto Ricans.

Field of Study. The student's undergraduate major field of study is considered here as an environmental variable, but the reader should keep in mind that it could also be considered as a student characteristic at college entry, since a student's choice of a major or career is, to a certain extent, an expression of the student's interests, personality, abilities, and so forth. The student's freshman choice of a major field shows relationships primarily to two types of outcomes: undergraduate GPA and career plans at the time of the longitudinal follow-ups.

The longitudinal analyses reveal a clear-cut pattern of the effects of major field on undergraduate grades. Minorities who major in the natural sciences, engineering, or premedical curricula tend to get lower grades than would be expected from their entering characteristics, whereas students majoring in the arts and humanities, social sciences, or education tend to get higher grades than expected. Given that the entering characteristics were controlled in these analyses, it would appear that the first group of majors are substantially more demanding academically than the second group. This general pattern of effects on undergraduate GPA appears to be fairly consistent across all minority groups.

Not surprisingly, the student's entering major field of study proves to be the most potent predictor of final field of study at the time of the follow-up. Entering majors also predict students' follow-up career choices, but the most potent predictors of follow-up careers are the students' initial career choices. In more than 90 percent of the regression analyses, the freshman career or major proves to be the most potent predictor of the corresponding follow-up career or major. It is also worth noting that minority students show a very consistent pattern of *change* in career choice between their freshman year and follow-up. For example, in the nine-year longitudinal sample, the largest gains in popularity between freshman year and follow-up occur in the fields of business and college teaching–scientific research. The percentages of students choosing these two career groups more than doubles between freshman year and follow-up. The largest declines in popularity occur in engineering and premedicine (which lost about half of their students between freshman year and follow-up) and in prelaw (which lost approximately 25 percent of its initial majors). Little or no change between freshman year and follow-up is observed for career choices in the fields of allied health, nursing, and elementary and secondary school teaching. It might be added here that Whites show very similar patterns of changes in careers and majors in the longitudinal data.

The most consistent pattern of relationships between the entering career choices and follow-up outcomes occurs with the career of elementary or secondary schoolteacher and undergraduate persistence. For all groups except Chicanos, aspiring to become a schoolteacher is positively related to persistence to the baccalaureate. Attainment of a doctorate or advanced professional degree (or being enrolled in pursuit of such a degree) is positively predicted from an entering major in prelaw for Blacks, Chicanos, and Whites, and positively predicted from an entering freshman major in premedicine for all groups except American Indians. In this regard, it is of interest to note that American Indians entering college as premedical majors are less likely to persist as undergraduates and are also more likely to be dissatisfied with their undergraduate institution.

Financial Aid. The most current and elaborate financial aid information was available from the 1975–1977 sample (this sample was, in fact, originally created in order to study the impact of financial aid on persistence during the first two undergraduate years; Astin and Cross, 1979). The 1971–1980 longitudinal sample contained much less detailed information on financial aid for the 1971 freshmen (information on participation in work-study programs, for example, was not available). It should also be noted that the actual financial situation prevailing in 1971 was not the same as that in 1975. The largest single federal aid program, the Basic Educational Opportunity Grant (BEOG), was not created until 1972. It is probably also safe to assume that the level of students' and counselors' sophistication about financial aid programs increased substantially between 1971 and 1975.

Given these differences in data sources and in financial aid programs, it is not surprising that the longitudinal analyses produced inconsistent and sometimes conflicting findings regarding the effect of financial aid on various types of student outcomes (see Table 34). Nevertheless, by combining results from the earlier financial aid studies (Astin, 1975; Astin, Christian, and Henson, 1975; Astin and Cross, 1979), it is possible to develop some tentative general conclusions about the relationship between financial aid and student progress:

• Support in the form of scholarships or grants tends to facilitate undergraduate persistence and also to influence students' choice of institutions. Students' decision making

Table 34. Effects of Financial Aid Variables on Student Persistence
(Partial Correlations After Control of Entering Freshman Characteristics)

1971 Freshman Sample

Financial Aid Variable	All Students					Two-Year College Entrants					Four-Year College and University Entrants				
	Blacks	Chicanos	Puerto Ricans	American Indians	Whites	Blacks	Chicanos	Puerto Ricans	American Indians	Whites	Blacks	Chicanos	Puerto Ricans	American Indians	Whites
Grants	-.02	.11[a]	-.03	.03	.03	-.02	.08[a]	.00	-.03	.03	.01	.05	.00	-.04	.00
Family Support	.01	.05	.01	.06	.06[a]	.02	.00	-.06	-.05	.00	.02	.06	.03	.05	.04[a]
Savings	-.01	.00	-.01	.00	.00	.00	-.03	.01	-.10	.01	.02	.00	.03	.00	-.02
Federal loan	-.03	.07[a]	.12[a]	.17[a]	.02	-.03	.04	.06	.04	.08[a]	.02	.07[a]	.08	.08	.00
Other loan	-.02	.01	.02	.01	.04	.03	.03	.08	.15	.01	-.01	.02	.04	-.02	.00

[a]Significant at the .05 level of confidence.

can apparently be positively influenced by an increase in the amount of grant money in a financial aid package.

- Work-study programs appear to facilitate student persistence, *provided* that the work is part time (less than twenty hours per week) and (preferably) located on the campus. Working more than twenty hours per week negatively influences undergraduate persistence, especially if the work is located off campus. Minority students who expect to work at outside jobs at the time they enter college are significantly less likely to persist to completion of the baccalaureate degree than students who indicate they will not have to work at outside jobs.
- Loans produce an inconsistent pattern of relationships to persistence among minority students.
- The effects of various types of financial aid packages on student persistence is unclear. The possibly negative effects of student loans appear to be greater if the loans are part of a financial aid package involving other forms of aid. Clearly, much more research on the effects of packaging needs to be done.

Place of Residence. A large body of earlier research (Astin, 1975, 1977a; Chickering, 1974) suggests that students benefit from the experience of going away from home and living in a residential hall on the college campus. Although the 1971 survey of freshmen did not inquire specifically about where the student planned to live during the freshman year, we considered the potential effects of the residential experience important enough to develop two surrogate measures based on other questionnaire items. First, the distance from the student's home to the college was utilized as a crude measure of place of residence. Two schemes for classifying residents were used: (1) students living 50 miles or more from home were considered residents; (2) students living 100 miles or more from home were considered residents. The second surrogate measure was based on students' stated reasons for attending college. Students who indicated that "living away from home" was a very important reason for choosing their particular college were considered to be residents, whereas students who checked this as a minor reason or not a reason were assumed to be living at home.

These alternative surrogate measures produced a similar pattern of results. Living away from home is positively related to persistence among Blacks, Chicanos, and Whites. (The distance from home to college turned out to be a better surrogate measure than did the student's stated reason for picking a particular college.) While the partial correlation coefficients for Puerto Ricans are also positive, they do not reach statistical significance because of the small sample size. Partial correlation coefficients for American Indians are both positive and negative, although none of them reaches statistical significance.

These surrogate measures of place of residence show a few scattered relationships to other student outcomes for particular minority groups, but no clear-cut pattern emerges.

Summary

Let us summarize the results presented in this chapter for five categories of outcome measures: undergraduate persistence, undergraduate GPA, undergraduate satisfaction, graduate attainment, and choice of major and career.

Undergraduate Persistence. The minority student with the best chance of persisting enters college with good high school grades, well-developed study habits, and relatively high self-esteem in terms of academic ability. The potential persister is also likely to have taken a college preparatory course in high school, to come from a relatively affluent and well-educated family, and to be relatively young at the time of college entry. Additional entering characteristics that apply primarily to black freshmen include high test scores, feeling well prepared in mathematics, having taken a large number of high school courses in science and foreign languages, having attended an integrated high school, and being a nonsmoker.

Environmental characteristics that facilitate persistence during the undergraduate years include attending a four-year college or university (rather than a community college), living on campus rather than at home, having financial aid in the form of grants or scholarships, not having to work at an outside job, majoring in education, and attending a relatively selective or prestigious institution.

Undergraduate GPA. By far the most important predictor of the student's undergraduate GPA is the student's high school GPA. Standardized test scores add nothing to the prediction except in the case of Blacks, where they add only slightly to the accuracy of the prediction. Other entering characteristics that add to the prediction of college GPA are having good study habits at the time of college entry and being a woman. Parental income also positively predicts grades for Blacks and Chicanos.

The most consistent environmental effects on GPA are related to the student's major field of study. Those who major in the arts or humanities, social sciences, or education do relatively well academically, whereas those minority students who major in engineering, natural sciences, or premedicine do relatively poorly. Minority students who attend highly selective or prestigious institutions tend to get somewhat lower grades than those who attend the less prestigious institutions. Among Blacks, coming from a predominantly black high school is negatively related to undergraduate GPA, but attending a predominantly black college has a positive effect on undergraduate grades.

Undergraduate Satisfaction. Only one entering characteristic of minority students shows consistently strong relationships to undergraduate satisfaction: the student's own estimate of how satisfied he or she would be with college at the time of initial entry as a freshman. The only other entering characteristic that predicts significantly for all groups (including Whites) is the type of high school curriculum in which the student had been enrolled: At the follow-up students were more satisfied with their undergraduate experience if they had taken a college preparatory curriculum in high school. For Blacks, Chicanos, and Whites, undergraduate satisfaction is also positively related to the income of the student's parents. Concern about finances at the time of college entry is negatively related to undergraduate satisfaction among Chicanos and American Indians.

Few environmental characteristics show any consistent relationships to undergraduate satisfaction. For Blacks and Chicanos, living at home is positively associated with undergraduate satisfaction. Also, for Blacks and Puerto Ricans, attending a selective or prestigious institution is positively associated with satisfaction.

Graduate Attainment. The several measures of graduate attainment used all produced similar results. The findings summarized here are derived from the analyses in which graduate attainment was defined as having completed (or currently being enrolled in pursuit of) a doctorate or advanced professional degree (M.D., J.D., and the like).

Minority freshmen with the best chance of eventually attaining a graduate degree are those who enter college with high aspirations or who plan to obtain the medical or law degree.

Among the environmental factors, the most important predictor of graduate attainment is the quality or prestige of the college initially entered. Those minority students who initially enroll at prestigious or selective colleges are substantially more likely to obtain graduate degrees eventually than are minority students who enter other institutions.

Choice of Major Field of Study and Career. By far the most important predictors of the minority student's major field of study and career choice nine years after college entry are the preliminary choices of a major and a career expressed at the time of college entry. These early choices, in other words, show some consistency over a relatively long time period. Pursuing a career as a doctor or dentist nine years after college entry is also more likely if the minority student's father is also a doctor or dentist. Minority students' choices of majors and careers are not consistently related to the various environmental measures employed in this study.

6

Government Programs

Governmental programs and policies play a central role in the higher education of minorities, not only because most minorities attend institutions that are supported and controlled by state governments but also because the policies of the federal government have important implications for most private as well as public colleges and universities.

A comprehensive first-hand evaluation of major federal and state policies and programs affecting higher education would have required more time and far greater resources than were available to us. However, the scope and potential significance of such programs for the higher education of minorities requires that they be subjected to some scrutiny. Accordingly, in this chapter, we briefly examine the history, substance, scope, and effect of governmental programs oriented toward minority college students.

Recent History

The tremendous expansion of higher education in the U.S. during the years following World War II is in part the result of an expanded governmental presence in higher education. This expansion has been marked by a major shift in the nature of the federal government's role: from purchaser and consumer of university research to supporter and underwriter of expanded access to and participation in postsecondary education. Similarly, the states' role in public higher education has changed dramatically, in part because of the growth of two-year colleges. Public higher education has evolved from a limited, low-cost, meritocratic system to one of open and potentially unlimited access for all citizens regardless of their ability to pay or their previous educational achievement.

The postwar commonweal concern for access to and equality of educational opportunity has been expressed in a number of government policy statements, judicial decisions, and legislative acts. The first strong expression was the 1947 report of the President's Commission on Higher Education. Another such strong statement was the historic *Brown* decision, based upon case law that evolved from judicial challenges to the "separate but equal" doctrine as practiced in higher education (Kluger, 1975; Preer, 1979). The great social upheavals stimulated by the civil rights movement, and the subsequent policy linkage forged between education and employment, had a tremendous influence on state and federal higher education policy.

At the federal level, the Great Society legislation engineered by President Johnson altered the course of American higher education by emphasizing federal support for college access and by directing federal dollars to students rather than institutions. Prior to 1965, "the federal role had been defined in terms of meeting national needs rather than advancing individual citizens' rights to an education" (Frances, 1980, p. 27). This change in federal policy—from the focus on "all who are able" in the National Defense Education Act of 1958 to the concerns for "all who can benefit" in the Higher Education Act of 1965—led eventually to the entitlement provisions of the Pell Grant program (formerly Basic Educational Opportunity Grant program) established by the Education Amendments of 1972.

The changing federal role in higher education is reflected in the rapid expansion of student aid and related support programs, coupled with the leveling-off of constant dollar funding for federal research and development projects, between 1965 and 1977. These two trends resulted in dramatic shifts in the allocation of federal higher education expenditures; thus, in 1967, 65 percent of these expenditures went for institutional support, largely in the form of funding for research and development, and student aid allocations amounted to only 35 percent of the total; by 1975, student aid totaled 72 percent of federal higher education outlays, and institutional support dropped to 28 percent (Carlson, 1978). In the 1976–77 academic year, federal student aid outlays accounted for almost one fourth of total (federal, state, and local) government expenditures for higher education, and just over 80 percent of total government student aid outlays (Carnegie Council on Policy Studies in Higher Education, 1980, table A-6).

The expanded federal presence in higher education tends to overshadow the primacy of the historical state role and responsibility for higher education. The Carnegie Commission on Higher Education (1972, p. 39) observed that: "The states have frequently functioned as educational entrepreneurs, financiers, and planners [while] the federal government has primarily been a purchaser of services [for example, research] and, through its student aid program, has encouraged others to become consumers of higher education." The states are the senior partner in higher education. Although the states and the federal government share the common goal of increasing access to and participation in postsecondary education, they have taken different approaches in their efforts to address these issues. The states have focused on the capacity for access and participation, encouraging the construction of more institutions and the development of more degree programs. In contrast, the federal government has focused on individual participation, and since 1965 federal policy has been primarily concerned with underwriting the individual costs of access and participation.

Despite the espoused similarity of goals, there are underlying tensions in the relationship between the federal and the
state governments. Disputes (and litigation) center on states'
policies, programs, and practices that are perceived to be detrimental to the interests of minority groups. The history of
American minorities' quest for equality of educational opportunity has often placed the states against the federal government.
Litigation is the most frequent method of redress, and, as Keppel
(1980) notes, the history of the past two decades shows "an
uneasy relationship between federal purpose and state performance" (p. 149). In the simplest terms, the continuing drama
played a benevolent federal government against the recalcitrant
states: Washington was the enforcer, wielding both carrot and
stick to ensure state compliance with court orders, legislative
acts, and administrative edicts.

Major Federal Programs

Federal programs that contribute to minority participation in higher education can be grouped into four major categories: institutional aid, student financial assistance, special
(categorical) assistance to promote access and persistence, and
support for professional training and human resource development (Table 35). Many of these programs, particularly those in
the last two categories, are, by statute, directed at minorities. In
some instances—for example, financial aid programs—minority
students are not the statutory beneficiaries, yet disproportionately
high minority participation in these programs provides clear
evidence of their significance to minority groups' goals and
interests. Both the number and funding levels of these programs
have increased rapidly during the past fifteen years.

Institutional Aid Programs. Federal support for institutions of
higher education began with the Morrill Land-Grant College Act
of 1862. Federal support for institutions serving minorities dates
back to the "separate but equal" provisions of the Second Morrill
Act of 1890 (Preer, 1979). Currently the federal government
funds three programs that provide direct financial assistance to

Table 35. Federal Higher Education Programs Assisting Minorities

	1980 Funding (millions of $)
Institutional aid programs	
Land-Grant College Appropriations	$ 2.9[a]
Tribally-Controlled Community Colleges	25.0[b]
Strengthening Developing Institutions	110.0
Student financial aid programs	
Pell Grants (formerly the	
Basic Educational Opportunity Grant/BEOG program)	2,414.4
Supplemental Educational Opportunity Grants	370.0
College Work-Study Program	550.0
National Direct Student Loan Program	300.8
Guaranteed Student Loan Program	1,609.3
State-Student Incentive Grants	76.8
Special programs (access and persistence)	
Upward Bound	57.5[b]
Talent Search	15.3[b]
Special Services for Disadvantaged Students	54.6[b]
Educational Opportunity Centers	7.7[b]
College Assistance Migrant Program	1.5[b]
Professional training and human resource development	
Minority Access to Research Careers	3.6[b]
Minority Biomedical Support	18.1
Legal Training for the Disadvantaged	1.0[b]
Bilingual Education Programs	166.0[b]
Indian Education—Fellowships for Indian Students	1.5
Health Professions Recruitment Program for Indians	1.1
Health Professions Preparatory Scholarship Program for Indians	0.8
Health Professions Scholarships for Indians	3.6
Prefreshman and Cooperative Education for Minorities and Indians	1.0[b]
Staff Training for Special Programs Staff and Leadership Personnel	2.4
Graduate and Professional Opportunities Program	8.6

[a] Includes only those funds administered by the U.S. Department of Education.
[b] Estimated.
Source. Green (1981b).

minority postsecondary institutions: Land-Grant College Appropriations, authorized by the Second Morrill Act, administered by
the Department of Education; the Strengthening Developing
Institutions program, Title III of the Higher Education Act of
1965, also administered by the Department of Education; and
the Tribally Controlled Community College program, established
in 1978 and administered by the Bureau of Indian Affairs. In
each instance, the federal government makes grants to eligible
institutions on the basis of their history or special characteristics.
These funds are intended to support general institutional activities, or, in the case of Title III, special programs that contribute
to development and improvement.

    Student Financial Assistance. The major federal student finan-
cial aid programs administered by the Department of Education
include Pell Grants (formerly Basic Educational Opportunity
Grants), Supplemental Educational Opportunity Grants (SEOG),
College Work-Study (CWS), National Direct Student Loan (NDSL),
State Student Incentive Grants (SSIG), and Guaranteed Student
Loans (GSL). While not specifically targeted to minorities, these
programs nonetheless play a critical role in facilitating minority
access to and participation in postsecondary education. Intended
to help low- and middle-income students manage the costs of
college attendance, these five programs have high rates of minority participation. Atelsek and Gomberg (1977b) report that while
fall 1976 minority enrollments constituted 13.7 percent of total
enrollments, minority students constituted 34.9 percent (undup-
licated count) of all federal aid program recipients, with minority participation ranging from 43 percent in the Pell Grant
program to 17 percent in the GSL program. Additional evidence
of how significant these federal aid programs are for minority
students comes from the 1978 freshman survey of the Cooperative Institutional Research Program (CIRP): 55 percent of all
minority first-time, full-time college students reported participating in at least one federal aid program (unpublished CIRP
data, 1978).

    Though not directly managed by the Department of
Education, the SSIG program is designed to increase state
funding for student financial aid programs by providing federal

challenge grants to states on a dollar-for-dollar matching basis, although in many states the ratio of federal to state contributions is much smaller.

In fiscal 1980, the total federal expenditure for these Department of Education programs (including SSIG) exceeded $5.3 billion (Table 35). A seventh student financial aid program, managed by the Bureau of Indian Affairs, provides additional support for American Indian students.

Special Programs—Access and Persistence. The federal government's special programs for the disadvantaged—Talent Search, Upward Bound, Special Services, Educational Opportunity Centers, and College Assistance Migrant Program—all seek to facilitate and encourage access to and participation in higher education by providing special interventions to identify, counsel, tutor, and otherwise assist academically able but educationally or financially disadvantaged students to complete high school and persist in college. Although the legislation does not specifically identify minority students as the intended target population for these programs, their legislative history as well as the high level of minority participation attest to their importance in helping minority students to enter and persist in higher education (Gordon, 1975).

Professional Training and Human Resource Development. Eleven federal programs provide funds to support minority participation in professional training and human resource development in selected disciplinary areas. Unlike most of the programs previously described, not all the professional training programs are managed by the Department of Education; four are under the jurisdiction of the Indian Health Service Office and one is coordinated by the Department of Energy. In general, these programs seek to increase the numbers of minority professionals in the sciences, engineering, and health fields.

The Role of the States

The rapid growth of federal higher education programs since 1965 has tended to overshadow the states' presence in higher education. The states—and not the federal government—

assumed the major costs and burdens of expanding the public sector of higher education in the years following World War II. Currently the states "contribute more to the total higher education budget than either the federal government, or students and their families" (Sloan Commission on Government and Higher Education, 1980, p. 14). In the academic year 1976–77, state governments contributed more than 40 percent of the $32-plus billion spent for educational and general purposes in American higher education (Carnegie Council on Policy Studies in Higher Education, 1980) In fiscal 1978, the states spent $2.42 for every dollar supplied by the federal government in the area of general institutional support (National Center for Education Statistics, 1980, p. 162). Consistent with constitutional intent, the states remain the senior partner among the three levels of government in relation to higher education.

Access and Educational Opportunity. State support for the expansion of public higher education during the postwar years implicitly addressed the issues of access and educational opportunity before these concerns rose to the federal policy agenda:

> The primary legal and financial responsibility for meeting the educational needs of the American people resides with the states. For the last two decades state energies and resources in higher education have focused on the expansion of opportunity in response to rapid growth of the college-age population, higher proportions of high school graduates, and increased participation rates. Since the 1960 California *Master Plan for Higher Education*, the first formal state commitment to provide education after high school to all who had the desire and motivation to benefit, the states have been at the forefront of the national movement to improve access. The state master plans developed during the sixties and early seventies were essentially blueprints for increasing access, and they led to dramatic increases in the numbers of programs and institutions of postsecondary education. The approaches used by the states have varied but generally have included some combination of ensuring geographic

proximity, enlarging institutions, developing new institutions and programs (most notably community colleges and vocational programs), providing student financial assistance, and increasing institutional support [Callan, 1978, pp. 54–55].

Callan adds that while the federal role has become increasingly important and financially significant, the states are primarily responsible for "the task for linking factors related to access— student aid, various forms of institutional support, and articulation between high schools and colleges . . . ideally working in collaboration with campuses." He notes that although the goal of equal access and opportunity has yet to be fully realized, the progress of the past two decades has been significant.

However, not all observers would agree with this assessment. Although the states did create the structures needed to accommodate increasing numbers of students, many critics argue that they have not been as successful in dealing with the real heart of the access issue, that is, the entry and retention rates of nontraditional students in all segments of public higher education. Federal incentives have been responsible for much of the movement of minority students into public colleges. Minority enrollments are greatest in those public institutions with the fewest educational resources, the two-year colleges (see Chapter Seven). And the *Adams* case, which in part addresses the role and mission of historically black public colleges in state systems of higher education, serves as a lingering reminder of the effects of previous segregational policies and practices in the states.

Public policy generally has focused on the issue of access to *any* postsecondary institution, assuming approximately equivalent effects and benefits of college attendance. This assumption is not supported by nearly three decades of research on college students and institutional effects (see Feldman and Newcomb, 1969, chap. 11; Astin, 1977a) nor by the analyses reported in Chapter Five. The meritocratic criteria frequently found in state master plans, criteria that link institutional and program quality with student attributes (for example, grades and test scores), can serve to restrict access, particulary among minorities.

Financial data suggest that one significant aspect of the

access issue relates to the distribution of educational resources—and the concentration of these resources in the "least accessible" institutions (see Chapter Seven). Clark Kerr (1963) was among the first to describe the potential conflict between access and excellence from the standpoint of the states, warning that state governments would find it difficult to satisfy the academic community's heightened expectations for program expansion and quality improvement and at the same time accommodate the increasing numbers of high school graduates who aspired to attain college degrees. Indeed, the states' interest in and responsibility for educational access and opportunity at all degree levels, and for all citizens—not just recent high school graduates—may well conflict with traditional notions of academic quality. However, in many states the definition of quality is broadening to include concern for the educational process as well as characteristics of students and faculty. This shift in perspective is in large part a response to the demands from a number of constituencies for an accounting of the resources allocated to public postsecondary education, and the availability and distribution of educational opportunities to various clientele (Callan, 1978). State program review, with its focus on accountability, equality, and quality—accountability for resources, equality of educational opportunity, and quality in education programs—also contributes to a new awareness of the nature of the states' responsibility for higher education (Green, 1981a).

Programs for the Disadvantaged. The size of and funding for state programs for the disadvantaged are small compared to the federal programs previously described. Some states operate sizable financial aid and support programs, while others have only recently begun to develop such programs. Several factors appear to affect a state's perspective on this issue: the size and the political influence of the state's minority population, legislative and gubernatorial interest (in part, perhaps, a reflection of minority political influence), the size and diversity of public and private higher education in the state, competition in and among both public and private institutions, and, of course, litigation and court orders. In recent years state governments have exhibited growing interest in and financial support for special minority programs. This trend may continue, as minorities become a larger proportion of the college-age cohort in the 1980s (Breneman and Nelson, 1980), although budget constraints and changing federal and state social program priorities could adversely affect these programs in the coming years. In their quest to maintain enrollments during the coming period of decline in the traditional college-age population, public institutions are likely to increase their efforts to recruit and retain minority students (see Frances, 1980). Additionally, federal incentives, such as the recent challenge-grant provisions of the revised Developing Institutions legislation, as well as judicial directives (for example, the *Adams* decision), will continue to affect state performance, programs, and funding decisions.

Like the federal government, the states have focused most of their programmatic efforts in the area of financial assistance, in part because of the federal incentives of the State Student Incentive Grant program. Although the federal government has shouldered the major costs of direct, need-based student aid since the 1958 National Defense Education Act legislation (Carnegie Council on Policy Studies in Higher Education, 1980, supplement A), state contributions to student financial assistance efforts are not insignificant. First, there are state subsidies that come indirectly in the form of low tuition, a sum that is difficult to estimate but surely amounts to several billion dollars annually. Second state contributions in the form of direct student assistance totaled $704 million in the 1977–78 academic year. Although SSIG funds are matching grants, the $60 million federal appropriation in 1977–78 accounted for only 5.9 percent of the total state funds awarded. Moreover, SSIG funds accounted for no more than 20 percent of the state aid dollars in twenty-one states and only fourteen states made only the minimum 50 percent contribution (U.S. Office of Education, 1979). Furthermore, while state financial aid programs traditionally have employed meritocratic or achievement criteria (for example, the New York State Regents Scholarships), of late these funds have been used to provide financial assistance to low-income students regardless of previous academic achievement.

In addition to financial aid programs, a number of states

(including California, Illinois, New York, New Jersey, and Wisconsin) have appropriated funds for campus-based affirmative action programs, recruitment efforts, and outreach activities. Although the terms and provisions vary from state to state, these programs, like other affirmative action efforts, seek to encourage minority access to public institutions, generally four-year colleges and universities with traditionally low minority enrollments. In the southern states affected by the *Adams* litigation, such efforts and programs are often part of state compliance plans (see Haynes, 1979b).

The Impact of Federal Programs

The underlying conceptual basis of current federal higher education policy rests on the link between education and economic opportunity. American higher education policy—the expansion of college access and the elimination of both the financial and nonfinancial barriers that impede matriculation and degree completion—is tied to a theory of social mobility and economic opportunity. Higher education has become the chosen vehicle of American social policy: Increased minority participation in American higher education is to yield increased minority participation in the American occupational structure, in the rewards of the American economic system, and in the mainstream of American life.

Since 1964, presidents, educational leaders, and government policy makers have espoused a broad and ambitious set of goals for the range of government programs that assist and support minority participation in higher education. Six complementary federal programs attempt to eliminate the financial barriers to college attendance. Four major intervention programs, a series of implicitly linked and dynamic support programs that address the nonfinancial barriers to access and persistence, begin in the junior and senior high schools and carry through the undergraduate years. One major institutional aid program assists colleges that have a history of service to low-income and disadvantaged students. Participants in this program include many of the historically black institutions and some tribal community colleges, among others. Other special federal programs assist and facilitate human resource development in various fields and specializations.

The Impact of Financial Aid Programs. The Higher Education Act of 1965 authorized several financial aid programs that subsequently altered the course of federal higher education policy. Currently five programs attempt to assist access and promote choice: access to higher education, and choice of higher education institutions. A sixth program provides federal incentives for the states to develop or expand financial aid programs to assist particularly needy students.

Several sources document the importance of federal aid programs to the goal of educational equity, equality of educational opportunity, and increased minority participation in higher education. Leslie (1977) observes that "perhaps as much as or more than equity by family income, considerations of racial equity were the driving forces behind the student aid programs of the later 1960s and early 1970s" (p. 29). Grants and related financial assistance cover a significant portion of college costs for minority students.

In Chapter Five we discussed evidence suggesting that minority student persistence is enhanced by grants and the work-study program. However, the question of how these massive programs have actually affected minority student access is more difficult to judge. Perhaps the best evidence comes from the trends in minority freshman enrollments discussed in Chapter Four: Black freshman enrollments began to increase during the late 1960s and continued to increase until the mid 1970s. Hispanic enrollments (which were not monitored until 1971) also showed increases during the early 1970s. If one wishes to argue that federal aid programs enhance minority access to college, then these increases are well timed; the major need-based federal student aid programs began in 1965 and were further supplemented in 1972 with the addition of the BEOG program. While the concurrence of the advent of federal aid programs and increased minority access does not necessarily prove causation, it is at least consistent with the hypothesis that need-based federal student aid increases minority access to higher education.

Interventions for Access and Persistence. Four related federal programs are designed to address the nonfinancial barriers to college attendance. Educational Opportunity Centers provide financial and academic counseling and related services in low-income areas to assist potential college attenders. Talent Search outreach programs attempt to identify financially or culturally disadvantaged high-potential students and encourage them to complete high school and go on to college. Upward Bound programs for junior high and high school students seek to build and further develop academic skills and motivation to overcome the effects of prior inadequate schooling. Special Services for Disadvantaged Students (SSDS) programs provide personal and academic counseling, and related support services for college students.

In the past ten years, federal, state, and institutionally supported, campus-based assistance and outreach programs for disadvantaged or high-risk students have proliferated. Roueche and Snow (1977) report that 86 percent of the nation's public institutions offer some sort of special services or programs for disadvantaged students: "Specifically, 95 percent of the [public] community colleges and 77 percent of the [public] senior colleges are providing a special service such as tutoring, counseling, and/or financial aid. In only four years we find a nearly 40 percent increase in special services for the academically disadvantaged student in higher education" (p. 19).

Regardless of their funding source (federal, state, institutional, or private), these programs are closely identified with minority interests and the goal of increased minority participation in higher education. These programs have ambitious goals and objectives: increased access, improved academic performance, and better persistence and degree completion rates. These programs have been extensively evaluated and, while the results are not always consistent or balanced, it appears that they are generally effective and do contribute to increased access and persistence (Burkheimer and others, 1980; Gordon, 1975; U.S. Office of Education, 1979).

Institutional Support. The Title III program of the Higher Education Act (as amended) is the largest institutional aid program in the federal higher education budget. The program is closely allied to and identified with minority interests, particularly those of the nation's historically black colleges. The program has been embroiled in some controversy for a number of years, in part because several evaluation studies have questioned both the purpose and the effectiveness of the program.

Despite its problems, Title III is a popular program, and a politically sensitive one as well. From its inception the program has been closely linked to the historically black colleges. Legislative amendments in the early years of the program also linked Title III to Hispanic and Indian interests. Four administrations have supported and expanded the program, perhaps in part because it was a visible way to demonstrate presidential support for black educational concerns.

While various evaluation studies (U.S. General Accounting Office, 1974, 1979; Hodgkinson and Schenkel, 1974; Weathersby and others, 1977) raise some questions about the overall effectiveness of the Title III program, grant recipients, their representatives, and their supporters are unequivocal in their support for this program. Participating and potentially eligible institutions want and, perhaps more importantly, feel they need Title III assistance to help sustain their institutions; to make some improvements in curriculum and administration; and to continue serving their low-income, disadvantaged, and poorly prepared students. Recipients' perceptions and assessments of the program's effectiveness unfortunately are not the kind of data that can be quantified and used to document qualitative improvement.

Federal aid does help Title III institutions maintain a baseline of academic and financial viability; the absence of such funds would adversely affect resources, expenditures, and ultimately the students attending these colleges.

Conclusions

In broad terms, the state and federal legislative agendas for the postwar development of American higher education are essentially complete (Breneman and Nelson, 1980). The state agenda, reflected in the level of state support for the expansion of the public sector during the past three decades, has placed some form of postsecondary instruction within geographical access of virtually all citizens. The ambitious federal agenda, first articulated in the Higher Education Act of 1965 (as amended), has also been realized. State and federal efforts have created a system of higher education unrivaled among the nations of the world, marked by an array of institutional diversity and the highest levels of citizen participation in postsecondary education.

The expanded federal presence in higher education tends to overshadow the primacy of the states' role and responsibility for higher education, but the states remain the senior partner in higher education. Despite the espoused similarity of goals, there has been some tension in the relationship between the federal and the state governments. Disputes (and litigation) center on state policies, programs, and practices that are perceived by federal officials to be detrimental to minority groups' interests. In simple terms, this drama seems to pit a benevolent federal government against the recalcitrant states: Washington has become the enforcer, wielding both carrot and stick to ensure state compliance with court orders and legislative edicts.

A review of state and federal programs and their effect on minority participation in higher education warrants the following conclusions:

- Government programs have had a positive effect on minority participation in higher education.
- Although the evaluative evidence is not conclusive, there is reason to believe that federal aid programs focused on the financial and nonfinancial barriers to access and participation in higher education contribute to increased access, improved persistence, and fuller participation.
- Institutional aid programs contribute to the maintenance of viable academic programs and financial stability in minority institutions.
- Although the rapid growth of federal categorical programs tends to overshadow states' roles and responsibilities, the individual states do support important programs that contribute to minority access and participation.

✤ 7 ✤

Equal Access and
Equal Opportunity

"Equal access" and "equal op-
portunity" are among the most popular catch phrases in the
contemporary jargon of postsecondary education. Virtually all
politicians and public figures, regardless of their political per-
suasion, claim to support equality of access in higher education.
In this chapter we carefully examine both the myth and the
reality of equal access.

One difficulty with the notion of equal opportunity lies in
the definition of the term itself. Many legislators and policy
makers are content to define access simply as the student's ability
to enroll in *some* postsecondary institution (California State
Department of Education, 1960; Executive Office of the President, 1979; National Commission on the Financing of Postsecondary Education, 1973; Willingham, 1970). If institutions
were roughly equivalent in their resources and offerings, this
definition would probably be acceptable. However, institutions
are by no means equivalent, and a minority student's future may

depend as much on the *kind* of institution attended as on attendance in itself. With the proliferation of public community colleges and the substantial financial aid now available to needy students, the real issue of access is not who goes to college, but who goes to *which* college.

Legislators, policy makers, and others concerned with expanding access for disadvantaged minorities would be well advised to resist any simple definitions. Rather, they should take a critical look at the diversity of colleges and examine the consequences of current admissions and financial aid policies in terms of such diversity.

It can be argued that higher education in the U.S. has evolved into a highly refined institutional status hierarchy (Astin and Lee, 1971). Like most status systems, it comprises a few elite and well-known institutions, a substantial middle class, and a large number of relatively unknown institutions. While most people are familiar with the hierarchical nature of private higher education—with a few prestigious private universities occupying the top positions—they do not always recognize that a similar hierarchy exists within many public systems. Unlike the private hierarchy, which evolved more or less by historical accident, the hierarchies within public systems were developed as part of a conscious plan. In the California Master Plan for Higher Education, for example, the hierarchical nature of public higher education is made explicit: "If the state colleges and the university have real differences of function between them, they should be exacting (in contrast to public higher education in most other states) because the junior colleges relieve them of the burden of doing remedial work. Both have the heavy obligation to the state to restrict the privilege of entering and remaining to those who are well above average in the college-age group" (California State Department of Education, 1960, p. 66).

Where Do Minority Students Enroll?

How are students from various racial and ethnic groups distributed among institutions at different levels in the hierarchy? Table 36 shows the distribution of Whites, Blacks, Hispanics,

Table 36. Percentage of College Students Enrolled in Different Types of Institutions, Fall 1978, by Racial or Ethnic Group

	Public Institutions			Private Institutions		
Group	Universities	Other Four-Year Institutions	Two-Year Colleges	Universities	Other Four-Year Institutions	Two-Year Colleges
Whites	19.7	24.8	33.2	6.5	14.6	1.3
Blacks	9.7	30.6	39.3	4.3	13.5	2.7
Hispanics	8.6	25.0	53.3	4.1	7.9	1.1
American Indians[a]	12.5	22.4	53.0	2.9	7.1	2.1
All students	18.4	25.2	34.5	6.4	14.1	1.4

[a]Includes Alaskan Natives.
Source. Dearman and Plisko (1980, table 3.5).

and American Indians among public and private two-year colleges, four-year colleges, and universities. By far the most significant pattern in Table 36 concerns the minorities: *Students from all minority groups shown tend to be concentrated in two-year public colleges.* (See also de los Santos and others, 1980; Dearman and Plisko, 1980; Olivas, 1979; Smartt, 1980.) In fact, more than *half* of all Hispanic and American Indian college students are enrolled in public community colleges, compared with only 39 percent of black students and 33 percent of white students. Whites, by contrast, are relatively highly concentrated in both the public and private universities at the top of the hierarchy. Indeed, Whites are twice as likely as either Blacks or Hispanics to be enrolled in a public university and about 50 percent more likely to be enrolled in a private university.

Table 36 also shows that Whites are more likely than minorities to enroll in some type of private institution. Thus, the proportion of Whites enrolling in private colleges (22.4 percent) is nearly twice as great as the proportion of American Indians (12.1 percent) and Hispanics (13.1 percent). Blacks are only slightly less likely (20.5 percent) than Whites to enroll in private colleges, a finding that is no doubt attributable to the fact that a large number of predominantly black institutions are private four-year colleges.

Every state has one or more flagship universities that generally are regarded as the most prestigious and influential public institutions within the state. Access to such public institutions is of considerable significance to disadvantaged minorities, since these institutions frequently serve as conduits to positions of power and influence within state government and private industry within the state.

To identify the flagship institutions within each of the fifty states, we utilized the typology of universities developed by the Carnegie Commission on Higher Education (1973). The commission presents a hierarchy of universities based on such factors as the amount of federal research money received and the total number of doctorates awarded. We used the top four categories of this typology (in descending order of prestige): Research Universities I, Research Universities II, Degree-Granting Universities I, and Degree-Granting Universities II. The university within each state that had the highest classification was designated as a flagship university. If more than one university received the highest classification, all such institutions were used. Following these guidelines, we identified sixty-five flagship universities. Most states contained only one flagship university, and only one state (California) contained more than two.

Minority representation was ascertained using racial enrollment data from the 1978 Higher Education General Information Survey conducted by the National Center for Education Statistics (NCES). An institution's representation of any minority group was determined by comparing the percentage of *undergraduate* enrollment for that group in the institution with the total enrollment of that group in institutions throughout the state. Note that total enrollment in the state (which was used because it was readily available) provides a conservative basis for estimating underrepresentation, since total enrollments include graduate and professional students (among whom minorities are known to be most severely underrepresented). In other words, the estimates of minority underrepresentation obtained by this procedure tend to underestimate the full degree of underrepresentation.

Table 37 summarizes the overall results for the sixty-five flagship universities. Not surprisingly, the results lean clearly in the direction of underrepresentation, with about 75 percent of the flagship institutions enrolling smaller proportions of minorities than would be expected from the total minority enrollment

Table 37. Representation of Minorities Among Undergraduates at Sixty-five Flagship Universities

Number of Universities in Which Group Is:	Minority Group		
	Blacks	Hispanics	American Indians
Overrepresented	6	9	10
Proportionately represented	3	8	9
Underrepresented	56	48	46

Note. Representation was determined by comparing the percentage of an institution's undergraduate minority enrollments with the percentage of total minority enrollments in all colleges and universities within the state. Representation was considered proportionate when the institution and state figures matched to the first decimal place.

within the state (which, of course, includes the flagship institution's enrollments). But these figures disguise an even more
significant fact: the *degree* of underrepresentation is much greater
than even the limited overrepresentation shown in Table 37. For
example, the median (absolute) degree of underrepresentation
of Blacks at fifty-six institutions (4.0 percent) is about *forty* times
greater than the median overrepresentation of Blacks at six
institutions (0.1 percent).

It is of some interest to examine the individual flagship
institutions that show the greatest degree of minority underrepresentation in their undergraduate student body. For this purpose
we identified those institutions that showed the highest *absolute*
rates of minority underrepresentation; an absolute rate is the
simple arithmetic difference between the percentage actually
enrolled and the expected percentage based on the total enrollment of that minority group in higher education institutions
throughout the state. We also computed for each of these
institutions a *relative* measure of underrepresentation by dividing
the institution's enrollment of each minority group by the
expected enrollment based on state figures. Thus, a relative rate
of underrepresentation of 50 percent, for example, indicates that
an institution enrolls only half as many members of that minority
group as would be expected from state figures. A relative underrepresentation figure of 75 percent indicates that an institution
enrolled only one fourth as many members of that minority
group as would be expected from state figures. Such an institution
would have to quadruple its enrollment of that group in order to
achieve proportionate representation.

Table 38 shows those institutions with the greatest (absolute) degree of underrepresentation of Blacks in the undergraduate student body. Not surprisingly, the flagship institutions at the
top of the list are located almost exclusively in the South, where
most public institutions of higher education were fully segregated
until the late 1950s and 1960s. It could also be argued, of course,
that using absolute rather than relative measures of underrepresentation biases the results in favor of those institutions located
in states whose black population is relatively small. Note, however,
that the *relative* degree of underrepresentation is very high in

Table 38. Flagship Universities with the
Greatest Underrepresentation of Black Undergraduates

	Percentage of Blacks Among:		Percentage of Underrepresentation	
Institution	Institution's Undergraduates	All Higher Education Students in State	Absolute	Relative
Mississippi State U.	7.6	29.6	22.0	74
Clemson U. [So. Carolina]	1.7	22.2	20.5	92
Auburn U. [Alabama]	1.9	22.4	20.5	92
Louisiana State U.	4.7	23.3	18.6	80
U. Georgia	4.4	19.0	14.6	67
North Carolina State U.	5.7	20.1	14.4	72
U. North Carolina	6.8	20.1	13.3	66
Virginia Polytechnic	1.8	14.6	12.8	88
U. Arkansas	4.6	15.0	10.4	69
U. Tennessee	5.5	15.7	10.2	65
U. Maryland	7.8	18.0	10.2	57
U. Virginia	5.3	14.6	9.3	64
U. South Carolina	13.0	22.2	9.2	41
Texas A&M U.	0.7	9.8	9.1	93
U. Illinois	3.9	12.8	8.9	70
U. Delaware	3.2	11.5	8.3	72
U. Texas, Austin	2.6	9.8	7.2	74
U. Florida	5.2	11.5	6.3	55
U. Missouri	3.3	9.3	6.0	65
SUNY Stony Brook	4.8	10.8	6.0	56
U. California, Davis	2.9	8.6	5.7	66
U. California, Berkeley	3.5	8.6	5.1	59
Michigan State U.	5.2	10.3	5.1	50
Pennsylvania State U.	2.4	7.4	5.0	68

almost all institutions in Table 38; indeed, for three of the institutions the degree of underrepresentation is over 90 percent (which means that these institutions would have to increase their black enrollments more than tenfold in order to achieve proportionate enrollments of Blacks).

It is also of interest that the four institutions with the greatest relative underenrollment of Blacks (Clemson, Auburn, Texas A&M, and Virginia Polytechnic Institute) are all technologically oriented universities. At least two factors may account for these extreme rates of underrepresentation: the avoidance by

Blacks of major fields in science and engineering (see Chapter Three), and the possibility that such institutions rely more heavily in their admissions practices on standardized tests (which tends to put Blacks at a considerable disadvantage when competing with others). The institution with the largest degree of overrepresentation of Blacks (2.9 percent) is the University of Pittsburgh. The only other institutions with overrepresentation beyond 0.2 percent were the University of Washington (1.1 percent) and the University of Minnesota (0.4 percent). All three of these institutions, it should be noted, are located in large urban areas and two of them (Washington and Minnesota) are located in states with relatively small black populations.

Table 39 shows the thirteen flagship institutions with the greatest underenrollments of Hispanics (the NCES surveys did not disaggregate Hispanics into Puerto Ricans, Chicanos, and so forth). These institutions represent all those with underrepresentation rates of at least 2.0 percent. Note that the absolute degrees of underrepresentation are smaller than those for Blacks, a finding which results simply from the fact that Blacks are more numerous than Hispanics. The location of the institutions clearly follows the population distribution of Hispanics: New York, Florida, the Southwest, and California. It is also of interest that the institution with by far the largest degree of underrepresentation (Texas A&M) is a technologically oriented university.

In nine flagship universities Hispanics are overrepresented, but it is difficult to argue that any of these display a significant degree of overrepresentation. At six institutions overrepresentation was 0.1 percent; at two, 0.2 percent; and at one (the University of New Mexico), 0.3 percent.

Table 40 shows the institutions with the largest absolute underrepresentation of American Indians. Because of the relatively small numbers of American Indians enrolled in postsecondary institutions in any given state, institutions are included in the list if their degree of underrepresentation was 0.8 percent or greater. As was the case with Hispanics, flagship universities showing the greatest underrepresentation of American Indians tend to be located in states with relatively large Indian populations: the Plains, Southwest, Far West, Montana, and the Dakotas.

Table 39. Flagship Universities with the
Greatest Underrepresentation of Hispanic Undergraduates

	Percentage of Hispanics Among:		Percentage of Underrepresentation	
Institution	Institution's Undergraduates	All Higher Education Students in State	Absolute	Relative
Texas A&M U.	2.3	12.4	10.1	82
U. California, Berkeley	3.5	9.2	5.7	62
U. California, Davis	3.5	9.2	5.7	62
U. Arizona	4.2	8.9	4.7	53
U. Texas, Austin	7.7	12.4	4.7	38
SUNY Buffalo	1.1	5.1	4.0	78
Colorado State U.	2.0	6.0	4.0	67
U. California, San Diego	5.8	9.2	3.4	37
U. California, Los Angeles	6.4	9.2	2.8	30
SUNY Stony Brook	2.7	5.1	2.4	47
U. Florida	3.9	7.3	2.4	47
U. Colorado	3.6	6.0	2.4	40
U. Hawaii (Manoa)	1.3	3.2	2.1	59

Although the relative degree of underrepresentation in most of these institutions is high, the relative degree of underrepresentation in two institutions — the University of New Mexico and the University of Oklahoma are quite low (less than 25 percent). As it happens, these institutions also have larger enrollments of American Indians in their undergraduate student bodies (both in numbers and percentages) than any other institutions in the United States. (The University of Montana is tied with the University of Oklahoma for second place, with American Indians accounting for 2.9 percent of the undergraduate enrollment; this institution is not shown in Table 40 because the overall state enrollment of American Indians is 2.8 percent.)

Of the ten institutions with an overrepresentation of American Indians among their undergraduates, one (the University of Alaska, Fairbanks) appears to have a significant degree of overrepresentation: American Indians accounted for 12.2 percent of that university's undergraduates but only 9.4 percent of enrollments in all institutions in the state, producing an overrepresentation of 2.8 percent. Apparently, those American

Table 40. Flagship Universities with the
Greatest Underrepresentation of American Indian Undergraduates

	Percentage of American Indians:		Percentage of Underrepresentation	
Institution	Institution's Undergraduates	All Higher Education Students in State	Absolute	Relative
South Dakota State U.	0.5	3.1	2.6	84
U. Arizona	0.6	3.2	2.6	81
Oklahoma State U.	1.7	3.8	2.1	55
Montana State U.	0.8	2.8	2.0	71
U. North Dakota	1.9	3.4	1.5	44
Kansas State U.	0.3	1.3	1.0	75
U. Kansas	0.4	1.3	0.9	69
U. California, Los Angeles	0.4	1.3	0.9	69
U. Oklahoma	2.9	3.8	0.9	24
U. California, Berkeley	0.5	1.3	0.8	62
U. California, San Diego	0.5	1.3	0.8	62
U. New Mexico	3.3	4.1	0.8	20

Indians in Alaska (a category that includes Alaskan Natives) who attend higher education institutions are disproportionately concentrated in the flagship institution in that state. Overrepresentation of American Indian undergraduates at Oregon State University measures 0.7 percent; at the University of Maine, Orono, 0.4 percent; and at the University of Arkansas, Main Campus 0.3 percent.

In short, our tables dramatize the underrepresentation of Blacks, Hispanics, and American Indians in the undergraduate student bodies of the flagship institutions in most states. In some states, particularly those in which a given minority group tends to be highly concentrated, the degree of underrepresentation is severe. Clearly, the public systems of higher education in most states are not organized so as to provide equal opportunities to those minorities who do enroll in higher education within the state.

We also compared the family background, academic preparation, and residence status of freshmen entering different types of institutions. As Table 41 shows, two-year colleges, four-year colleges, and universities follow a perfect hierarchical ordering with respect to the six background characteristics we examined. In the public sector, freshmen entering universities are twice as likely to report annual parental income of $30,000 or more than are freshmen entering two-year colleges. Conversely, the parents of freshmen entering two-year colleges are twice as likely to have an annual income of less than $15,000 than are the parents of freshmen entering public universities. On both attributes, the students entering four-year institutions fall in between those entering two-year colleges and those entering universities. Comparable but even greater differences exist within the private sector.

An identical pattern occurs with respect to the educational level of the parents of freshmen. In the public sector, both the mothers and the fathers of the students entering universities are twice as likely to have a college degree as are the mothers and fathers of students entering two-year colleges; the parental education reported by students entering public four-year institutions falls midway between the other two groups. An identical hierarchical pattern exists within private institutions, although once again the differences are even more pronounced.

With respect to academic preparation, students entering public universities are more than twice as likely to have ranked in the top fifth of their high school class as are students entering public two-year colleges. Within private institutions, those entering the universities are *three times more likely* to have ranked in the top fifth of their class than are those entering private two-year colleges. Once again, students at the four-year colleges fall midway between those at the two-year colleges and those at the universities in terms of academic preparation.

The final item in Table 41 shows the proportion of freshmen living in college dormitories. This freshman characteristic was included because a considerable body of research (Astin, 1975, 1977a; Chickering, 1974) suggests that a student's educational development is enhanced if he or she lives in a dormitory during the freshman year. Once again, we find a hierarchical pattern, except that differences are sharper in the public than in the private sector. A freshman at a public university is more than three times as likely to live in a dormitory than is a

Table 41. Selected Attributes of First-Time, Full-Time Freshmen Enrolled in Different Types of Institutions, Fall 1980

Percentage of Freshmen with Attribute

	Public			Private		
Attribute	*Universities*	*Four-Year Colleges*	*Two-Year Colleges*	*Universities*	*Four-Year Colleges*	*Two-Year Colleges*
Annual parental income						
$30,000 or more	43.4	29.1	21.7	55.8	38.2	24.5
Below $15,000	18.0	31.0	35.1	14.1	24.4	38.1
Parental education						
Fathers hold college degrees	47.0	32.2	23.6	60.8	45.1	27.7
Mothers hold college degrees	29.9	20.7	15.5	42.5	31.8	19.4
Rank in top fifth of high school class	54.3	39.9	23.6	69.0	49.1	22.0
Live in college dormitories	74.4	61.5	21.1	82.1	77.1	61.4

Source. Astin, King, and Richardson (1980).

freshman entering a public two-year college. Within the private sector, dormitory living appears to be the mode, although the three types of institutions still form a hierarchical arrangement with respect to dormitory residence.

As the data shown in Tables 36 and 41 demonstrate, different types of students are by no means randomly distributed among different types of institutions. The community colleges, which represent the bottom of the institutional hierarchy within public systems, have a disproportionate share of minority students, underprepared students, and students from poor and relatively uneducated families. The universities, in contrast, have relatively few minority students and a high concentration of well-prepared students and students from well-educated and affluent families. The four-year colleges within public systems fall about midway between the two-year colleges and the universities with respect to these various freshman characteristics. An identical pattern exists within the private sector, with the differences within the hierarchy even more pronounced than is the case in the public sector.

The Distribution of Resources

While it is probably no great surprise that minority students, poor students, and underprepared students tend to be concentrated in the public community colleges, most policy makers have probably not considered the possible *consequences* of such a distribution for the minority students themselves. What difference does it make, for example, if a minority student attends a selective private university rather than a two-year college? Do students in both types of institutions receive an equivalent educational experience? Are the student's chances of completing a degree program about the same in each type of institution? In Chapter Five we considered the educational *outcomes* associated with attending various types of institutions. In the remainder of this chapter, we examine the educational *resources* available in each type of institution.

Financial Resources. We compared the six different types of institutions on nine measures of their financial resources, expressed in expenditures per full-time student. To adjust for differences between full- and part-time students, each part-time student is counted as one third of a full-time equivalent; to compensate for the greater cost of graduate and professional education, each graduate or professional student is counted as the equivalent of three full-time undergraduate students. Our results are shown in Table 42.

Our first resource measure involves expenditures for educational and general purposes, an attribute usually regarded as the best single measure of an institution's investment in its educational program. This measure does *not* include funds from externally funded research projects, auxiliary enterprises, and so on. These per-student expenditures follow the hierarchical pattern exactly, with the lowest expenditures occurring in the two-year colleges and the largest in the universities. Within the public sector, universities spend approximately 60 percent more per student than do the two-year colleges. Differences in the private sector are even greater, with the universities spending nearly three times as much as the two-year colleges.

Our second measure includes resources specifically targeted to support instruction (instructional expenditures represent a subset of educational and general expenditures). Once again we find the typical hierarchical ordering, except that the relative differences are somewhat smaller than those for educational and general expenditures. Within the public sector, universities spend about 20 percent more per student for instruction than do the two-year colleges. Within the private sector, the universities spend more than twice as much as the two-year colleges.

Per-student library expenditures, the third resource measure listed in Table 42, also differ substantially in ways consistent with the hierarchical pattern. Public universities spend about 50 percent more on libraries than two-year colleges; in the private sector, universities spend over 250 percent more than two-year colleges. Four-year colleges in both sectors fall about midway between the universities and two-year colleges.

Figures for the fourth resource measure—per-student funded research—follow the expected pattern: Universities spend

Table 42. Educational Resources per Student, by Type of Institution, 1977–78

Resource	Public			Private		
	Universities (N=119)	Four-Year Colleges (N=379)	Two-Year Colleges (N=923)	Universities (N=65)	Four-Year Colleges (N=881)	Two-Year Colleges (N=224)
Expenditures for Educational and general purposes	$4,638	$3,251	$2,909	$ 7,456	$ 4,161	$2,901
Instruction	1,761	1,487	1,464	2,171	1,492	979
Libraries	166	150	110	273	164	105
Funded research	924	90	6	2,342	72	4
Financial Aid	160	149	71	470	456	183
Student Services	192	227	233	217	358	286
Subsidy[a]	4,074	2,753	2,474	5,677	2,197	1,319
Endowment	834	128	87	15,387	3,570	1,399
Physical plant[b]	9,224	8,163	6,014	15,500	11,706	9,424

Note. The greater cost of graduate and professional education has been compensated for by weighting each graduate or professional student by a factor of 3.00; part-time students were weighted by a factor of .33.

[a]Educational and general expenditures plus financial aid minus tuition.

[b]Value of buildings, land, and equipment.

Source. Unpublished data from the National Center for Education Statistics, Higher Education General Information Survey (1973, 1978).

more than ten times as much per student as the other types of institutions.

The fifth expenditure measure, per-student financial aid, also produces substantial discrepancies that follow the hierarchical pattern. Within the public sector, universities spend more than twice as much per student on financial aid as do the community colleges. In the private sector, differences are even greater. Considering that low-income students (including many minority students) are highly concentrated in the two-year colleges and underrepresented in the universities, it is ironic that universities spend more than twice as much per student on financial aid as two-year colleges. Of course, the greater financial-aid expenditures of universities may be justified on the grounds that the student costs are higher at such institutions than at four-year and two-year colleges. A comparison of the average tuition at various types of institutions tends to support this argument. Within the public sector, the average tuition costs per year were as follows: universities, $724; four-year colleges, $647; two-year colleges, $506.

The sixth measure—per-student expenditures for student services—is the only one that does not follow the hierarchical pattern. Several explanations for this result are possible. Perhaps student services have relatively low priority in elite institutions, or perhaps students who enter the less selective institutions require more support services (see, for example, Cross, 1971).

Our seventh resource measure is called "subsidy" and constitutes an alternative way of looking at the issues of costs and student aid by quantifying the extent to which different types of institutions subsidize a student's educational costs. Subsidy was estimated by adding the amount expended for educational and general purposes to the amount expended for student financial aid and subtracting tuition. The net difference represents the amount to which an institution subsidizes a student's educational costs. Once again, results follow precisely the hierarchical ordering, with the smallest subsidies found in the two-year public colleges and the largest by far found in the universities. Given the substantial differences in parental income (Table 41), we note that the subsidy is smallest in those institutions enrolling the poorest students (including the bulk of minority students), and greatest in those institutions enrolling the most well-to-do students (and relatively few minority students).

More important, these data show clearly that educational opportunity, as measured by the amount contributed to a student's education through public funds, is by no means equivalent in different types of public institutions. Here we have another example of how the hierarchical public systems based on selective admissions serve to deny an equal opportunity to minorities. Those minority students who attend two-year colleges receive substantially less public subsidy for their postsecondary education than do the students (most of whom are white) who qualify to enter the more selective public colleges and universities.

Our last two resource measures, per-student endowment and per-student value of the physical plant, once again exactly follow the hierarchical pattern.

Other Resources. We earlier pointed out that most freshmen entering public universities and private institutions of all types live in residence halls, a decided asset in terms of student development (Astin, 1975, 1977a; Chickering, 1974). A second nonfinancial asset of a college or university that affects student development is the quality of faculty. Is there any evidence that the faculty in the universities are superior to those in the two- and four-year colleges? Although direct measures of faculty quality are not available, it is possible to argue that the best faculty generally command high salaries. A recent study (Astin, 1977a) shows that the average faculty salary paid in public universities is approximately 38 percent higher than the average salary paid in community colleges and about 22 percent higher than the average paid in public four-year colleges. Thus, once again, the evidence suggests that equal opportunity, here defined as the quality of faculty, is denied to those minority students who have no option but to attend a community college.

One final measure of opportunity, and perhaps the most significant one, concerns the likely *outcomes* of attendance at various types of institutions. As we saw in Chapter Five, a student's chances of completing a baccalaureate program are substantially reduced if he or she initially enrolls at a community college rather than a four-year institution. Even greater discrepancies are apparent when the various types of four-year institutions are further subdivided in terms of their selectivity (Astin, 1977a). Thus, since admissions test scores and high school grades are the primary criteria used by the most selective institutions in accepting applicants, and since minority students tend to fare poorly in comparison to Whites on both criteria, the hierarchical institutional arrangement of American higher education has even greater negative consequences for minorities than the data in Table 42 suggest.

Institutional selectivity represents perhaps the best single index of the quality of an institution's educational resources (Astin, 1962; Astin and Henson, 1977). Since the selectivity of a college has a strong negative relationship to the proportion of minority students it enrolls (Astin, King, and Richardson, 1980), it is important to understand which background characteristics of students affect their chances of being admitted to a selective institution. According to a recent analysis (Karabel and Astin, 1975), a student's high school grades and test scores are by far the most important determinants of the selectivity of the college he or she attends. Although socioeconomic measures (parental income and education) are moderately related to the selectivity of the college attended, this relationship appears to be mediated chiefly (though not entirely) by test scores and grades. In other words, the positive association between students' social class and the quality of the college attended is explained in large part by the fact that students from high socioeconomic backgrounds have better academic preparation than those from lower socioeconomic backgrounds. This finding once again underscores the importance of academic preparation as a determinant of which colleges minorities attend.

Why a Hierarchy?

Educators have developed elaborate rationales for institutional hierarchies based on selective admissions; for example, some argue that the system offers an institution for every type of student. However, the system is perpetuated less for educational reasons than for reasons connected with competition and status. University professors support selective admissions because high achievers are better students and thus easier to teach. Alumni, legislators, faculty, administrators, and probably a great many students support selective admissions because the enrollment of highly motivated and talented students is likely to yield distinguished and affluent alumni. Many secondary school educators support the track system that results from selective admissions because they see it as a reward or incentive to motivate their students; high school teachers and guidance counselors frequently tell their students to study hard so that they will be able to attend a good institution.

There are also important *educational* defenses for a tiered system. Perhaps the most common justification is that students will develop better academically if they are grouped with students of similar ability. This assumption has several important corollaries: (1) Bright students need the stimulation and competition of other bright students to realize their full potential; (2) bright students will become bored and apathetic if grouped with students of lesser ability; and (3) mediocre students will become intimidated and discouraged if forced to compete with bright students. Although little research has been done to test these assumptions, the evidence that is available does not support them. Thus, as far as learning outcomes are concerned, there seems to be little or no interaction between the selectivity of the institution and the ability of the student (Astin, 1968; Nichols, 1964; Rock, Centra, and Linn, 1970). Although this evidence is by no means exhaustive, it does suggest that certain widely held assumptions about tracking may be wrong.

Another argument used to defend selective admissions is that any relaxation of admissions standards would lower an institution's academic standards. While this is indeed possible, it is by no means inevitable. The traditional view is that academic standards are determined primarily by the abilities of the students who are admitted. This bit of folklore may apply to institutions that grade strictly on the curve, but there is no reason that colleges cannot set any standards they wish, independent of their admissions practices. Academic standards specify the performance levels required of students in order to pass certain courses or complete requirements for a degree. Even though fewer students are likely to succeed if performance levels remain high while admissions criteria are relaxed, such standards can still be defined and maintained, independent of changes in the admissions process.

If one accepts the idea that colleges exist to *educate*, the model of selective admissions based on test scores and prior grades makes little sense. If an institution exists to educate students, its mission is to produce certain desirable changes in students or, more simply, to make a difference in the student's life. This "value-added" approach to the goals of higher education suggests that admissions procedures should be designed to select students who are likely to be *influenced* by the educational process, regardless of their entering performance level. (See Chapter Eight for a fuller discussion of this issue.)

Too often college admissions officers tend to operate like personnel managers in a commercial enterprise, rather than like educators. Picking winners is an appropriate activity for businesses and industries, whose goal is to hire the best talent in the interests of maximizing productivity and profit. Similarly, competition among rival companies for the pool of available talent is consistent with the very nature of business. But the business model, which has been adopted by the most selective institutions, is not appropriate to education. The mission of the college is *not* simply to maximize its output of distinguished alumni by enrolling as many talented students as possible. Such a static process reduces the college to a funnel: What comes out is purely a matter of what goes in. Colleges and other educational institutions exist to change the student, to contribute to personal development, to make a difference.

Perhaps the strongest justification for selective admissions can be made in the case of advanced professional education, where very high absolute levels of performance are needed to protect the public (law and medicine are perhaps the most obvious examples of such professions). Even if current graduation or certification standards in these professions were maintained, one could argue that a more open admissions policy would be extremely costly because many relatively poorly prepared students would either take an inordinately long time to reach minimum performance standards or drop out of advanced training because the academic demands were simply too great. While such arguments have some validity, these issues are relative rather than absolute. That is, if special admissions standards for professional education were to be established for minorities, the important questions are *how much* additional time the less well-prepared minority student will need to reach certification standards, *how much* the dropout rate will increase, and *how much* will be needed in additional resources. These interrelated quantitative issues, which tend to be obscured by rhetoric about "maintaining standards" and "protecting the public," merit serious analysis.

Another argument frequently advanced to support selective admissions relates to the traditional *criteria* of test scores and grades. The use of such measures is usually defended on the grounds that they *predict* performance in college. As we show in Chapter Eight, the prediction argument is fallacious.

Perhaps the most important hidden assumption underlying the prediction argument is that a student's grade-point average is a reflection of what he or she has *learned*. Indeed, the concept of flunking students is based on the assumption that those who get low grades are not "profiting" from their educational experience. Little evidence supports this assumption, and some recent evidence actually contradicts it (Harris, 1970). For example, in terms of pretest-posttest gains on the College Level Examination Program (CLEP), students who get failing or near-failing grades show gains comparable to those of students with high grades. Similarly, in a study of the open admissions program at the City University of New York (Rossmann and others, 1975), students with initially low levels of reading competency (including many Blacks and Puerto Ricans) made gains in reading skill comparable to the gains made by students with initially high scores. These findings suggest that students at all levels of ability are capable of profiting from higher education, and that admissions test scores and grades in college may not accurately reflect what a student can learn or has learned.

Still another argument used to support a hierarchical admissions policy focuses on the "selecting and sorting" function of colleges. By excluding the less able people at the point of admissions, the selective public universities can be reasonably sure that the students they graduate four years later will be of reasonably high quality. Flunking those admitted students who later perform poorly also ensures high-calibre graduates. Colleges assume that the more stringent the initial selection criteria and the more severe the grading practices applied to those admitted, the higher the quality of the graduates.

Graduate and professional schools and employers rely heavily on the hierarchical system to perform this sorting and selecting. If the criteria of the selective universities are stringent enough, a prospective employer or graduate school can virtually ignore other information and still be reasonably confident that a graduate of a selective university will be bright and highly motivated. That such selecting and sorting have proved useful is difficult to deny. What has not been considered is how the college's educational function is affected when it also accepts responsibility for selecting and sorting. For example, when a college does not admit a minority student or when it chooses to flunk a minority student whose grades are poor, the college precludes the possibility of its having any further educational effect on that student. By selectively screening out the low-performing minority student, the institution implicitly takes the position that the education of that student is not a worthwhile endeavor for that institution.

A more telling criticism of institutional selecting and sorting is that these functions can probably be performed better by the employers and graduate schools. What really matters to these "consumers" of higher education's "products" is the candidate's level of competency at graduation. Note that reliance on undergraduate *admissions* criteria, as reflected in the hierarchical arrangement of institutions, freezes students in their relative order of performance at graduation from high school. Such information is not only outdated and therefore of dubious value to the employer or graduate school, but also it penalizes the "late bloomer" and gives an unfair advantage to those students whose initially high performance deteriorates during the college years. As long as employers and graduate schools have sufficient information (for example, through interviews, recommendations, performance on Graduate Record Examinations) about the prospective candidate at college graduation, undergraduate admissions information seems of limited value and may even be misleading.

Perhaps the most important single justification for hierarchical public systems is economic. In the minds of many legislators and planners, the two-year college is an appealing way to expand access because it is much less expensive than other types of institutions. At the same time, expanding the community college sector gains support from the more selective universities because it allows them to preserve their selectivity and prestige and to avoid the pedagogical difficulties associated with teaching less well-prepared students. A dramatic example of this attitude is found in the 1960 California *Master Plan for Higher Education* which states that "[the] quality of an institution and that of a system of higher education are determined to a considerable extent by the abilities of those it admits and retains as students" (California State Department of Education, 1960, p. 66).

The pressure to accommodate enrollment increases by building more commuter institutions, particularly two-year or community colleges, presents a special dilemma to the educational planner and policy maker. Commuter institutions presumably provide low-cost, easy-access higher education for the residents of a particular geographical region. Members of the community can attend these relatively inexpensive colleges with relatively little interference in their everyday activities. Further, many of these institutions schedule classes during the late afternoon and evening, which permits people to hold full-time jobs and attend college full time. But one pays a certain price for this easy access to postsecondary education. Disruption in the student's outside life is minimized but, by the same token, the student's involvement in the educational process is decreased. Students merely have to show up on campus for an hour or so to attend classes and find some time at home to complete assignments and study for examinations. There are no peers to meet with during meals or in the evening, no encouragement to participate in extracurricular activities, and often no campus of the type found at residential institutions. This lack of collegiate experience is perhaps of minor importance to so-called nontraditional students: those who are married, older, or attending part time. However, for the traditional student—the eighteen-year-old who has just completed high school and is pursuing a baccalaureate on a full-time basis—attending a commuter institution that has limited educational resources and provides few chances for involvement may not be the ideal undergraduate experience. Commuter institutions clearly do not offer the educational opportunities to minorities that residential universities and colleges offer.

It is probably true that, were it not for community colleges, many minority students would not attend college at all. These institutions have expanded access to a large segment of society. But they tempt some students who otherwise might go to a residential college to live at home and commute. The real questions are whether educators and policy makers are content to perpetuate differential admissions policies that leave many minority students with no alternative but the community college, and whether they are prepared to reexamine the current pattern of resource allocation that favors other institutional types by so great a margin.

Conclusions

An analysis of the institutional structure of American higher education with respect to the opportunities provided to disadvantaged minorities warrants the following conclusions:

- Both the public and private sectors of higher education are characterized by a hierarchical ordering of institutions, with research universities occupying the top position in the hierarchy, four-year colleges in the middle, and two-year colleges at the bottom.
- In this three-tiered arrangement, the universities have substantially superior educational environments as represented

by the following resources: educational expenditures, libraries, financial aid, research, endowments, physical plants, faculty salaries, and residential facilities. The two-year colleges are at the bottom with respect to these resources, and the four-year colleges fall in the middle.

- Minority students (Hispanics and American Indians, in particular) are disproportionately concentrated in those institutions with the fewest resources (especially community colleges). These facts suggest that the educational opportunity provided to the typical black, Chicano, Puerto Rican, or American Indian student is not the equivalent of the opportunity provided to the typical white student.
- Given the great disparities in institutional resources and the uneven distribution of disadvantaged minorities among various types of institutions, the traditional concept of equal opportunity needs to be expanded to take into account the *type* of institution attended.
- Since hierarchical systems of institutions are supported in some states by a policy of selective admissions that forces disproportionate numbers of minority students into community colleges, these states would be well advised to reexamine their policies in the interests of maximizing equal opportunity for disadvantaged minorities.

❧ 8 ❧

Standardized Testing
and the Meritocracy

Many of the obstacles impeding the progress of disadvantaged minorities in American higher education can be traced to the meritocratic character of the higher education system. Meritocratic values not only underlie a wide range of time-honored practices such as testing, grading, admissions, and ability tracking but also shape the very structure of the institutional system itself, with a disproportionate share of resources being concentrated in the institutions at the top of the hierarchy.

The thesis of this chapter is that meritocratic practices can be contrary to the fundamental purposes of education and that continued reliance on meritocratic values in American higher education poses the single most serious obstacle to the educational progress of disadvantaged minorities. We further argue that the abandonment of meritocratic values in favor of purely educational values will benefit not only minorities but all stu-

154

dents by improving substantially the overall quality of education in the U.S.

The Development of Meritocratic Values

The term *meritocracy*—popularized by British sociologist Michael Young in his book *The Rise of the Meritocracy* (1958)—was coined in contrast with the term *aristocracy*, a concept that has characterized British society during much of its history. In an aristocratic society, rewards such as money, power, and status are allocated on the basis of family and bloodline. In a meritocracy, however, these rewards are allocated on the basis of performance: The greatest rewards go to those who perform best. Thus, in a meritocratic society, competition plays a central role.

Given American society's rejection of aristocratic values and its emphasis on competition, it is understandable that meritocratic values should be so pervasive, underlying most areas of American life, including our higher education system. The most obvious societal manifestation of these meritocratic values is, of course, in the field of business, where free enterprise implies that the greatest material rewards will be bestowed upon those entrepreneurs who are the most clever, creative, and highly motivated. In addition, meritocratic thinking reflects a peculiarly American preoccupation with measuring, ordering, and ranking in order to make explicit and public the meritocratic nature of various social phenomena. The "Fortune 500" grouping is perhaps the best-known example within corporate business. However, this fascination with meritocratic rankings has permeated almost all sectors of our society, as manifested in such diverse activities as rankings of television shows, collegiate and professional athletic teams, political candidates, and colleges and universities.

While it is not entirely clear how and why American higher education came to embrace meritocratic values so uncritically, the popularization of intelligence testing seems to have played a major part. The individually administered intelligence tests, developed early in this century, served as a model for the group-

administered tests used in higher education today. While the IQ
score was not, strictly speaking, a normative measure, it prompted
the use of normative jargon with strong meritocratic connotations:
genius, superior, normal, dull, and so forth. Large-scale group
testing was conducted first by the military services, which, during
the two world wars, wanted to screen out the illiterate and the
"mentally defective" and to identify candidates for officer training.
These applications of group testing were basically meritocratic,
intended to label the "best" and "worst" candidates.

Following World War II, when the number of college
applicants threatened to overwhelm existing campus facilities,
many colleges adopted group testing—which could be conducted
on a large scale at relatively low cost—with the similar intention
of selecting the most desirable applicants and rejecting the
"undesirables." Normative scores provided a simple and seem-
ingly fair means of identifying the "best" students. This meritocratic view of testing was reinforced by the competitiveness of
the colleges themselves; educators accepted the notion that the
"best" colleges are those that enroll the highest-scoring students
(Astin and Solmon, 1979).

In the late 1950s and the 1960s, this meritocratic orientation was reinforced by competitiveness at the international level.
The launching of Sputnik led many Americans to believe that the
U.S. had slipped behind the U.S.S.R. because some of its
"brightest" students were not going to college. One manifestation of this belief was the landmark National Defense Education
Act, which sought to increase the number of highly able students
entering higher education, especially in the fields of science and
technology. Another manifestation was the National Merit Scholarship Corporation, which annually tests close to one million
students just to identify the 1,500 or so with the highest scores
and offer them scholarships to assure their college attendance.
Colleges became highly competitive in their quest for Merit
Scholars, and the number of such scholars in the student body
was widely regarded as a sign of academic quality. A similar
competition developed among the high schools to "produce"
the most Merit Scholars.

Standardized Testing

The widespread use of standardized testing is one of the most pervasive results of the meritocratic standard, and perhaps no issue related to the higher education of minorities has generated more controversy. Various types of tests have come to play an extremely important role in at least four critical areas of higher education: admissions, grading, counseling, and institutional tracking. Our review of standardized testing has led us to conclude that these time-honored uses of testing are inconsistent with the ostensible purposes of higher education and detrimental to the progress of minorities.

Most of the debate over standardized testing centers on what is called the construct validity of these instruments. Are they culturally biased? Do they accurately measure the academic abilities of people from other than white, middle-class backgrounds? This debate over the tests' bias (see, for example, Educational Testing Service, 1980) has been heated and has tended to obscure a much more fundamental problem: The *way* in which tests are used is basically inappropriate to the purposes of education. This misuse of tests, in turn, poses special obstacles to the educational development of minorities.

Before we examine specific objections to current uses of tests in admissions, grading, counseling, and tracking, we emphasize that the arguments presented are predicated on one fundamental assumption: A major purpose of higher education institutions is to *educate* students, to produce certain desirable *changes* in the student or, more simply, to make a difference in the student's life. In the simplest terms, the measure of an institution's success in educating its students is the difference between the students' performance or abilities upon leaving the institution and that upon entry. This conception of the purpose of higher institutions very closely resembles the economist's notion of "value added."

Admissions. What is the rationale for the use of standardized tests in traditional admissions practices? One obvious answer is that tests provide an inexpensive quantitative index that facilitates the admissions decision-making process (Manning, 1977). Many admissions officers and faculty members argue that test scores predict grades in college. Let us defer for the moment the adequacy of college grade-point average as a measure of student learning and consider the educational implications of this argument. People with high scores on admissions tests are preferred over those with low scores on the grounds that they will subsequently earn higher grades in college. This prediction argument represents a weak justification for the use of *any* selection device, because prediction may have little, if any, relationship to the educational mission of the institution defined in terms of value added. This objection is not to suggest that standardized test scores do not reflect a student's level of preparation or that such tests should not be used to place a new student in college courses appropriate to that student's current level of performance. The objection here is to the use of such devices to deny the student entry to the institution.

To illustrate the fallacy inherent in the prediction argument, suppose that a college admitted a group of students who proceeded to learn absolutely nothing from their college experience. Even in such an extreme case, the admissions tests could still *predict* grades, but the college would be an abysmal failure in its mission. Although admissions tests may predict grades, they do not measure the educational experience the student has in achieving those grades, that is, the value that education has added to that student's life. Since different students are likely to learn at different rates, the greatest student learning may be occurring at those colleges where tests have the poorest predictive "validity."

Grading. A possible rejoinder to this criticism of the prediction argument is that the criterion used to justify admissions testing—the college grade-point average—is indeed an accurate measure of what the student has learned in college. While little research has been done to test this assertion, the evidence that does exist fails to support it. Harris (1970) examined pretest-posttest gains on the College Level Examination Program (CLEP) administered before and after enrollment in various courses. Students who got failing or near-failing grades in the courses showed test score gains comparable to those of students with high grades; in other words, both groups received a similar value from having taken the courses. This research suggests that standardized testing on a pretest-posttest basis might offer a better means of assessing student progress than course grades. Again, the question is not the use of standardized tests but rather the uses to which such tests are put.

The problem with traditional grading practices, of course, is that a grade in a course is a *relative* measure that simply ranks students from best to worst without any necessary reference to what the student has learned as a result of the educational program. That institutions have not relied more on standardized tests to assess cognitive learning is puzzling. Many professors object to such tests as somehow inadequate: superficial, incomplete in coverage, culturally biased, and so forth. But their heavy reliance on these same tests to determine undergraduate admissions, advanced placement, and admission to graduate and professional schools belies these objections. If institutions are willing to use standardized tests in evaluating the performance of *prospective* students, how is it that, once the student is admitted, such tests suddenly become inappropriate measures of learning? Perhaps the answer to this question lies more in professors' reluctance to be evaluated than in the tests themselves.

The minimal-competency testing now being introduced into the public schools of most states represents a large-scale effort to assess student performance through standardized tests. Whether testing will facilitate learning or simply pose another obstacle to students' progress depends entirely on how the tests are used. If they are given only at the end of secondary school, as a type of quality-control measure of the high school diploma, they will probably be of little educational value and may, in the case of minorities, represent another serious barrier to college access. However, if these tests are first administered early in the student's career (as a pretest at the beginning of high school), the results may be of considerable educational value to both students and teachers. Early test scores can be used to guide a student's educational program in a productive direction. Unless the schools are willing to use early pretests as a diagnostic aid and as a baseline measure for evaluating subsequent learning, however, minimal-competency testing in the public schools should probably be resisted.

One difficulty with using standardized tests to monitor student development is the way in which they are scored. Virtually all test results report student performance in normative terms: percentiles, standard scores, stanines, and so on. These norm-based scores only show how the individual performs in relation to others. Such scores are useful for selecting and screening (identifying the "best" students), but they are almost worthless in measuring an individual's change or growth over time. Lacking any absolute referent, one cannot know from successive administrations of such tests if, or how much, the student's performance has improved. (The traditional letter-grade system suffers from the same limitation, of course, particularly if students are graded on the curve.)

Standardized tests could be used to provide information on changes in a student's *absolute level* of performance; for example, the number or percentage of items answered correctly. In addition, performance data on individual test items could be provided to diagnose particular strengths and weaknesses or to measure growth in more specific areas of skill or knowledge. Psychometricians have discouraged testing companies from reporting results for individual test items on the grounds that such information is unreliable. However, data on individual items can be highly reliable if they are reported for *groups* of students. (Data on performance on individual test items have been used, with considerable success, in the *International Study of Achievement in Mathematics* [Husen, 1967].) If the colleges and universities that use standardized tests were to demand that raw scores be reported and that item data be included, the testing companies would probably provide them. Such demands could be made for most of the tests now widely used: the achievement and advanced placement tests of the College Entrance Examination Board (CEEB), the College Level Examination Program tests, the undergraduate program of the Graduate Record Examination, and the various tests to select students for graduate and professional schools. In view of the good use that teachers and students could make of this additional information, the cost of providing it would be trivial. Given that so much care is devoted to writing and pretesting items and that these activities account for a major share of the cost of standardized test construction, the potential benefits from these developmental efforts should not be lost in the construction of scales and the computation of percentiles, standard scores, and other normative measures.

Why does the test industry persist in limiting score reports to normative measures when such information is of limited value to students and institutions? There seem to be at least two explanations. First, the psychometricians who control the technical aspects of the test industry are overly concerned with the statistical properties of standard scores and the elegance of the normal distribution, the cornerstone of classical test theory. Thus, raw scores (number of questions answered correctly, or the number wrong subtracted from the number right) are converted to normative scores, a procedure that eliminates the original units of measurement. Because any individual item may be statistically unreliable, items are aggregated in sufficient numbers to produce scales that form the appropriately shaped distribution with the proper degree of classical statistical reliability.

A second, and more important explanation, is that normative measures are consistent with the competitive and meritocratic values that permeate so much of American society. Thus, a student's test score is more a reflection of his or her standing *relative* to student peers than a measure of what the student actually knows or what the student's actual competencies are.

Today, most academics take for granted the normative-meritocratic nature of testing. As a consequence, their concern with fostering student change, growth, or development is subordinated to their concern with ranking students from best to worst. This bias has infected grading practices: Grades primarily reflect how students perform, compared with one another, at a given point in time rather than what students have learned during a course or during their college careers. Because students' grade-point averages are a convenient means of identifying the "best" students, employers and graduate schools further reinforce these grading practices. Aside from habit and tradition, colleges have no reason to persist in these practices. Using results from individual items or absolute or raw scores requires little additional effort, whether the test is a nationally standardized instrument or an individual classroom examination.

Since colleges and graduate and professional schools have only a limited number of available spaces, *some* kind of process is obviously needed to screen applicants. The value-added approach to education suggests that admissions procedures should be designed, at least in part, to select those students who are likely to be *influenced* by the educational process. The responsibility of an educational institution should not be to identify just those students who are likely to be the best performers but also those most likely to be most affected by their college studies.

The discussion so far advances two basic proposals for change: First, that the meritocratic model of admissions be abandoned in favor of a value-added approach; and second, that test scores, together with item and raw score data, be used to provide both students and teachers with information about student growth and development. While this second proposal could probably be implemented tomorrow if the academic community were prepared to abandon its traditional grading system, the value-added approach in the admissions process poses a number of unresolved problems, the most important being that no existing selection devices adequately reflect the student's *potential* to benefit from the collegiate experience. It could be argued that, lacking such measures, we should retain traditional admissions tests until something better is devised. The problem with this argument is that the effects of tests in college admissions are not neutral or benign; they operate to the particular disadvantage of Blacks, Chicanos, Puerto Ricans, and American Indians.

To illustrate the severity of the disadvantage posed by the use of tests in admissions, the staff of the Higher Education Research Institute recently conducted a simulation survey (Astin, Fuller, and Green, 1978). For example, when application rates are so high that only one out of ten applicants can be admitted (a situation similar to that found in many medical and law schools), a school relying solely on test scores to determine selection would admit only 1 percent of the black applicants and 3 percent of the Chicano applicants, compared to 10 percent of the white applicants. In other words, a white student is three times more likely to be selected than a Chicano student, and ten times more likely than a black student. Clearly, if these minority groups are ever to approximate educational parity, some other approach to admissions must be found.

Counseling. Standardized tests are used in counseling at virtually all levels of education. At the secondary level, results of standardized tests are frequently the basis for channeling students into various courses of study. Students who do poorly on such tests may be encouraged by their counselors and teachers to enroll in vocational curricula on the grounds that they lack the academic skills to cope successfully with a college-preparatory program. Among those college-bound students who take college admissions tests, those with relatively low scores are often discouraged from applying to any except the least selective institutions, while students with high scores are generally urged to apply to the most elite or selective institutions.

To use tests in this way is to view the student's academic potential as *fixed* at the time of the test. Thus, rather than being taken as evidence that a student needs more work or special educational programs to improve performance, low scores are frequently interpreted as *limiting* the educational options that students should pursue.

In marked contrast to this situation, some colleges and universities use standardized tests to guide new students and to place them in courses appropriate to their particular level of academic development. In effect, such a practice seeks to *remedy* academic deficiencies rather than to force students to accept such deficiencies as irremediable; it does not impose limits on their future educational options. Clearly, the educational interests of minorities will be greatly enhanced if this practice becomes more widespread.

Institutional Tracking. Another educational practice that involves the use of standardized testing is the tracking of students into different types of institutions. In Chapter Seven, we noted that public higher education in many states is arranged hierarchically, with the major public university occupying the top rung, the state colleges and universities (many of which are former teachers colleges) in the middle, and the open-door community colleges at the bottom. In some states, tests play a major role in determining which of these three tiers is available to a high school graduate. Generally speaking, the highest-scoring students can avail themselves of all three tiers, whereas the lowest-scoring students are allowed to enter only the community colleges. We have already seen that minority students tend to be underrepresented in the universities and heavily concentrated in the community colleges. Given that the educational resources of the public universities are superior in almost all respects to those of the community colleges, these hierarchical public systems based on selective admissions deny equal educational opportunity to Blacks, Chicanos, Puerto Ricans, and American Indians.

How can the inequality of opportunity implicit in hierarchical public systems be eliminated? The problem can be approached in at least two ways. The first, and certainly the most unrealistic approach, is to equalize resources and expenditures among the different types of institutions. Certainly legislators and taxpayers are unlikely to support increases in the total higher education budget within the state to achieve such parity, and any proposal to take resources from the universities to upgrade the community colleges would divide the higher education community and would be opposed by the universities with every political means at their disposal. The second approach, which involves modifying admissions policies, is a much simpler and certainly less expensive solution. Nevertheless, if the (more selective) universities change their policies to admit larger numbers of underprepared minority students, additional resources will almost certainly be required to provide adequate remedial assistance and other special support services.

Shortcomings of the Meritocratic System

We believe that a heavy reliance on competitive and meritocratic values in American higher education not only penalizes minorities disproportionately but also serves to undermine the educational mission of the system as a whole. We emphasize that this argument applies solely to the practices of testing, admissions, grading, and the development of public higher education systems. It is not our purpose to argue that meritocratic values have no place in American society, that employers should not make meritocratic assessments in deciding which prospective job applicants to hire, or that students should not have to compete with one another once they enter the labor force. While a thorough critique of the role of meritocratic values and competitiveness in American society is beyond the scope of this book, we cannot ignore meritocratic values because they so directly affect American higher education.

Advocates of a meritocratic higher educational system are inclined to view education as a kind of open competition, analogous to an intellectual footrace. All contestants are permitted to enter the race, and the spoils go to the swiftest. This view, however, distorts certain important realities about the competition:

- Many minority-group members never even get to the starting line because they have already dropped out of secondary school.
- Many minority-group members fail to show up at the right place or at the right time because they lack reliable information about the race.
- Many minority-group members who start the race do not run well because they are not fully familiar with the rules or do not understand the subtle tricks of the game.
- The idea that college attendance is a single track offering exactly the same competitive conditions to all contestants is simply untrue. A community college, for example, is not the equivalent of an Ivy League college. Thus, one may participate in the race, run well, but end up with a tin trophy.

But a more fundamental difficulty with the competitive-meritocratic view of American higher education is that it severely limits the available opportunities by presupposing that there will

be "winners" and "losers." And this is perhaps the basic ideo-
logical flaw in the relativistic or meritocratic model when it is
applied to education: Not everyone can "succeed," and *one
person's achievement is another person's failure.*

An Alternative Model

If one rejects the meritocratic model and accepts the
premise that educational institutions exist primarily to facilitate
students' learning and personal development, there is simply no
reason why *all* students cannot learn and why one student should
be penalized because another student learns more or learns at a
faster pace. As a matter of fact, in actuality the opposite should
happen; that is, a student should learn most in a school environment where other students are also learning a lot. Conversely, a student should not learn as much in a school where
fellow students are learning very little. In other words, the
success of any student and the quality of the student's educational
program should be measured primarily in terms of whether, and
by how much, that student grows and develops.

To reject a meritocratic approach to testing, admissions,
grading, and the design of public higher education systems is not
to argue that higher education must set itself entirely apart from
other meritocratic aspects of the larger society. Indeed, the
selective application of meritocratic and competitive values at
the exit point in higher education serves the interests of the
general society in at least two instances. The first is professional
certification: The public has a reasonable right to assume that
those college-trained professionals who directly serve the public
(for example, physicians, lawyers, accountants, civil engineers,
and allied health professionals) possess certain minimal skills and
competencies. The second involves those situations in which an
employer seeks to hire the most competent or most qualified
from among a group of college-trained applicants; clearly, being
able to rank or otherwise compare applicants in terms of job-
related skills facilitates this selection process.

Note that in both these instances—professional certification and hiring—the issue of competence is central. The first instance requires assessment of the individual's minimal or *absolute* level of competence, and the second instance requires assessment of *relative* competence among a group of individuals. In neither instance, however, is the development or enhancement of competence a matter of concern; rather, the emphasis is on the assessment or measurement of absolute or relative competence.

Thus, a fundamental distinction must be made between the proper functions of educational institutions and the proper functions of certification and licensing agencies and employers. In education, the primary purpose is to develop or increase competence, whereas in certification and hiring, the principal concern is merely to assess competence in either absolute or relative terms. More important, certification is needed only *after* the person's education is completed.

Viewed in this way, there is no real conflict between the pedagogical values of higher education and the meritocratic values of employers. As long as higher education is effective in carrying out its mission to develop students' competence, the needs of prospective employers will be met. Thus, in professional education, where minimal competence levels must be maintained, an effective higher education program not only will increase the numbers of persons who attain these levels but will also maximize the "margin of safety" by which people exceed these minimal levels. In the more competitive instance where employers seek to hire the most qualified person from among a group of applicants, the absolute potential of the *entire group* of applicants will be greater if they have attended truly effective educational programs. In short, the legitimate meritocratic interests of society are well served by an educational system that emphasizes its *educational*, or value-added, function.

If competency *development* is accepted as a legitimate and important function of higher education, then what is the proper role of competency *assessment*? Clearly, American higher education should strive to make its competency-assessment activities complement or advance competency development; any other use of competency assessment should be questioned, particularly if it compromises or otherwise conflicts with the educational function and if it tends to deny opportunity.

What, then, is the educational purpose served by our current meritocratic testing and grading practices? Those who defend such practices argue that one major function of the higher education system is to select and sort, to screen candidates for the various types of jobs they will hold once they leave college. In this view, higher education serves to weed out incompetent persons who are likely to perform poorly on the job and to identify and certify those more talented ones who are likely to perform well.

This argument is fallacious in at least two ways. First, it overlooks the fact that, since the employers rather than the educational institutions need to assess competency, the principal responsibility for carrying out these assessments should not be assigned to the institutions. Second, it assumes that employers depend on institutions to perform competency assessments of their students, when in fact virtually all employers make their own competency determinations (through job interviews, tests, and so forth), regardless of any assessments the institutions may provide in the form of grades, course credits, and degrees. But our most serious objection is that competency assessment as currently practiced in American higher education does not serve well the system's educational mission, does not promote the development of competency.

Summary

Higher education in the U.S. has come to embrace many of the competitive and meritocratic values that characterize American society. Thus, testing, admissions, and grading are designed not to facilitate the educational development of the student but rather to rank, sort, and select students. Such practices not only operate to the special disadvantage of minorities but also tend to subvert the institution's educational mission.

Employers have a legitimate concern with meritocratic assessment of an institution's graduates, and the general public has a right to expect meritocratic quality controls to be applied in the certification of professionals. Meritocratic competency assessment thus has a legitimate role to play at the termination point in higher education. However, since the principal function of educational institutions is competency *development* rather than competency assessment, any other uses of competency assessment should be designed to enhance the educational process. By emphasizing the development of competency and by subordinating all other functions to that primary mission, higher educational institutions can best serve the interests of students, employers, and the public at large.

Specifically, institutions should replace traditional grading practices with a system that reflects what students are actually learning and that shows how students are changing as a result of their educational experiences. Furthermore, institutions should question their use of standardized tests as a means of screening and selection and reconsider their potential for evaluating student progress, for placing students in appropriate courses, and for assessing the effectiveness of educational programs at all levels. Tests should be used more as measures of educational *outcomes* than as *predictors* of future performance. The predictive model of admissions should be abandoned in favor of a value-added model. Selective institutions in the public sector may want to consider experimenting with alternative selection procedures that identify students who have the greatest potential for *growth* or *learning*. Another alternative is to utilize a lottery system in those public institutions in which the number of applicants exceeds the number of places. The ideal solution, of course, would be to reshape public systems of higher education such that student demand and the supply of available places in various types of institutions would correspond more closely. If the types of institutions that are particularly popular were expanded, the need for selective admissions could be obviated. But until such a utopian system is achieved, the standardized test and the predictive model of admissions will continue to represent serious barriers to the educational development of minority students.

❧ 9 ❧

Summary
of Findings

As previously stated, the principal purposes of the project were to examine the past gains, current status, and future prospects of Blacks, Chicanos, Puerto Ricans, and American Indians in higher education and to formulate recommendations aimed at furthering the educational development of these groups. To provide a strong empirical basis for policy recommendations, the study was originally designed to concentrate on two areas: first, on a description of the current and recent situation of the four minority groups with respect to their access to higher education, choice of institutions and of fields of study, and degree attainment; and second, on an analysis of the factors that influence the access and attainment of these minority groups. During the course of the study, the commission overseeing the project added a third major area of activity: an analysis of controversial issues relating to the higher education of minorities.

The specific questions addressed under each of these three major categories of research activity are as follows:

Educational Access, Choice, and Attainment

- To what extent are Blacks, Chicanos, Puerto Ricans, and American Indians represented at various points in the educational pipeline between secondary school and completion of advanced training? Where are the major leakage points in this pipeline?
- What is the representation of each of these four minority groups by field of study and type of institution?
- How has the representation of each minority group changed since the mid-1960s?

Factors Influencing Educational Development

- How are the educational access and attainment of minority students influenced by family background, socioeconomic status, and personal characteristics?
- What features or characteristics of educational institutions and programs (for example, type of high school, type of higher education institution, student peer groups, faculty attitudes, special institutional programs) are most critical in affecting the progress of minority students?
- How is the progress of minority students affected by the type of financial aid they receive during undergraduate and graduate training?
- Which governmental programs seem to be the most effective and which the least effective in facilitating minority progress in higher education?

Controversial Issues

- To what extent are minorities afforded equal access to higher education? Is "equality of access" more a myth than a reality?
- How valid is the current popular stereotype of the "overeducated American"? What implications for minority progress

in higher education does acceptance of this stereotype have?
- In what way does standardized testing, as currently used, impede the educational development of minorities? How can standardized testing be employed to contribute to educational development?
- How do the meritocratic aspects of the U.S. higher education system affect minority progress?

The first two categories of research activities—"educational access, choice, and attainment" and "factors influencing educational development"—were approached by means of a series of analyses of empirical data. While considerable use was made of existing data sources, a substantial amount of new data was also collected. The third major category of project activity—"controversial issues"—was accomplished by means of a series of essays drawing upon the existing literature and, in some instances, upon relevant empirical data.

The Limits of Higher Education

Higher education was chosen as the focus of this study because the Ford Foundation and the persons associated with the project believe that it contributes to the social and economic well-being of individuals and to the political resources and strength of groups within U.S. society. Blacks, Chicanos, Puerto Ricans, and American Indians all suffer from powerlessness, and higher education is clearly one of the main routes whereby individuals can attain positions of economic and political power. Further, the quality of life in general can be improved through higher education, which expands employment options and contributes to greater geographic mobility. Finally, higher education can enrich leisure by exposing the individual to a wide range of experiences in the arts, music, literature, history, science, and technology.

But higher education is by no means a panacea for all the problems that confront disadvantaged minorities in the United States. Vestiges of prejudice may persist in the minds of many Americans for years to come, no matter how many minority students complete higher education programs. Perhaps more significant is the fact that many of the educational problems facing these groups occur prior to higher education, at the elementary and secondary levels. Indeed, the results of this study dramatize the need for a much more concerted national effort to upgrade the quality of elementary and secondary education for minorities. Although it is true that higher education can play some role in this process through the selection and training of administrators and teachers in the lower schools, many of the problems of minority education are probably beyond the control of higher education. While the commission believes that this reality does not relieve the higher education system of the responsibility for doing the best job possible with those minority students who manage to enter academic institutions, it also recognizes that solving the problems of precollegiate education for minorities will require the sustained efforts of federal, state, and local governments.

The Educational Pipeline

Much of the technical effort of the project was directed at gathering and synthesizing the best available data on the representation of minorities in higher education. As was pointed out in the discussion of data limitations, several problems arose in connection with this effort. For instance, some of the sources used report data for the general category "Hispanic," rather than separately for different Hispanic subgroups. Therefore, many of the figures for Chicanos and Puerto Ricans reported here are estimates based on the known fact that the former constitute 60 percent of the Hispanic population in the United States, and the latter 15 percent. Another problem is the paucity of data on American Indians; thus, estimates for this minority group may not be accurate and should be treated with caution.

Given these strictures, the following sections give the best estimates possible of the representation of the four racial and ethnic minority groups by level in the educational system, their representation by field of study, and recent trends in the representation of minorities.

By Level.

If one views the educational system as a kind of pipeline leading ultimately to positions of leadership and influence in our society, it is possible to identify five major "leakage" points at which disproportionately large numbers of minority group members drop out of the pipeline: completion of high school, entry to college, completion of college, entry to graduate or professional school, and completion of graduate or professional school. The loss of minorities at these five transition points accounts for their substantial underrepresentation in high-level positions. Figure 1 gives an overview of the educational pipeline for all four minority groups under study and for Whites.

High School Graduation. A substantial proportion of minority students leave the educational system before they even complete secondary school, thus severely handicapping their efforts to attain higher levels of education and to avail themselves of a greater range of career options. For instance, the high school dropout rate for Blacks is approximately 28 percent (compared with a rate of about 17 percent for Whites), and this attrition occurs throughout the high school years. Close to half (45 percent) of Chicanos and Puerto Ricans never finish high school, and this attrition begins in the junior high school years and continues through the high school years. Finally, although data are sparse, it appears that approximately 45 percent of American Indian students leave high school before graduation.

College Entry. With the exception of American Indians, those students who manage to complete high school enter college at about the same rate as Whites. Among high school graduates of each racial and ethnic group, approximately 45 percent of Whites and Puerto Ricans, 40 percent of Blacks and Chicanos, and 31 percent of American Indians enroll in college. (The figure for Puerto Ricans may be inflated, because it is based on data from the years when the City University of New York had a more open admissions policy. Since a majority of the Puerto Ricans who are residents of the continental United States live in New York City, they benefited particularly from this policy, which has since been modified.)

Figure 1. The Educational Pipeline for Minorities

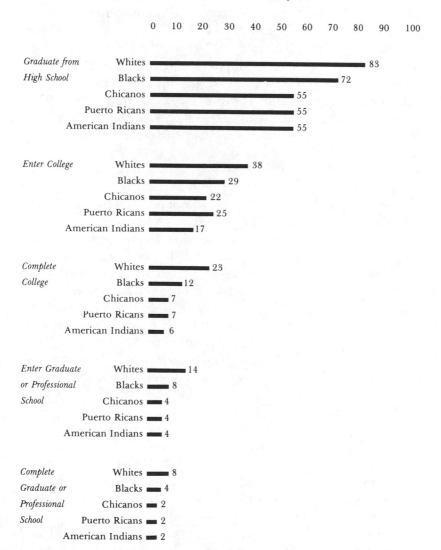

Percent of Cohort

		0	10	20	30	40	50	60	70	80	90	100

Graduate from High School
- Whites — 83
- Blacks — 72
- Chicanos — 55
- Puerto Ricans — 55
- American Indians — 55

Enter College
- Whites — 38
- Blacks — 29
- Chicanos — 22
- Puerto Ricans — 25
- American Indians — 17

Complete College
- Whites — 23
- Blacks — 12
- Chicanos — 7
- Puerto Ricans — 7
- American Indians — 6

Enter Graduate or Professional School
- Whites — 14
- Blacks — 8
- Chicanos — 4
- Puerto Ricans — 4
- American Indians — 4

Complete Graduate or Professional School
- Whites — 8
- Blacks — 4
- Chicanos — 2
- Puerto Ricans — 2
- American Indians — 2

Baccalaureate Attainment. Of those who enter college, Whites are much more likely to complete the baccalaureate within the traditional four-year period than are minority students. According to the National Longitudinal Study, 34 percent of the Whites, 24 percent of the Blacks, 16 percent of the American Indians, and 13 percent of the Hispanics who entered college in 1972 had completed the baccalaureate by 1976. In all likelihood, these differences are attributable in part to the high concentration of both Hispanics and American Indians in community colleges. Although three fourths of community college entrants indicate as freshmen that they intend to get at least a bachelor's degree, (Astin, King, and Richardson, 1980) their chances of actually transferring to a senior institution and completing the baccalaureate are slim. Even after taking into account their generally poorer academic preparation, one finds that regardless of race and ethnicity community college students are substantially less likely than are four-year-college entrants to complete four undergraduate years (Astin, 1975; see also Chapter Five of this volume).

Looking at baccalaureate completion rates beyond the four-year span, one finds that approximately 56 percent of White freshmen, 51 percent of Black freshmen, 42 percent of Puerto Rican freshmen, 40 percent of Chicano freshmen, and 39 percent of American Indian freshmen eventually receive the bachelor's degree. Again, the high concentration of American Indians, Chicanos, and Puerto Ricans in community colleges during the early undergraduate years contributes significantly to their higher baccalaureate attrition rates.

Graduate and Professional School Entry. According to recent data from the U.S. Office for Civil Rights, the transition from undergraduate college to graduate or professional school does not seem to be a major leakage point for minorities; the ratio of the number of first-year graduate students to the number of baccalaureate recipients during the same year was roughly similar for all groups. It should be emphasized, however, that the first-year graduate enrollment figures for minorities may be inflated by delayed entrants (that is, those who do not enroll for advanced training directly after completing the baccalaureate but delay their entry for some period) and the very large proportion of minority students who pursue master's degrees in education.

Advanced Degree Attainment. Although minority students who manage to complete the baccalaureate may not be at a disadvantage when it comes to enrolling in graduate or professional school, they are less likely than White students to complete their advanced training. Approximately 45 percent of Blacks, 52 percent of Chicanos and Puerto Ricans and 48 percent of American Indians drop out before completing their graduate or professional degrees. The comparable figure for Whites is 41 percent.

Summary. The following conclusions can be drawn about the educational pipeline for minorities:

- All four of the minority groups under consideration in this study are increasingly underrepresented at each higher level of degree attainment: high school completion, baccalaureate attainment, and advanced degree attainment.
- Minority underrepresentation is attributable not only to greater than average attrition rates from secondary school, undergraduate college, and graduate and professional school, but also to disproportionately high losses in the transition from high school to college.
- Blacks fall midway between Whites and the three other minority groups in terms of their ability to survive to the end of the educational pipeline.
- The single most important factor contributing to the severe underrepresentation of Chicanos, Puerto Ricans, and American Indians is their extremely high rate of attrition from secondary school. The second most important factor is their greater than average attrition from undergraduate colleges (particularly community colleges).

By Field

To examine the representation of the four minorities in various fields of study at successive degree levels, the project staff defined ten categories of major fields. Each category was selected either because it is a prerequisite for a high-level career, because it is chosen by a large proportion of students, or because it fulfills both these criteria. The ten categories, which together accounted for about 90 percent of the baccalaureates awarded in the United States in 1978–79, were: allied health; arts and humanities; biological science; business; education; engineering; prelaw; premedicine and predentistry; physical sciences and mathematics; and the social sciences.

It should be pointed out that all four minority groups will tend to be underrepresented in all fields at all levels, because the total proportion who survive to each level is low; and that the underrepresentation in a given field will be even greater if relatively few survivors choose that field.

Among entering freshmen, minorities are underrepresented in all ten categories of fields except the social sciences and education. In addition, Black freshmen are only slightly underrepresented among those naming allied health as a probable major, and are overrepresented among those naming business as a probable major. Moreover, the underrepresentation of minorities increases at each higher level of the educational pipeline. Thus all four minority groups are substantially underrepresented among both baccalaureate recipients and doctorate recipients in all fields. (The only possible exceptions to this generalization are education and the social sciences, where Blacks seem to be only slightly underrepresented, and American Indians do not seem to be underrepresented.)

The field categories in which the four minorities are most severely underrepresented are engineering, biological science, and physical science and mathematics. To achieve proportionate representation in these fields at the doctorate level, the number of minority doctorates would have to increase from four- to sevenfold. The field categories in which minorities are least severely underrepresented (other than education) are the social sciences, law, and medicine. Proportionate representation in these fields could be achieved by doubling the number of minority degree-recipients.

Generally speaking, the factor that best explains minority

underrepresentation in various fields—especially the natural sciences, engineering, and the social sciences—is the poor academic preparation that minority students receive at the precollegiate level.

Recent Trends

Although minority underrepresentation increases at each higher level of the educational pipeline and is especially severe in the sciences and engineering, the last two decades have witnessed dramatic increases in minority representation at all levels of the educational pipeline and in virtually all fields. These increases are attributable in large part to the civil rights movement of the late 1950s and the 1960s, to the Civil Rights Act of 1964, and to the initiation during the 1960s of a number of social programs aimed directly at increasing minority enrollments. The trend data on minority enrollments, although sparse (especially for Chicanos, Puerto Ricans, and American Indians), warrant the following conclusions:

- Between 1970 and 1977, Blacks were much less likely to drop out of high school than previously, while Whites, especially 16- and 17-year-olds, were more likely to drop out. Nonetheless, attrition prior to completion of secondary school is still about a third higher among Blacks than among Whites.
- Both the absolute numbers of the four minority groups entering two-year and four-year colleges and their proportions among entering freshmen increased between the mid 1960s and the mid 1970s; the proportions have since stabilized at about 12–13 percent.
- The proportion of Blacks in the 25–29 age group who had completed four or more years of college increased from 10 percent in 1970 to 15 percent in 1975. Between 1976 and 1979, the proportion of Blacks, Chicanos, and Puerto Ricans among baccalaureate recipients increased slightly, while the proportion of American Indians remained relatively stable.
- Between 1973 and 1977, the share of doctorates awarded to

members of all four minority groups increased substantially, from 3.8 percent to 6.3 percent. Since 1977, however, the share has declined slightly.

- In the late 1960s, students from the four minority groups constituted only about 3 percent of first-year medical school enrollments; by the 1974–75 academic year, they constituted 10 percent. Since that time, the minority proportion of enrollments stabilized at 9 percent.
- The proportions of the four minorities among total law school enrollments increased from about 3.8 percent in the late 1960s to 6.4 percent in the 1976–77 academic year. Since that time, the proportions of Blacks, Chicanos, Puerto Ricans, and American Indians among law students have changed very little.

In summary, minority representation at all levels of higher education increased substantially between the mid 1960s and the mid 1970s. In more recent years, however, their proportions have stabilized, and few gains have been made since the mid 1970s.

Factors Influencing Educational Progress

Analyses of the two-year (1975–1977) and nine-year (1971–1980) longitudinal samples yielded a wealth of findings, which are summarized here. For simplicity, the results are presented under two major headings: *entering student characteristics* and *college environmental characteristics*.

Entering Student Characteristics

The quality of academic preparation in secondary school is a major factor in the student's academic performance in college and baccalaureate attainment. Academic performance in secondary school, as measured by the student's grade average or class rank, was a much more important predictor of undergraduate grades and persistence than were standardized test scores, although in the case of Blacks, such scores did contribute to the prediction of college grades and persistence.

Study habits and type of high school curriculum were also closely associated with undergraduate grades and persistence. Those students who took a college preparatory curriculum in high school and who entered college with well-developed study skills were more likely to do well academically and to attain the baccalaureate than were those students who took some other type of program (for example, vocational or secretarial) and whose study habits were poor.

As expected, certain family background characteristics indicative of socioeconomic status proved to be related to college grades and persistence. Minority students whose parents were better educated and had higher incomes were likely to perform more successfully than were those whose parents were relatively poor and uneducated. Parental income alone predicts persistence and achievement for all four minority groups but is unrelated to the college performance of Whites. This finding implies that although financial aid (especially grants) has a positive impact on both access and persistence, it cannot compensate for all the negative effects of poverty on the minority student's academic achievement.

In addition, those minority students who gave themselves high self-ratings on academic ability and who were relatively young at the time they entered college tended to make good grades in college and to persist to baccalaureate completion. Among Blacks, scoring high on standardized college admissions tests, feeling well prepared in mathematics, and taking a relatively large number of secondary school courses in science and foreign languages predicted achievement and persistence; among Blacks and Chicanos, attending an integrated high school had positive effects on these outcomes.

College Environmental Factors

The longitudinal analyses examined four general categories of college environmental factors: institutional characteristics, field of study, financial aid, and place of residence.

Institutional Characteristics. Initial enrollment in a community college substantially reduced the student's chances of persisting to baccalaureate completion. This finding, which replicates findings from earlier longitudinal studies, suggests that in those states with hierarchical systems of public higher education—where high school graduates with the best academic records can choose from the full range of postsecondary options, while those with relatively poor academic records are consigned to community colleges—many minority students are in effect being denied an equal educational opportunity.

The quality of the undergraduate college (as measured by such indexes as the institution's prestige, per-student expenditures, and admissions selectivity) was consistently related not only to baccalaureate completion but also to attainment of a doctorate or an advanced professional degree. In short, the higher the quality of the undergraduate institution attended, the greater the minority student's chances of persisting to the baccalaureate and of enrolling in a program of study for the doctorate, medical degree, or law degree. (The only exception to this generalization occurred in the case of American Indians, where the effects of quality measures were mixed.) These findings suggest that one way to increase the number of minority students who successfully complete advanced training is to increase the number who enter the more prestigious and elite institutions as freshmen. Such institutions apparently serve as conduits for students who will eventually go on to graduate and professional schools. These findings have at least two policy implications: first, prestigious institutions should intensify their efforts to recruit more minority students; and second, those institutions in which minority students are now concentrated should be strengthened so that they will be more effective in encouraging their minority undergraduates to enter graduate and professional training.

Field of Study. The student's undergraduate grades are significantly affected by the course of study pursued. Those students, both minority and White, who major in natural science, engineering, and premedical curricula get lower grades than would be expected from their entering characteristics; those who major in the arts and humanities, the social sciences, and education get higher grades than expected. Apparently academic standards in the sciences and engineering are more stringent than those in the other major fields.

During the undergraduate years, there is a substantial loss of minority students who aspire to become physicians, engineers, or lawyers and a concomitant increase in the number who aspire to careers in business and in college teaching. With certain exceptions, these shifts in career plans tend to exacerbate the underrepresentation of minorities in natural sciences and engineering. (It should be noted, however, that White students show similar changes in interests during the undergraduate years.)

Financial Aid. Perhaps the most consistent finding with respect to financial factors is that holding a full-time outside job while in college has unfavorable effects. Minority students who enter college expecting to work full time at an outside job are much less likely to persist to baccalaureate completion than those who enter college with no such expectation. On the other hand, part-time work seems to facilitate persistence, especially if the job is located on campus.

The type of financial aid received is also important. The effects of grants or scholarships are generally positive, but the effects of loans are mixed.

Place of Residence. Students who live away from home while attending college are more likely to persist to baccalaureate completion than those who live at home with their parents; this is especially true for Blacks and Chicanos. The positive effects of the residential experience are consistent with a body of earlier research (Astin, 1975; Astin, 1977a; Chickering, 1974).

Views of Minority Educators

The commission's survey of 311 minority educators, whose past experiences and current positions make them a rich resource of information, also contributed to our understanding of factors influencing the educational progress of minorities. Participants in the survey first completed an open-ended instrument asking them to respond freely to questions about facilitators of and barriers to the educational attainment of people from their racial and ethnic backgrounds. Their responses were compiled and categorized to produce a second questionnaire in a forced-choice format. The findings from this second instrument can be summarized as follows:

Asked about factors that facilitated their completion of the baccalaureate, respondents were most likely to mention the encouragement and support of their families and their own educational goals and interests. These factors also motivated their enrollment in graduate or professional school, as did career-related or economic goals and the receipt of financial aid. The chief barriers at both the undergraduate and graduate levels were financial concerns (including problems connected with having to work while in college) and faculty composition and attitudes. In addition, respondents indicated that institutional indifference to minority students was a barrier to their completion of college, and that family responsibilities were often a burden during graduate school.

Despite their high academic attainment (66 percent of the sample of 311 respondents had earned a doctorate, and 26 percent held a master's degree), minority educators feel that they face special problems as professionals. Among the most serious of these problems are the lack of institutional commitment to minorities, difficulty in gaining the acceptance and respect of their colleagues, institutional ethnocentrism that ignores the perspectives and values of other cultures, and being stereotyped and exploited as "minority experts" in ways that limit opportunities for professional advancement. Generally, Blacks were least likely to cite these problems, probably because many of them are employed at historically black institutions.

Another section of the questionnaire asked respondents for their views about obstacles to the educational attainment of young people of their racial and ethnic background. Close to two-thirds cited poor educational preparation. Financial problems were also seen as constituting an obstacle, especially for Chicano and Puerto Rican males. American Indian respondents said that young people of their racial and ethnic background are particularly subject to self-concept and identity problems. In addition, some respondents believed that minority women face problems not encountered by their male counterparts: namely, sex-role stereotypes and conflicts engendered by multiple-role demands.

According to respondents, the barriers encountered by minority students differ somewhat by educational level. Poor teaching and poor educational preparation are major problems at both the elementary and secondary levels. In addition, elementary school children (especially American Indians and Blacks) face barriers related to the home environment (lack of resources in the home, poor health and nutrition, parents who are not able to help their children with schoolwork or who do not become involved in their children's schooling), the lack of effective instructional programs designed to promote cultural awareness and identity and to develop bilingual skills (mentioned most often by Chicano, Puerto Rican, and American Indian respondents), and the lack of transitional instructional programs for students with limited English-language skills (mentioned most often by Puerto Rican respondents). Inadequate academic and career counseling was identified as a particularly serious barrier for minority high school students.

At the undergraduate and graduate levels, financial difficulties loom large, especially for Puerto Ricans. Moreover, poor educational preparation is an obstacle for minority undergraduates, whereas minority students in graduate and professional schools are hindered by the lack of minority faculty, mentors, and role models.

Chicano, American Indian, and Puerto Rican respondents believe that the greatest strength of their young people is strong cultural identity. In addition, Chicanos and American Indians mention strong family and communities as strengths, while Puerto Ricans cite bilingual skills. Blacks, on the other hand, feel that their young people are distinguished most by intelligence, curiosity, resilience, and flexibility.

Asked to indicate what higher education institutions could do to better serve minorities, respondents tended to emphasize these areas of action: the hiring, promotion, and tenuring of minority faculty, counselors, and administrators; the encouragement of college attendance through outreach and recruitment programs to inform students and parents about college benefits, opportunities, and choices; the provision of access through conditional or open admissions; and the improvement of articulation between community and four-year colleges.

⚔ 10 ⚔

Recommendations on the Higher Education of Minorities

Given the current pressure for fiscal stringency, the Commission on the Higher Education of Minorities was faced with a critical decision. Would it be more judicious to exercise restraint by selecting and concentrating on just a few recommendations for action, with the hope that cost-conscious government and institutional policy makers would thereby be more willing to consider these recommendations? Or should a broader-based approach be taken?

Several considerations prompted us to choose the second alternative. First, while recognizing that indifference and even hostility to minority concerns has been growing in certain quarters, the commission is strong in its belief that redressing inequality in higher education must become a first-ranked national priority, for both practical and moral reasons. Second, while large financial outlays might be required to implement some of these recommendations, others call for a reexamination of current policies and practices and a restructuring of certain

187

components of the educational system—painful, perhaps, but not expensive. Finally, we welcome the opportunity to address a number of issues that have surfaced in the course of the project and to speak to a number of audiences that have some responsibility for and some interest in making changes. It should be emphasized that many of these suggested changes would benefit not only students from the four minority groups under consideration but all college students, U.S. higher education as a whole, and, ultimately, society at large.

Implementation of the Value-Added Model

The commission recommends:

- That educational institutions revise their testing and grading procedures to reflect and enhance the value-added mission. Such a revision requires, first, that current normative or relativistic measures be replaced by measures that assess the learning and growth of the individual student and, second, that these measures be administered periodically to assess the individual's growth over time. Results from both local and national tests should be routinely fed back to individual students and teachers on an item-by-item basis. Such revised testing and grading procedures will better serve the educational process by providing students, teachers, institutions, and policy makers with feedback on the nature and extent of student learning and growth over time. This feedback will be useful not only in evaluating the effectiveness of educational programs but also in diagnosing the educational progress and needs of individual students.
- That educational institutions use standardized tests for course placement, evaluation, and counseling rather than just for the selection and screening of students.
- That educational institutions enlarge their concept of competency measures to include the assessment of growth in the noncognitive realm: personal development, interpersonal skills, and self-esteem.

Rationale. The principal function of all educational institutions should be to change people: to increase the competence of students, to enhance their personal development, and to help them lead more productive and fulfilling lives. Ideally, testing and grading procedures should be designed to facilitate this value-added mission of institutions.

Typically, testing and grading procedures in higher education are used not to measure student growth or change but to rank students in relation to each other. Because current practices emphasize the screening and certification of students, tests and grades not only fail to contribute to the learning process, but also pose special obstacles to the development of minority students.

Precollegiate Education

The commission recommends:

- That school counselors and teachers make special efforts to assist minority students in understanding the relationship between their education and their future careers and other life options.
- That secondary school counselors and teachers encourage minority students to enroll in college preparatory curricula and to take courses in mathematics, languages, natural science, and social science.
- That schools routinely test new and continuing students, as a basis for undertaking any remedial efforts that may be required to correct for the effects of earlier educational deficiencies.
- That secondary school teachers and administrators, working in close collaboration with faculty from nearby colleges and universities, define those intellectual competencies that are crucial to effective performance in college and develop tests to measure such competencies.
- That such tests be administered on a repeated before-and-after basis to assess student progress and program effectiveness, in accordance with the value-added model.
- That the results of such periodic testing and retesting be a

major element in the accountability of school teachers and administrators, and that those who are demonstrably effective in assisting minority students should be more adequately compensated.

- That the school leadership make greater efforts to ascertain and respond to the concerns of minority parents, to involve them in the operation of the schools, and to assist them in understanding the objectives, procedures, and practices of the schools.
- That the per-student formula now used to allocate resources among public elementary and secondary schools within a school district be revised so that predominantly minority schools receive a greater share of these resources, some of which should be used to develop rigorous academic programs and associated support services for their students.
- That higher education institutions, schools, and departments concerned with the training of elementary and secondary school teachers develop stronger academic programs designed, among other things, to increase the prospective teacher's awareness of and sensitivity to minority cultures and values.

Rationale. A body of research shows that the quality of precollegiate education is critical in determining whether young people go on to college, what kinds of higher education institutions they attend, how they perform in college, and whether they are able to complete their college education. While disagreeing on the causes, most observers agree that in recent years the quality of public schooling at both the elementary and secondary levels has deteriorated, and that the weaknesses of the public education system are borne most heavily by minority students, especially those attending predominantly minority schools located in the inner city and in isolated rural areas. Such schools typically have fewer resources (finances, facilities, high-quality teaching, administrative leadership, community involvement and support) than do middle-class white schools. Moreover, whereas middle-class White students usually have resources and support systems outside the school to compensate for deficiencies in the system, many low-income minority students have no such resources to fall back on.

The consequences of this situation are clear. As data from the project show, high school dropout rates are much higher among minority youth (especially Chicanos, Puerto Ricans, and American Indians) than among white youth. Largely because of their poorer secondary school preparation those minority students who do go on to college are less likely to complete the baccalaureate than are white undergraduates. Moreover, minority students tend to major in education and the social sciences; relatively few choose engineering or the natural sciences as major fields of study.

Community Colleges

The commission recommends:

- That community colleges revitalize their transfer function by establishing as one option a "transfer-college-within-a-college," wherein all students aspiring to a baccalaureate can be brought together and exposed to the same kinds of intensive educational and extracurricular experiences commonly available to students at residential institutions. Funding formulas may have to be revised to strengthen the "college-within-a-college."
- That the transfer program staffs of community colleges work closely with their counterparts at senior institutions to improve articulation.
- That transfer programs within community colleges offer intensive remediation and academic counseling.
- That senior institutions make more effort to facilitate the transfer of community college graduates by setting aside an appropriate amount of financial aid for these students and by offering orientation and counseling to meet their special needs.
- That in areas where senior institutions and community colleges are located close to one another, young people aspiring to a baccalaureate be encouraged to enroll in the senior institution, without prejudice to the continuing op-

portunity of students in two-year colleges who may wish to transfer to the senior institution.

Rationale. Because they are geographically accessible, relatively inexpensive, and flexible in admissions policies and scheduling, community colleges have opened postsecondary access to many people who otherwise might not have gone beyond high school. Community colleges have succeeded in providing vocational training and adult education for many Americans. The relatively recent American Indian community college movement demonstrates how effective these institutions can be in responding to the immediate needs of that community by offering career associate-degree programs in such areas as range management, animal husbandry, and practical nursing.

Community colleges have been less successful, however, in performing their transfer function. Our data indicate that whereas three in four community college freshmen intend to get the baccalaureate, only one in four actually does so. What makes the attrition problem especially severe is the heavy concentration of minority students in community colleges, particularly in states like California and Texas that have a hierarchical, three-tier system of public higher education. Because many minority students do not meet the admissions requirements of four-year institutions, they are forced to enroll in community colleges. For some of these students, the community college's open door leads to a dead end. Moreover, many of those community college entrants who succeed in transferring to a senior institution find themselves as students with advanced standing but without the resources and services that are ordinarily available to entering freshmen—for example, financial aid and orientation.

Academic and Personal Support Services

The commission recommends:

- That colleges and universities strengthen their efforts to help underprepared minority students improve their study habits and develop their basic skills, by offering tutoring, developmental courses, and academic counseling. Such efforts will not only benefit the individual student but will also help institutions financially by reducing student attrition rates.

- That colleges and universities provide resources to establish centers where minority students can meet together for social and educational exchanges. Such centers can promote a sense of community, can help new students learn about the system, and can foster cultural identity, pride, and strength in such a way that minority students will be able to challenge as well as to enrich and broaden the traditional values of the institution.

- That minority students themselves, as well as local minority communities, be used as a resource in providing leadership and initiatives for the organization of such academic and personal support services, and that they be given a responsible role in decisions concerning the operation and management of minority services.

- That the trustees, administrators, and faculties of colleges and universities give strong and visible support for the development of ethnic studies programs, so that the perspectives added by such programs will be available for the benefit of all students, minority and majority.

Rationale. Data indicate that minority freshmen represent the entire spectrum of academic ability and preparation, but that a substantial proportion enter college lacking good study habits and feeling poorly prepared in reading, writing, and computational skills. Moreover, longitudinal data show that students who lack these skills are less likely to persist in higher education. Both these points are confirmed by respondents to the commission's survey of minority educators, many of whom cited lack of preparation in basic academic skills as a major barrier to educational attainment. Other barriers mentioned frequently were social isolation and loneliness, "culture shock," and institutional ethnocentricity and lack of commitment to minority students.

In recent years, some slight gains have been made through the establishment of ethnic studies—including Afro-American studies, Black studies, Hispanic studies, Chicano studies, Puerto Rican studies, Asian American studies, and Native American studies—on some of the nation's college campuses. Ethnic studies were born out of the campus unrest of the 1960s, when students in general were pressing for more relevant curricula and when minority students in particular were demanding that institutions address their needs. The almost exclusive focus on Western culture and civilization of the traditional liberal arts program was under attack. Minority students complained justifiably that not only was consideration of minority cultures and values absent from the curriculum, but support-service mechanisms were unavailable to them. As a result of these pressures, ethnic studies were introduced in various forms. On some campuses, courses on one or more minority groups are taught under the aegis of existing departments (for example, sociology, anthropology, history, literature). At others, an interdisciplinary major in ethnic studies is offered. At still others, separate departments of ethnic studies have been established. Although the numbers of students graduating with ethnic studies majors is small, these arrangements have the advantage of allowing other students to minor in, or at least sample, such courses and thus to gain some knowledge or awareness of ethnic studies. On some campuses, ethnic studies programs go side by side with an ethnic center, which attempts to address some of the social and personal needs of minority students and faculty in predominantly white institutions. In addition to giving both minority and majority students a new perspective on the total American experience, ethnic studies have contributed to the college community's enriched awareness of minority literature, art, and music. Over the past decade or so, scholarly inquiry into the presence, experience, and contributions of the various minority groups in the United States has produced fruitful results. Nonetheless, ethnic studies still have not gained respectability in the eyes of many academics, and their very survival is now threatened by fiscal exigency and by growing indifference to minority concerns.

The Myth of Equal Access

The commission recommends:

- That educational policy makers and planners revise their

traditional concept of equality of access to take into account the type, quality, and resources of the institution entered.

- That the more selective institutions—including the "flagship" (major) universities in each state—review their recruitment and admissions procedures and where necessary revise them to attract and admit more minority students.
- That these selective institutions make clear their commitment to the goal of increasing minority enrollments by providing support services, presenting minority perspectives in the curriculum, and hiring, promoting, and tenuring more minority faculty and administrators.
- That institutions reexamine the educational rationale underlying traditional selective admissions practices. Ideally, the predictive model of admissions should be replaced with a model that focuses on the institution's value-added mission.
- That those institutions using the predictive model of admissions examine the validity of their formulas separately for minorities, with special attention to the possibility that standardized test scores, which pose a far greater handicap to minorities than high school grades, add little to the prediction of college performance.

Rationale. Aggregate statistics on college enrollments mask the fact that minority students are overrepresented in the less selective institutions and underrepresented in the more selective schools—especially the major public universities of most states. Given that the more selective public and private institutions tend to have greater financial resources, more residential facilities, larger libraries, better physical plants, more varied curricula, and more highly trained faculty, it follows that those students who must attend the less selective institutions are denied equal educational opportunities.

Selective admissions based on high school grades and standardized test scores have been justified on the grounds that grades and tests predict college performance. While this predictive model may be appropriate for businesses, it is inappropriate for public higher education, where institutions exist for the benefit of students. Furthermore, the results of our longitudinal analyses show that test scores add little beyond high school grades in predicting the academic performance and persistence of minority students during the undergraduate years.

Financial Aid

The commission recommends:

- That whenever possible students with significant financial need be given aid in the form of grants rather than loans.
- That students be given enough aid so that they do not need to work more than half time.
- That if students are given financial aid in the form of work-study support, it be packaged in such a way that they work less than half time and, whenever possible, at on-campus jobs.
- That federal and state legislators and policy makers support expanded grant and work-study programs.

   Rationale. Minority students often start college with heavy financial responsibilities. For example, two fifths of minority freshmen entering college in the mid 1970s said they had major expenses and debts; close to a third of the Chicano and Puerto Rican freshmen contributed to the support of their parents; and 16 percent of Blacks and Chicanos, as well as 10 percent of Puerto Ricans, were single parents or heads of households. Even though large proportions of these freshmen (90 percent of the Blacks, 83 percent of the Chicanos, 84 percent of the Puerto Ricans, and 59 percent of the American Indians) received financial aid, many of them still had to work at outside jobs. Half the American Indians, a third of the Chicanos and Puerto Ricans, and a fifth of the Blacks worked more than half time while in school. The implication of these two sets of figures is that minority freshmen who do not get financial aid must find outside jobs. Research evidence indicates that working more than half time has a negative effect on persistence, whereas working less than half time, particularly at an on-campus job, has a positive effect (Astin and Cross, 1979).

Our analyses further indicate that receiving a grant not only contributes to the student's persistence but also gives the student a wider range of institutional options. Finally, the findings with respect to the effects of loans were inconsistent, perhaps because loan programs for college students have changed drastically since the early 1970s.

Bilingualism

The commission recommends:

- That federal and state policy makers examine the goals and outcomes associated with current bilingual education policy and practice, recognizing that no child should be forced to choose between educational opportunity and cultural identity.
- That along with pedagogical considerations, the historical and juridical facts supporting group claims to language rights and cultural continuity should be kept clearly in view. The right of minorities to establish language and cultural objectives for themselves should be recognized in public policy, and processes should be fostered through which informed and responsible decisions about language and education can be made by the communities concerned.
- That colleges and universities more actively promote the broad-gauged, interdisciplinary, and historically grounded research necessary to inform a more rational, efficacious, and humane national policy concerning language and education.
- That elementary and secondary schools provide the instructional services and resources necessary to maintain and develop the language skills of children who enter school speaking Spanish or an Indian language, if these students or their parents request such services. This recommendation in no way relieves the schools of their responsibility for providing these students with a complete training in English.
- That researchers seek to identify the instructional methods, materials, and programs at both the precollegiate and postsecondary levels that contribute to student performance in school and promote the development of bilingual skills.

- That researchers seek to identify the barriers faced by college students whose command of English is limited as a result of poor instruction in the elementary and secondary schools or of recent migration to this country and to explore ways in which the educational achievement of these students can be facilitated. (The lack of research related to the needs and experiences of bilingual college students frustrated the commission's efforts to understand the dynamics of bilingualism at the postsecondary level.)
- That postsecondary educators recognize their responsibility for and commit themselves to furthering the development of bilingual skills among college students and, through their roles as teacher trainers, support and improve the job training of teachers already working at the elementary and secondary levels.
- That colleges and universities acknowledge and utilize the linguistic talents of bilingual students by providing them with the training and opportunities to work part time on community liaison and on student recruitment and orientation programs; by employing upper-division or graduate students to provide academic tutoring and personal counseling for new bilingual students who need such services; and by hiring and training students as tutors and teaching assistants in foreign language courses and as research assistants on projects concerned with studying language-related issues or with collecting data within bilingual communities. These kinds of opportunities benefit students as well as the institution by enhancing student involvement in the college experience and by providing on-campus employment that is likely to be of greater interest and value than many other work-study jobs.

Rationale. Language is a vital component of personal identity, cultural continuity, and community cohesion for Chicanos, Puerto Ricans, and American Indians. While the commission recognizes that the acquisition of English-language skills is a prerequisite for full and effective participation in most aspects of U.S. life, including higher education, it fails to see why the acquisition of these skills should preclude a parallel acquisition of competency in the language of one's culture and community. Indeed, the commission would endorse the goal of achieving genuine bilinguality not just for Chicanos, Puerto Ricans, and American Indians, but for all U.S. citizens. The apparently learned disability with languages other than English that affects so many Americans is destructive of cross-cultural and international understanding and relationships.

It is important as well to acknowledge the roots of present language conflicts affecting Indians, Chicanos, and Puerto Ricans. The hostilities with Mexico, Spain, and various American Indian nations generally ended in formal treaties that in almost every case promised to respect these peoples' property, political rights, culture, and language; over the years, however, these peoples have often been exposed to unequal systems of education where English has been imposed as the language of instruction and where native languages have been excluded from the schools. This historical background needs to be kept in view, along with emergent international norms regarding minority language rights, in considering the legal bases for bilingual schooling and other public services in the United States.

Spanish is spoken in and is a vital feature of many U.S. communities and will be for decades to come (Macias, 1979). The Hispanics are the fastest growing minority in the country, with an increasing number of dispersed regional concentrations. Substantial migration to the U.S. from Mexico, Puerto Rico, and other Spanish-speaking countries will continue, and the lives of many migrants will be characterized by a complex circulation pattern between the U.S. and their home countries. Survey results indicate very strong support for preserving Spanish and for bilingual education within Chicano and Puerto Rican communities. Knowledge of Spanish provides a concrete link to a rich and creative intellectual and political tradition of worldwide scope and, on a more immediate and practical level, allows people to be active and effective participants in their communities. The demand for young college-trained professionals, business persons, government employees, and service workers with a command of both Spanish and English is steadily growing.

   Although an estimated 206 Indian languages and dialects
have survived as living languages and a half dozen have 10,000
or more speakers, fifty or so have fewer than ten surviving
articulators of the traditions they embody (Medicine, 1979).
Because each Indian language is a product and expression of a
distinctive culture, recording and teaching an Indian language
represents the preservation and transmission of a whole way of
life—a particular mode of viewing and ordering the world and
experience. Separated from the living cultures, the languages
become essentially meaningless; separated from the languages,
the cultures cannot long survive in depth. Thus Indian communities have repeatedly urged that their languages be taught in
the schools and that the traditional mechanisms of transmitting
these languages be revitalized where they have broken down.
Indians in the United States today stand poised before the
prospect of a new era in which a recovery of sovereignty and self-
determination may be coupled with the command of resources
that have the potential to put great wealth in the hands of some
tribal governments. The opportunity and need to come to grips
creatively with problems of education and language have never
been greater.
   Federal support for bilingual education dates from the
late 1960s and addresses only the most elemental problem of an
officially monolingual but linguistically diverse society: how to
teach children who enter school with little or no knowledge of
English. The Bilingual Education Act (1967) and subsequent
state statutes allowed such children to receive instruction in their
own language for a transitional period. Thus Spanish and Indian
languages are permitted in the schools, but only as a means of
facilitating the first steps toward learning English. The child who
is proficient in a language other than English, but not in English,
is summarily labeled as "language deficient." By 1980 nearly a
billion dollars had been spent on remedial and compensatory
programs that narrowly define eligibility for bilingual instructional services and seek to return students to regular classrooms
as rapidly as possible.
   The commission recognizes that government and school
provisions for bilingual education, even in their most rudimen-

tary form, are highly controversial, and that there are divisions of opinion about them within the Spanish-speaking and Indian communities. It does not pretend to have greater insight into the best resolution of this controversy, nor does it recommend enforced bilinguality for students from these communities. It wishes to affirm its opinion that bilingualism is a strength, and that students who enter the nation's schools speaking some language other than English bring a talent to be developed, not a disability to be overcome. As stated in their value premises, the commission firmly believes that full access to and participation in education and in U.S. social and economic life is an incontestable right of each of these groups, and that exercising this right should under no circumstances require individuals to surrender their cultural distinctiveness, including language.

Graduate and Professional Education

The commission recommends:

- That federal, state, and institutional policy makers increase financial aid for minority students at the graduate and professional levels. In particular, every effort should be made to expand the number of assistantships available to minority graduate students, since this form of aid seems to intensify student involvement in graduate study, promote professional development, and strengthen the bond between student and faculty mentor.
- That federal, state, and private agencies consider implementing challenge grant programs, since such programs seem likely to increase the amount of financial aid available for minority graduate students as well as to strengthen institutional commitment to the goal of increasing minority enrollments.
- That graduate faculties be more sensitive and responsive to the need of minority graduate students to have more freedom and support in selecting research topics, choosing methodologies, analyzing data, and interpreting results, consistent with graduate standards.

- That graduate and professional schools make special efforts
  to increase their pools of minority graduate students and the
  presence of minority members on their faculties.
- That federal and state policy makers give increased attention
  to the nation's long-term needs for highly skilled academic,
  research, and technical workers. We believe that recent cuts
  in funding for advanced training programs based on actual
  or presumed short-term surpluses of personnel in certain
  fields are short-sighted, and that they disproportionately and
  unfairly reduce the opportunities of emerging minority
  scholars to contribute to the general good.

Rationale. Advanced education is an important route to
positions of leadership in U.S. society. Despite some gains in the
past decade, minority enrollments in graduate and professional
schools remain low, lagging behind minority undergraduate
enrollments and falling far short of White enrollments at the
graduate and professional levels.

Data from the current project contribute to our understanding of the problems confronting minority students who
pursue advanced degrees. Five factors were found to affect
minority access to, participation in, and satisfaction with graduate
and professional education.

First, financial aid is terribly important to minority graduate students and has become a critical issue because of declines
in federal and private financial support in recent years. Our
analyses revealed that financial aid facilitates entry to and persistence in graduate school. Respondents to the commission's
survey of minority educators identified financial concerns as a
major obstacle to graduate school attendance. A large proportion
of the Ford Fellows said that receiving the fellowship award
enabled them to attend the graduate schools of their choice and
to stay in school once they had enrolled. The 1980 follow-up of
1971 freshmen indicated that minority respondents who had
attended graduate school were far less satisfied with the financial
aid counseling they had received than were their White counterparts. Almost as important as the availability of financial aid was
its form. Teaching, administrative, and research assistantships

that promote professional development are preferable to loans, which do little to encourage students to participate in the apprenticeship that is such an important aspect of the graduate experience.

A second important factor is the type of undergraduate institution attended. Analyses of the 1971–1980 data indicated that the minority student who completes the baccalaureate at a high-quality (that is, selective, prestigious, affluent) college has a much better chance of enrolling in and completing graduate and professional study than the minority student who attends a low-quality college.

Third, the environment of the graduate institution has a major impact on the minority student's participation in and satisfaction with graduate education. Survey respondents indicated that they were often uncomfortable with the cool, somewhat alien, environments of academic departments and research universities. Low minority enrollments and lack of institutional concern for minority students contributed to their sense of isolation and impeded their adjustment. A number of Ford Fellows commented that the inhospitable atmosphere of academic institutions, along with the prospect of taking a low-paying faculty position, contributed to their decision to seek employment in the private sector rather than in academe following degree completion.

Fourth, faculty expectations and attitudes constitute a significant part of the graduate and professional experience of minority students. A large proportion of the Ford Fellows and of the minority educators said that they entered graduate programs feeling stigmatized by their race and ethnicity; minority respondents felt that faculty members all too often assumed that they had been admitted to satisfy affirmative action requirements and that they were less competent than White graduate students. The continual need to prove themselves angered them and contributed to their dissatisfaction with graduate study.

Finally, survey respondents and Ford Fellows reported that majority faculty often failed to acknowledge, let alone support, minority-oriented research interests and associated cultural values. As graduate students they faced constraints in their choices of research subjects and approaches and in drawing implications from their studies, because of negative attitudes, very specialized concerns, and methodological rigidity on the part of faculty. These sources of conflict contributed to the sense of alienation pervading these accounts of the graduate experience.

Minority Faculty and Administrators

The commission recommends:

- That colleges and universities seek to recruit and hire more minority faculty members, administrators, and student services personnel and make every effort to promote and tenure minority educators. Actions do indeed speak louder than words: no amount of rhetorical commitment to the principles of equal opportunity, affirmative action, and pluralism can compensate for or justify the current degree of minority underrepresentation among faculty, administrators, staff members, and students in higher education.

- That top administrators demonstrate their clear and unequivocal support of efforts to recruit, hire, promote, and tenure minorities. In many respects, the administration establishes the campus atmosphere or "tone." Thus, a visible personal commitment to change on the part of one or two senior officials can be critical in effecting increased minority representation on a campus.

- That colleges and universities make every effort to ensure that minority faculty members, administrators, and student personnel workers are represented in all types of positions at all levels within the institution. An unfortunate side effect of the effort to provide better services to minority students has been the creation of positions that are perceived and labeled as "minority" positions; often, minority staff are hired for part-time, short-term, nontenure-track jobs that are supported by "soft" funds from outside the institution's line-item budget. Because they are isolated from the institutional mainstream, the incumbents of such jobs have little opportunity to influence institutional policies and practices, limited interaction with majority students, and few prospects for advancement.

- That colleges and universities revise their hiring and promotion criteria so as to recognize and reward a wider variety of accomplishments and types of service. Although we are certainly not the first to advocate change in the current review and promotion system, continued adherence to narrowly defined criteria tends to penalize minority staff members who, in trying to fulfill the multiple roles demanded of them, often have little time or energy left to devote to scholarly research and other traditional functions. Institutions that emphasize scholarly activity as a major criterion for promotion should consider establishing a junior faculty research leave program for those young faculty members who have taken on special advising and counseling duties.
- That state legislatures and state boards support administrative internship programs (such as the current state-funded program in the University of California and California State University and College systems) to develop and promote minority and women administrators in public colleges and universities.

Rationale. The commission's survey of 311 minority educators asked respondents to indicate what higher education institutions could do to better serve minority students. The most frequently endorsed recommendation was: hire, promote, and tenure minority faculty members, administrators, and counselors. We believe that this response reflects a recognition of the important functions that minority academics serve as role models; as advisors; as student advocates; as monitors of institutional policies and practices; as dedicated educators committed to educational excellence and equity; as scholars approaching traditional subjects and research questions with new perspectives or laying the intellectual foundations in emerging fields of inquiry; as ambassadors to the minority communities; and, in many cases, as newcomers unwilling to accept the status quo at face value. We also believe that their ranks are thin in number and junior in status and that the foothold they have gained in academe is threatened by institutional retrenchment, the "tenuring-in" of academe, union protectionism of seniority, and rising political, social, and economic conservatism.

In 1976, the National Center for Education Statistics reported that 92 percent of all full-time faculty and 95 percent of full-time faculty at the rank of professor were White. Just over a fourth (27 percent) of the White full-time faculty hold positions below the rank of assistant professor (for example, instructor, lecturer), compared with 44 percent of Black and Indian educators and 41 percent of Hispanic educators. According to recent survey results reported by Florence Ladd, minorities are dramatically underrepresented among college and university presidents, executive vice-presidents, and academic deans of predominantly White institutions (Ladd, 1981).

Government Programs

The commission recommends:

- That the federal government continue to play its leadership role in emphasizing access to higher education for all segments of society. In particular, federal programs in the areas of student aid, institutional support, and special interventions deserve continued support.
- That state and local policy makers, planners, and educators devote more attention to the factors that impede full minority participation in higher education. Federal funding should supplement, not supplant, state and local efforts to support a range of programs and interventions responsive to the needs of minority students.

Rationale. During the past fifteen years, the federal government has assumed major responsibility for the educational equity issues often overlooked by state and local governments. Evidence indicates that federal leadership in this area has contributed to increased minority participation in higher education, and that federal categorical programs—financial aid, institutional aid, and special interventions—have helped to move the higher education system somewhat closer to the goal of equal access.

The success of federal efforts often depends upon the willingness of state and local officials to administer and implement federally funded programs. Unfortunately, state and local performance has not always been consistent with federal priorities, and this discrepancy has had important consequences for minority groups. Local, state, and federal governments have a collective and equal responsibility for minority participation in higher education—a responsibility that does not diminish during times of fiscal stringency.

Minority Women

The commission recommends:

- That colleges and universities provide counseling services and personal support groups to assist minority women in overcoming the barriers that result from double standards and sex-role stereotypes.
- That colleges and universities provide science and mathematics clinics and special courses to help minority women make up for deficiencies in preparation in these subjects, so that these women will be able to consider a wider range of careers. These efforts should be additional to particular interventions at the precollege level.
- That institutions hire and promote more minority women as faculty, administrators, and staff.
- That institutions provide child care services on campus.
- That institutions make an effort to involve those minority women who live at home more fully in campus life—for example, by providing dormitory space or other facilities where these women can spend time interacting with other students.

Rationale. Sex differences in the choice of major field and in career aspirations transcend racial and ethnic differences, but in some instances, are more pronounced among minorities than among Whites. At all degree levels, women are more likely to major in allied health fields, the arts and humanities, and education, whereas men are more likely to major in business, engineering, the physical sciences, and mathematics. Further, although women tend to make better high school grades than men do, more female than male freshmen—and especially minority female freshmen—express a need for special remedial assistance in science and mathematics. Data on earned degrees indicate that minority women are even more poorly represented than White women among those receiving degrees in engineering, physical sciences, and mathematics.

Minority women are heavily concentrated in the field of education. In 1975–76, 8 percent of White women receiving baccalaureates were education majors, in contrast to 24 percent of Hispanic women, 31 percent of Black women, and 32 percent of American Indian women. At the master's level in 1978–79, half of the White women (52 percent) and the Hispanic women (53 percent), 57 percent of the Indian women, and 66 percent of the Black women received their degrees in education. At the doctorate level, about a third of the White and Hispanic women, half of the Indian women, and two fifths of the Black women earned their degrees in education. Clearly, if minority women are to have access to a wider range of positions and occupations, their current patterns with respect to undergraduate majors must change.

Finally, responses to the survey of minority educators indicate that minority women suffer from sex-role stereotypes and conflicts engendered by multiple-role demands.

Data Pertaining to Minorities

The commission recommends:

- That all federal, state, and other agencies concerned with collecting and reporting data on minorities replace the "Hispanic" category with specific categories that separately identify Chicanos, Puerto Ricans, and other Hispanic groups.
- That, wherever possible, data on Puerto Ricans residing in the United States be reported independently of data on those whose homes are in Puerto Rico.
- That since the designation "American Indian" is ambiguous, and since survey respondents who identify themselves in this

way frequently change their response on subsequent surveys, persons who indicate that they are American Indians be asked for further specific information—that is, to specify their tribe or band.

- That all sample surveys strive to oversample minorities, especially the smaller groups—for example, Chicanos, Puerto Ricans, and American Indians.
- That the U.S. Bureau of the Census hire and train more minority census takers and researchers to develop and administer questionnaires and to analyze and interpret the results of Census Bureau surveys.
- That the officials responsible for public higher education in each state institute a comprehensive data system for tracking and monitoring the flows of minority and nonminority students through the community colleges, baccalaureate-granting institutions, and graduate institutions in the state.

Rationale. The success of any attempt to understand the educational problems of minorities or to develop appropriate remedies for these problems is heavily dependent on the quality of the available data. Most sources of data used in this project were seriously flawed; in certain instances, data pertaining to a given issue were simply not available.

Considering the importance of minority issues in our society and the fact that the special educational problems of minorities are far from solved, the costs of improving the quality of existing data and of filling gaps where additional data need to be collected are trivial. With no or very modest funding, the recommendations listed above could be implemented immediately.

Evaluation of Minority-Oriented Programs

The commission recommends:

- That public and private agencies funding minority-oriented programs require that all proposals for such projects include an evaluation component, and that they earmark a certain fraction of the project funds for such evaluation.
- That funding agencies view the results of evaluation studies

as a means of improving and strengthening programs, and that they communicate this view to those involved in operating the programs.

Rationale. Evaluation should be a key component of any minority-oriented program, not only because well-designed evaluative research provides vital feedback to guide both program personnel and funding agencies but also because objective evidence of program efficacy can serve to protect the most effective programs in times of budgetary austerity.

It is an understatement to say that the commission was frequently frustrated by the lack of hard evidence concerning the effectiveness of the many programs that have been undertaken to facilitate the progress of minority students in higher education. While impressionistic and anecdotal evidence supplied by the people responsible for running the programs suggests that many of these programs have been useful, systematic objective evidence on program impact is rarely available.

The commission believes that better data on program outcomes will be helpful to funding agencies as they develop plans for future support of minority-oriented programs. Even more important, it will help program personnel as they strive to improve existing programs and design new ones.

The people responsible for operating minority-oriented programs are often indifferent or resistant to systematic evaluation. These attitudes have some basis in reality. In the first place, program staff generally lack the expertise needed to design and implement evaluative studies. Further, evaluation tends to consume limited resources. And finally, program staff are inclined to view evaluation as a threat because it can generate data that might lead others to conclude that the program is not worthwhile. Considering that program staff are almost by definition committed to the belief that their programs are useful and effective, they see themselves as having little to gain and potentially much to lose from program evaluation.

Unfortunately, these defensive attitudes prevent many funding agencies, as well as program personnel, from viewing evaluation as a potential benefit—a source of information to

guide them as they develop and refine their programs and as
they strive to develop proposals for new programs. Ongoing
evaluations, for example, can be very useful in providing funding
agencies with information on such matters as the following:
elements of the program that might be expanded or elaborated
because they seem to be most effective; elements of the program
that seem to be least effective and thus need to be changed or
eliminated; types of students who benefit most from the program; unforeseen or unplanned outcomes of the program; and
the effectiveness of the program compared with the effectiveness
of traditional or standard programs.

Further Research on Minorities

The commission recommends:

- That officials in private and state agencies, as well as in the
  federal government, give priority to minority-oriented research in allocating their increasingly limited funds. These
  funding sources should aim to establish a process whereby a
  broad-based and sustained consultation about information
  needs and issues in higher education can take place within
  minority communities. Scholars from these communities
  should have a leading role in efforts to combine imaginatively
  the talents and energies present within these communities
  for the purposes of generating research agenda and priorities,
  carrying out research, and implementing the action implications flowing from these studies.
- That the following specific topics be given much more
  thorough study:
  a. factors affecting attrition from secondary school;
  b. the quality of education received in secondary schools
     with predominantly minority enrollments;
  c. the effectiveness of programs for improving articulation be-
     tween secondary schools and higher education institutions;
  d. factors affecting minority students' decisions to pursue
     careers in natural sciences and engineering;

    e. factors affecting minority access to the more prestigious institutions;
    f. factors affecting minority attrition from undergraduate study;
    g. the impact of alternative financial aid programs on the achievement and persistence of minority students;
    h. factors affecting the success of community college students who aspire to the baccalaureate;
    i. the importance of sex differences within minority groups;
    j. ways to develop the talents and skills of adults living in minority communities who have not had prior access to educational opportunities.

- That public and private funding agencies give serious consideration to providing relatively long-term support for programmatic research on minorities. Given the importance of longitudinal research in furthering our understanding of issues related to the higher education of minorities, what is specifically needed is a periodic longitudinal study that will make it possible to monitor the flows of minorities through the educational system and into the workforce, to evaluate the impact of special minority-oriented programs, and to identify educational policies or practices that facilitate or inhibit minority progress through the system. Such a study should begin during the secondary school years (or at the latest by college entry) and should be replicated on a regular basis at least every four years.

Rationale. These recommendations are based on the commission's understanding of prior research efforts as well as on its direct experience in conducting research for this project. They are meant to complement the recommendations regarding data and evaluation. Given the current efforts to reduce federal support for research in education and in the social and behavioral sciences, pressures for funding further research on minority education will fall heavily on private and state agencies.

℀ *Appendix A* ℀

Assessment of the Quality of Data

In this appendix we evaluate the quality of the data used by the HERI research team to assess the educational progress and current status of American Indians, Blacks, Chicanos, and Puerto Ricans. We assess the data, the problems posed by the available data, and the gaps in the available data by examining the racial and ethnic definitions and categories used to collect and report data, discussing the major data sources we used, and describing the populations covered by these different data sources (for example, undergraduates, graduate students, faculty). We then review the data by each of the four minority groups that are the study's focus and summarize the strengths and weaknesses of these data.

Racial and Ethnic Categories and Items

The categories and items that various survey instruments use in collecting data on the respondent's race or ethnicity pose three problems. The first problem stems from lack of clarity or of comprehensiveness in definitions. For example, instruments that employ the categories Hispanic or Spanish-surnamed American aggregate diverse populations and thus create a problem for researchers concerned with specific subgroups of this population.

The second problem arises when items on a particular instrument are revised. Over the past ten years, racial and ethnic categories have been redefined between data collection efforts. Until the mid 1970s, these changes uniformly represented improvements insofar as they involved adding or redefining categories so that finer and more useful distinctions could be made among various groups. For example, in 1971, the Cooperative Institutional Research Program (CIRP) added the categories Mexican-American/Chicano and Puerto Rican–American to the Student Information Form (SIF), which is used to collect data on a national sample of first-time, full-time freshmen. Prior to 1971, Chicano and Puerto Rican freshmen completing the SIF may have classified themselves as White, Black, American Indian, or other, depending on their racial background, sense of ethnic identification, and political consciousness.

When categories change from one administration of an instrument to the next, longitudinal analysis of the data may become more difficult. Further, since about 1975, categories on several important instruments have been revised in such a way as to eliminate distinctions among groups. For example, from 1973 to 1976, the National Research Council (NRC) used an item with seven response categories to collect data on the race or ethnicity of doctoral degree recipients. In 1977, the item was reduced to five response categories: Puerto Rican–American and Spanish American/Mexican American/Chicano were collapsed into Hispanic, and "other" was dropped from the response options. Thus, it is impossible to know whether the increase in the number of Hispanic doctoral degree recipients in 1977 represents actual gains made by Puerto Ricans and Chicanos or whether it merely reflects the inclusion in the Hispanic category of people who would previously have classified themselves as White, Black, or other.

The third problem is that, because different instruments use different racial or ethnic categories, data are often not comparable—certainly not easily comparable—across instruments. For example, while the October Current Population Surveys (CPS) collect data on first-time, full-time freshmen, neither their categories nor, until very recently, their data collection procedures were similar to those used by the CIRP to collect data on the same population.

The need to coordinate the development of common racial and ethnic definitions and to collect comparable and nonduplicative racial and ethnic educational data was recognized by the federal government as a result of the recommendations made by the Federal Interagency Committee on Education (FICE) Subcommittee on Minority Education and their report *Higher Education for Chicanos, Puerto Ricans, and American Indians* (1973). Encouraged by Caspar Weinberger, then Secretary of Health, Education and Welfare, FICE created an Ad Hoc Committee on Racial and Ethnic Definitions in June 1974. All federal agencies with major responsibilities for either collecting or using racial and ethnic data were invited to participate in the committee's deliberations.

By majority—not consensus—opinion, the committee selected and defined five racial and ethnic categories:

- *American Indian or Alaskan Native*: A person having origins in any of the original peoples of North America.
- *Asian or Pacific Islander*: A person having origins in any of the original peoples of the Far East, Southeast Asia, or the Pacific Islands. This area includes, for example, China, Japan, Korea, the Philippine Islands, and Samoa.
- *Black/Negro*: A person having origins in any of the black racial groups of Africa.
- *Caucasian/White*: A person having origins in any of the original peoples of Europe, North Africa, the Middle East, or the Indian subcontinent.
- *Hispanic*: A person of Mexican, Puerto Rican, Cuban, Central or South American, or other Spanish culture or origin, regardless of race.

The FICE endorsed the committee's recommendation that these five basic categories be used by all federal agencies to collect and report racial and ethnic data.

The annual October Current Population Surveys (CPS), conducted by the Bureau of the Census, collect educational data but have some significant definitional and procedural problems. They provide only three options for race: White, Black, and other. Moreover, until 1978, respondents were classified on the basis of observer identification; that is, the data collector made a judgment as to the race of the interviewee and checked the corresponding box. Beginning with the 1974 CPS, respondents were asked to indicate their own "origin or descent" or that of some other household member by selecting one from a flash card list of ethnic origins. Although the documentation is poor, it appears that the choices which are collapsed to create a "Spanish origin" category are: Mexican American, Chicano, Mexican (Mexicano), Puerto Rican, Cuban, Central or South American, and other Spanish. At their most detailed, CPS reports based on these data give figures for (1) All races, (2) White, (3) Black, (4) Spanish origin, (5) Mexican origin. Obviously, the responses of people of Mexican origin are also included in the figures for Spanish origin. Using CPS public use data tapes, the HERI staff has been able to examine separately the responses of Puerto Ricans and Chicanos from 1974 on. No identifiable data are available for American Indians, and pre-1974 data for Blacks and Whites include responses of Hispanics who selected or were placed into these classifications and who cannot be identified and selected out through data analysis procedures.

Analyses of longitudinal files from CIRP suggest that student responses to racial items are highly reliable. Opportunities to examine reliability were provided by three longitudinal follow-up surveys in which racial or ethnic items were repeated. The follow-ups, which covered periods ranging from three months to four years, produced very high agreement in self-identification for three groups: White (from 96 to 98 percent), Black (96 to 97 percent), and Oriental (92 to 94 percent). Agreement on the category American Indian, however, was extremely low (from 21 to 63 percent).

Another source of information on the reliability of self-reported race or ethnicity was provided by the nine year follow-up of 1971 entering freshmen conducted in 1980 as part of the current project. In the 1980 follow-up an attempt was made to overcome some of the problems associated with the American Indian category by asking those respondents who identified themselves as American Indian also to report their tribe or band. Of those 1971 freshmen who returned the 1980 questionnaire, the following degree of agreement was obtained:

Response in 1980	Agreement with 1971 CIRP (Percentage)
White	99.1
Black	98.1
Chicano	98.5
Puerto Rican	90.8
American Indian	90.3

Again, the rate of agreement is high, but of particular interest is the fact that the American Indian category showed a much higher level of agreement in this follow-up than in the CIRP follow-ups. Apparently, most actual American Indians check that category when they enroll as freshmen.

Data Sources

A review of the data resources, the instruments, and the ways in which racial and ethnic data are collected by these instruments illustrates both the strengths and the limitations of the various sources of data.

Cooperative Institutional Research Program (CIRP). The principal purpose of the ongoing CIRP longitudinal surveys is to determine the effects of college on students. Each fall since 1966, the Student Information Form (SIF) has been administered to the incoming freshman class at a representative sample of the nation's colleges and universities. Although some part-time students and some students previously enrolled in college are also surveyed, only data from first-time, full-time freshmen are used in computing each year's national norms, which thus constitute important baseline information about this particular student population. Follow-up surveys of subsamples from particular entering cohorts yield longitudinal data about student experiences.

The CIRP represents the most longstanding and most frequent monitoring of minority enrollments and provides the most detailed information about minority students: their personal and educational backgrounds, their academic and career aspirations, their beliefs and attitudes.

From 1966 to 1970, SIF respondents were asked to mark one of five racial or ethnic options, though the precise wording of two categories was revised in 1969: Negro was changed to Black/Negro/Afro-American, and, for the sake of consistency, Caucasian was changed to White/Caucasian. The other three categories were American Indian, Oriental, and other. In 1971, the categories Mexican-American/Chicano and Puerto Rican–American were added in response to requests from the Hispanic community. These two new options were selected by a total of 1.3 percent of the first-time, full-time freshmen in 1971; one cannot ascertain how such students chose to identify themselves in earlier surveys. Since 1971, the instrument has collected data using these seven response options, although the category Oriental was redefined as Asian-American/Oriental in 1976.

Since the CIRP was designed primarily as a study of institutional influence on student development, the original sampling of institutions was designed to minimize sampling error with respect to *student* characteristics. Major stratification variables included: the average academic ability of the entering freshmen (which was also called "selectivity"), race (predominantly black or predominantly white institutions), religion (Protestant colleges, Catholic colleges, nonsectarian colleges), sex, control (public or private) and the level of highest degree offered (university, four-year college, two-year college). Thirty-seven stratification cells based on these characteristics were formed (see Astin, King, and Richardson, 1980, fig. 1).

The original sample of participating institutions was selected in 1966 such that there were at least five participants within each stratification cell. Certain cells had larger numbers, primarily because it was believed that the institutions within those cells were more heterogeneous than the institutions in other cells. Increasing the actual sample size in such cells would tend to reduce institutional sampling errors. When institutions were initially invited to participate in 1966, the acceptance rate from those initially selected was 91 percent. The acceptance rate in community colleges was somewhat lower (about 80 percent) than in other types of institutions. Nonparticipants were replaced by randomly selected institutions within each cell.

Since 1966 the repeat participation from year to year has been approximately 90 percent. This loss of participants has been compensated for each year by the addition of several randomly selected institutions within the appropriate cells, and some institutions that have dropped out of the sample have returned in subsequent years. All losses or gains of participants within sampling cells are compensated for in any given year by the weighting procedure for generating national norms (see Astin, King, and Richardson, 1980).

Between 1966 and 1970 a number of additional institutions were allowed to participate at their own request, although their data were not included in the computations of the national norms. After 1970, however, a decision was made to encourage all institutions in the population to participate at a nominal fee. Although this decision runs the risk of some nonrepresentativeness within sampling cells, it has the advantage of reducing the likelihood of sampling errors by increasing the proportion of participants in each cell. In effect, the decision to include the paying institutions in the normative computations represents a trade-off: decreased sampling errors against the possibility of some nonrandomness within sampling cells.

The Student Information Form for entering freshmen is typically administered during registration, freshman orientation, or the first few weeks of classes. Institutions are strongly advised to administer the form under a proctored situation rather than by mail or other methods. Each year a decision is made about which institutions to include in the computation of national normative data. Briefly, a decision not to include an institution is based on two considerations: how the form was administered and what proportion of the first-time, full-time entering freshmen actually completed it. Thus, if a high percentage (say 90 percent) of the entering freshmen actually complete the form, then the method of administration is normally not an issue (except, of course, for those few institutions who administer the form rather late during the first academic term). If the percentage of participants is marginal (say, for a four-year college, between 80 and 90 percent), then the decision as to whether or not to include the data in the normative computations is based upon an analysis of the method of administration. Basically, if there is reason to believe that the omitted students are not self-selected but rather randomly or accidentally left out of the sample, then the data will be included in the normative computations. Approximately 90 percent of the institutions administer the questionnaire to proctored groups during freshman orientation or registration.

The possible nonrandom effects of including paid participants tended to be minimal during the 1971 survey, since this was the first year in which paying institutions were included. Thus, of the 487 participants in the fall of 1971, only 72 institutions were paying participants.

In assessing the quality of the data provided by the CIRP and in particular in evaluating its appropriateness for use in the current project, two somewhat different but related questions arise. First is the question as to whether or not the CIRP sampling of *institutions* produces a representative sampling of *minority freshmen*. This question concerns any given freshman survey, as well as the *trends* over time that might be affected by variations in institutional sampling from year to year. The second basic question concerns the nonrespondents in the follow-up of any given cohort of freshmen. In particular, it is important to determine the nature of the biases in responding to the 1980 follow-up of 1971 freshmen and to ascertain whether various follow-up and weighting procedures can provide a reasonably trustworthy estimate of the persistence rates of each minority group over the nine-year interval.

First let us consider the representativeness of the institutional and student samples who participate in the CIRP annual freshman survey. Since there are four separate stratification cells for predominantly black institutions, errors in estimating enrollments of black students are to some extent controlled by the weighting procedures. However, since no stratification is provided by the *number* of Blacks or other minority groups enrolling at predominantly white institutions, the possibility of institutional sampling errors is increased and the estimates of racial enrollments obtained through these surveys are necessarily open to some question. The principal source of errors in institutional sampling is caused by the fact that some institutions enroll very large proportions of minorities; estimates of minority enrollments can thus be substantially affected by whether or not such institutions happen to be included in the sampling. Moreover, if an institution enrolls a very high proportion of, say, Chicanos (the University of Texas at El Paso, for example), population estimates of Chicano enrollments may vary from year to year according to whether or not such institutions happen to be in the participating sample. However, as noted earlier, repeat institutional participation from year to year approximates 90 percent.

One way to assess the representativeness of the CIRP sample of institutions with respect to minority enrollments is to compare the participating sample's minority enrollments with those of the entire population. The U.S. Office of Civil Rights surveyed racial enrollments in the entire population of higher educational institutions in the fall of 1972. (Since these surveys are done in even-numbered years, it was not possible to obtain population enrollment figures for 1971.) Using OCR data, the HERI staff computed enrollment figures in the entering freshman class for the three minority groups that are relevant to this particular study: Blacks, Hispanics, and American Indians. The basic question we sought to answer was, To what extent does the CIRP sample include institutions that enroll relatively high proportions of these three minority groups?

Of the thirty-five U.S. institutions of higher education that have the largest numbers of Blacks in their entering freshman class in 1972, ten (29 percent) were CIRP participants in 1971, although CIRP participants represented only 20 percent of the total institutional population in 1971 (Cooperative Institutional Research Program, 1971). This overrepresentation of institutions enrolling large numbers of black freshmen is to be expected, since the predominantly black institutions have been deliberately over-sampled in the CIRP stratification design. In any case, it appears that institutions enrolling large numbers of Blacks are well represented in the 1971 CIRP sample.

Of the thirty-five institutions enrolling the largest numbers of Hispanics, eight (23 percent) were CIRP participants in 1971, a figure that compares favorably with the proportion of the total population represented by the CIRP sample (20 percent in 1971). Thus it would appear that institutions enrolling high proportions of Hispanics are adequately represented in the 1971 CIRP sample.

Of the thirty-five institutions enrolling the largest numbers of American Indian freshmen in 1972, only three (8 percent) were CIRP participants in 1971, a figure substantially below the expected rate of 20 percent. While it is not clear whether this is a systematic or random sampling deviation, it should be noted that two of these three CIRP participants are among the top four institutions in terms of the number of American Indian freshmen. In fact, the number of Indian freshmen accounted for by just these two institutions ($N=551$) is more than the total enrolling at the seven institutions at the end of the list of thirty-five ($N=495$).

In summary, it appears that the 1971 sample of CIRP participating institutions includes adequate proportions of institutions with large enrollments of Blacks and Hispanics, whereas the representation of institutions enrolling relatively large numbers of American Indians is below expectation.

How valid are the estimates of racial enrollments obtained through CIRP surveys? Of course, any method of evaluating the validity of one fallible data source involves comparison with one or more other fallible data sources. With this caution in mind, let us first compare the CIRP estimates with estimates obtained by the Office of Civil Rights (OCR) surveys that began in 1968. Since the OCR surveys are done in even-numbered years, the year 1972 was selected for comparison. The percentages of entering freshmen represented by each of the four groups from the two surveys are:

Group	1971 CIRP	1972 OCR
Blacks	8.7	9.50
Chicanos	1.5	1.77
Puerto Ricans	0.6	0.44
American Indians	1.1	0.64

This comparison indicates that CIRP surveys a reasonably representative proportion of each of the groups, with the possible exception of American Indians, for whom the CIRP estimate is substantially higher than the OCR estimate. Possibly, this larger figure results from the inclusion in the 1971 CIRP sample of two of the four institutions with the largest number of American Indian freshmen. Also, the use of self-report tends to greatly exaggerate the number of American Indians; the OCR estimates might include self-report measures, since each institution uses its own method for estimating.

OCR estimates for the two largest minority groups— Blacks and Chicanos—tend to be slightly higher than the CIRP estimates. However, OCR data include part-time students, and Blacks and Chicanos account for a disproportionate share of part-time students.

How reliable are these estimates from year to year? Table 43 shows the CIRP estimates of minority enrollments for the past fifteen years. In general the data reflect growth that is consistent with other sources of data. However, a good example of the influence of one institution on the data is the rise in enrollment figures for Chicanos between 1979 and 1980. The increase from 1.2 percent to 2.1 percent of the entering freshmen is accounted for entirely by the inclusion in 1980 of an institution that was not included in 1979 (East Los Angeles College, a community college with a majority of Chicano students).

The data in Table 43 were recast in the form of three-year moving averages (see Chapter Four, Table 22). The representation of Blacks among entering college freshmen grew regularly

Table 43. Annual Estimates of First-Time, Full-Time Freshmen Enrollments from the Cooperative Institutional Research Program

								Year							
Group	1966	1967	1968	1969	1970[a]	1971	1972	1973	1974	1975	1976	1977	1978	1979	1980
Whites	90.7	98.9	87.3	90.9		91.4	87.3	88.5	88.6	86.5	86.2	87.9	88.5	86.3	86.0
Blacks	5.0	4.3		6.0		6.3	8.7	7.8	7.4	9.0	8.4	8.8	8.1	9.2	9.2
Chicanos						1.1	1.5	1.3	1.5	1.7	1.7	1.4	1.0	1.2	2.1
Puerto Ricans						0.2	0.6	0.4	0.6	0.7	0.5	0.9	0.9	1.0	0.9
American Indians	0.6	0.7	0.7	0.3		0.9	1.1	0.9	0.9	0.9	0.9	0.8	0.8	1.0	0.8
Orientals	0.7	0.8	1.1	1.7		0.5	1.1	1.1	0.9	1.5	2.0	1.1	1.1	1.4	1.4
Other	3.0	4.4	5.1	1.1		1.2	1.8	1.5	1.7	1.9	1.8	1.8	1.7	2.0	1.7

[a] Data for 1970 are not available because of weighting errors in the original report.
Source. Cooperative Institutional Research Program (1966–1980).

and substantially between 1966 and 1975 (from 5 percent to 9.2 percent). Growth rates for the other three groups were also gradual and consistent. The substantial jump for American Indians between 1970 and 1971 is in all likelihood accounted for by the introduction of multiple response categories in 1971. Although only 3 percent of the students chose to classify themselves in this way, a disproportionate share of those who did chose American Indian as one of their multiple categories.

In short, the results of the comparisons with OCR data and the data shown in Table 43 and Chapter Four (Table 22) suggest that institutional sampling variations in the CIRP have not caused erratic fluctuations in the estimates of racial enrollment obtained from CIRP, even though no stratification procedure is provided in the sampling design to control such errors directly (except in the case of predominantly black colleges).

Now we turn to the second technical issue: the bias created by nonrespondents to the 1980 longitudinal follow-up of the 1971 freshmen. The original sample selected for follow-up included all American Indians ($N=2,336$), Chicanos ($N=2,682$), and Puerto Ricans ($N=768$) who participated in the 1971 entering freshman survey, together with a sample of approximately 50 percent of all Blacks ($N=11,045$) and approximately 10 percent of all Whites ($N=31,421$). Approximately 20 percent of these students responded to a long questionnaire mailed in 1980; approximately 25 percent of those who did not respond to the mailing were contacted by phone. Finally, about 65 percent of the institutions completed rosters giving the following information about all students in the follow-up sample: highest degree obtained, number of years completed, and whether transcripts were forwarded to another institution. The institutions that responded appeared to be representative of all institutions in the original sample.

Comparisons of the questionnaires, phone surveys, and roster data suggest that—as expected—students who returned the questionnaires are not a representative sample of the follow-up group. Those who responded to the phone survey, however, are a reasonably representative sample of nonrespondents to the mailed questionnaire.

Through a complex series of statistical analyses, we arrived at what appear to be reasonably valid estimates of college completion for the follow-up sample.* The results, shown in Table 30 in Chapter Five, indicate pronounced differences among the various racial and ethnic groups in terms of overall baccalaureate completion rates. Not unexpectedly, Whites show the highest persistence rate (55.6 percent), but the rate for Blacks is almost as high (50.9 percent). There does not appear to be any single explanation for this slight difference, since Blacks' persistence rates are slightly lower at all three types of predominantly white institutions. (The number of Whites enrolling at predominantly black institutions was not sufficient to provide separate estimates for this group; consequently, the persistence rates in four-year colleges were used to account for those few Whites, American Indians, Puerto Ricans, and Chicanos who enroll at predominantly black institutions.)

Chicanos, Puerto Ricans, and American Indians all show comparably low overall rates of baccalaureate degree completion (around 40 percent). For Chicanos and Puerto Ricans, these relatively low rates appear to be primarily attributable to their high concentration in two-year institutions. Thus, nearly 60 percent of the Hispanics entering colleges in the fall of 1971 enrolled in two-year institutions, compared to only about 40 percent of Blacks and Whites. Chicanos show slightly higher baccalaureate attainment rates in four-year colleges (70.4 percent) than do Blacks (66.6 percent), and rates nearly as high as those of Whites (72.7 percent). Puerto Ricans show a similarly high persistence rate in predominantly white universities.

American Indians show substantially lower persistence rates than all other groups in predominantly white institutions, particularly in the universities. While there is no immediate explanation for this result, results of earlier research on dropouts (Astin, 1975) suggest that students who come from relatively small towns and rural areas have a harder time persisting in large universities than do students from urban areas.

---

*For an account of the analyses and procedures, readers are invited to write the Higher Education Research Institute, Room 320, Moore Hall, UCLA Campus, Los Angeles, CA 90024.

Office for Civil Rights (OCR). In 1968, the Office for Civil Rights of the Department of Health, Education and Welfare began collecting biennial data on minority enrollments from all higher education institutions that received federal financial assistance. This data collection effort was part of the larger effort to monitor compliance with Title VI of the Civil Rights Act of 1964. The compliance report that institutions must complete has grown increasingly detailed over the years.

In 1968, each institution was asked to provide enrollment data, by ethnic group, on its undergraduate, graduate, and professional students. The user's guide to the data file suggests that the 1968 survey closely resembles the 1970 instrument, which asks for institutional enrollment data by level for five racial and ethnic groups (American Indian, Negro, Oriental, Spanish-surnamed American, and all other students) and for all students. Enrollment figures were reported for full-time undergraduates by year (first year, second year, third year, fourth year and beyond, and total) and for full-time graduate *and* professional students by year (first year, second year and beyond, and total). No data on part-time students were collected.

In 1972, the compliance report requested these same data but indicated that graduate enrollments should be reported separately from professional program enrollments, as in 1968. For the first time, data on part-time students were also collected, by level: undergraduate, graduate, first professional. In 1972, however, the reporting unit was no longer the institution but rather each undergraduate, graduate, and professional school on campus.

Procedures for collecting the data are left to the discretion of the institution, and the instructions state that a student may be classified in the minority group "to which he appears to belong, is regarded in the community as belonging, or categorizes himself as belonging." Self-identification by students is acceptable, although verification of such data for completeness and accuracy is strongly recommended. Further breakdowns of the categories into subgroups and the substitution of *Black* or *Negro* are also acceptable in developing forms to collect the required data from students through self-identification. The instructions specify that the category Spanish-surnamed Americans is intended to include people of Mexican, Central American, South American, Cuban, Puerto Rican, Latin American, or other Spanish origin.

In 1974, the reporting unit again changed: The institution was required to file a compliance report for each major field of study (up to twenty-six separate reports) and an institutional summary. The racial and ethnic reporting categories remained the same, except for some cosmetic alterations (Negro became Black, and Oriental became Asian American), but within each category, data were to be reported by sex. The categories for reporting enrollment data also changed. An item was added to determine how many of the full-time undergraduates were first-time community or junior college transfer students. A new category for full-time unclassified students was added; full-time graduate students were to be reported by program (master's, doctorate, and total) rather than by year; and full-time students studying for their first professional degree were to be reported simply by total enrollment in each racial or ethnic category. Part-time enrollments were to be reported as in 1972.

In 1976, the OCR compliance report was incorporated into the Higher Education General Information Survey (HEGIS), and the National Center for Education Statistics (NCES) assumed responsibility for collecting the data. The six racial and ethnic categories were: Black non-hispanic, American Indian or Alaskan Native, Asian or Pacific Islander, Hispanic, White non-Hispanic, and nonresident alien. Enrollments were to be reported by sex within these six categories. Institutions were asked to provide enrollment reports for eleven major fields and a summary report. Again, the enrollment categories changed somewhat: First-time, first-year students were distinguished from all other first-year students among undergraduates; and the item on community and junior college transfers was dropped; full-time unclassified students were to be reported by level (undergraduate, postbaccalaureate); and the reporting categories for full-time graduate students were first year and second year and beyond. Data on part-time students were to be reported using a format parallel to that used for full-time students. The institution was also asked to calculate and report total part-time and full-time enrollments.

The OCR data are important because they provide an institution-by-institution count of enrollments, by level, using the same instrument. The basic problem with these data is that one cannot know how institutions defined and calculated their enrollments by race and ethnicity, particularly for the first several reports. Brown and Stent (1977) found that OCR information on Blacks and Asian Americans compared favorably with that collected by the Bureau of the Census and by the American Council on Education but that enrollment reports on Hispanics and, especially, American Indians were less reliable.

Through the HEGIS program, in 1976 the OCR also began collecting data on degrees conferred from all academic institutions. Prior to 1976, it had collected some data on degrees conferred from selected states. Data for the period July 1, 1975, to June 30, 1976, were reported by sex for the six racial and ethnic categories used in the 1976 HEGIS enrollment reports. Data were collected by race and ethnicity for ten specified professional degrees; for bachelor's, master's, and doctor's degrees in twenty-four major fields of study; for interim master's-doctorate degrees or certificates; and for seven types of prebaccalaureate degrees and awards. The general instructions for completing the survey noted that many institutions awarded degrees in 1975 before learning of the need to collect racial and ethnic data on degree recipients. Data on degrees conferred are essential to any assessment of minority educational progress. These 1975–1976 data provide the first comprehensive national picture of the race and ethnicity of degree recipients.

Bureau of the Census. It is commonly agreed that past decennial censuses substantially undercounted racial and ethnic minorities. The problem is compounded by multiple responses: for example, people who identify themselves as white or black Puerto Ricans or who report mixed heritage.

The annual Current Population Surveys (CPS) are important to this study because the annual data provide a clear picture of age cohorts within the general population. (The limitations of these data are discussed earlier in this appendix.)

National Longitudinal Study (NLS) of the High School Class of 1972. The NLS, a large-scale, long-term program supported by NCES, initially surveyed a national representative sample of

1972 high school seniors. These students have subsequently been followed up four times, and a fifth follow-up survey is scheduled for 1985. The data provide a highly detailed longitudinal profile of a particular cohort of students who completed high school in 1972; some of them attended college, others did not. Data on respondents' race and ethnicity were collected in the base-year survey, and the item was repeated on the 1974 follow-up. The categories used were: White/Caucasian; Black/Negro/Afro-American; American Indian; Mexican-American/Chicano; Puerto Rican; other Latin American; Asian-American/Oriental; and other.

National Research Council (NRC). The NRC annually collects data from doctoral degree recipients. Although the first published annual summary report covers degrees awarded in fiscal year 1967, a race and ethnicity item was not included on the survey instrument until 1973. This seven-category item was repeated on the 1974, 1975, and 1976 instruments. The categories were: White/Caucasian; Black/Negro/Afro-American; American Indian; Spanish-American/Mexican-American/Chicano; Puerto Rican–American; Oriental; and other. Although one could take issue with the wording of some categories, they are basically clear and make useful distinctions among groups. In 1977, however, the survey directions asked respondents to choose among the following categories: American Indian or Alaskan Native; Asian or Pacific Islander; Black, not of Hispanic origin; White, not of Hispanic origin; and Hispanic. Unfortunately, the use of the Hispanic category not only aggregates Mexican Americans and Puerto Ricans but also includes people who previously would have chosen another racial or ethnic category.

❧ *Appendix B* ❧

Description of Dependent or Outcome Variables Used in Regression Analyses

Two-Year (1975–1977) Panel

College grade-point average (GPA). The student's cumulative undergraduate grade point average as reported at the time of the two-year follow-up. Grades were on an eight-point scale, ranging from 1 (D or lower) to 8 (A or A+).

Undergraduate persistence. A dichotomous variable reflecting whether or not the student was still enrolled full-time and in pursuit of the bachelor's degree at the time of the follow-up. Only students who aspired to at least a bachelor's degree at the time of initial entry to college were included in these analyses.

Satisfaction with the undergraduate college. A composite measure combining the student's reported degree of satisfaction with eighteen aspects of the undergraduate experience (for example, quality of teaching, counseling, financial aid).

1971–1980 Panel

Attainment of a baccalaureate. Students who indicated, on the follow-up questionnaire, that the highest degree they currently hold is a bachelor's, master's, or professional degree or a doctorate were counted as having attained a baccalaureate. Only students who aspired to at least a bachelor's degree at college entry were included in this analysis.

Attainment of an advanced degree. Students who indicated, on the follow-up questionnaire, that the highest degree they currently hold is a master's or professional degree or a doctorate were counted as having attained an advanced degree. Only students who aspire to at least a bachelor's degree at college entry were included in this analysis.

Enrollment in graduate or professional school. Students who listed the name of their current or most recent graduate or professional school on the follow-up questionnaire were counted as having enrolled in a graduate or professional school. Only students who aspired to at least a bachelor's degree at college entry were included in this analysis.

Attainment of a doctorate or advanced professional degree. Students who indicated, on the follow-up questionnaire, that the highest degree they currently hold is a professional degree or a doctorate were counted as having attained a doctorate or advanced professional degree. Only students who aspired to at least a bachelor's degree at college entry were included in this analysis.

Attainment or current pursuit of a doctorate or professional degree. Two types of students were counted as having attained or currently pursuing a doctorate or professional degree: (1) those who indicated that the highest degree they currently hold is a doctorate or professional degree, and (2) those who are currently enrolled in graduate or professional school and are working on a doctorate or professional degree. Only students who aspired to at least a bachelor's degree at college entry were included in this analysis.

Undergraduate grades. Students were asked to indicate the average grade they earned as undergraduates. Only students who aspired to at least a bachelor's degree at college entry were included in this analysis.

Satisfaction with undergraduate college. Students were asked how satisfied they were with the college they entered in 1971 with possible responses ranging from "very satisfied" to "not at all satisfied." Only students who aspired to at least a bachelor's degree at college entry were included in this analysis.

Career as a businessperson. A career as a businessperson includes accountants, business executives, business owners, and salespersons or buyers. Persons currently enrolled in a professional school and majoring in business are assigned a career as a businessperson rather than the career they listed on the follow-up questionnaire. Only students who aspired to at least a bachelor's degree at college entry were included in this analysis.

Career as an engineer. A career as an engineer includes engineers and persons currently enrolled in graduate school and majoring in engineering. Only students who aspired to at least a bachelor's degree at college entry were included in this analysis.

Career as a medical professional. A career as a medical professional includes physicians, dentists, veterinarians, and optometrists. Persons currently enrolled in professional schools and majoring in medicine are assigned a career as a medical professional rather than the career they listed on the follow-up questionnaire. Only students who aspired to at least a bachelor's degree at college entry were included in this analysis.

Career as an allied health professional. A career as an allied health professional includes dieticians, home economists, laboratory technicians, laboratory hygienists, pharmacists, and physical, occupational, and speech therapists. Persons currently enrolled in a professional school and majoring in allied health are assigned a career as an allied health professional rather than the career they listed on the follow-up questionnaire. Only students who aspired to at least a bachelor's degree at college entry were included in this analysis.

Career as an elementary or secondary school teacher. A career as an elementary or secondary school teacher includes elementary and secondary school teachers, and school counselors and administrators. Persons currently enrolled in graduate school and majoring in education are assigned a career as an elementary or secondary school teacher rather than the career they listed on the follow-up questionnaire. Only students who aspired to at least a bachelor's degree at college entry were included in this analysis.

Career as a college teacher or scientific researcher. A career as a college teacher or scientific researcher includes college professors and scientific researchers. Persons who are currently enrolled in graduate school and majoring in the arts, humanities, social sciences, physical sciences, or mathematics are assigned a career as a college professor or scientific researcher rather than the career they listed on the follow-up questionnaire. Only students who aspired to at least a bachelor's degree at college entry were included in this analysis.

Career as a lawyer. A career as a lawyer includes lawyers and persons currently enrolled in law school. Only students who aspired to at least a bachelor's degree at college entry were included in this analysis.

Career as a nurse. A career as a nurse includes nurses and persons currently enrolled in a graduate program in nursing. Only students who aspired to at least a bachelor's degree at college entry were included in this analysis.

Undergraduate major in biosciences. An undergraduate major in biosciences includes biology, biochemistry, biophysics, botany, zoology, and other biological sciences. Only students who aspired to at least a bachelor's degree at college entry were included in this analysis.

Undergraduate major in physical sciences and mathematics. An undergraduate major in the physical sciences and mathematics includes chemistry, earth science, mathematics, physics, statistics, and other physical sciences. Only students who aspired to at least a bachelor's degree at college entry were included in this analysis.

Undergraduate major in premedicine. An undergraduate major in premedicine includes predentistry, premedicine, and preveterinary medicine. Only students who aspired to at least a bachelor's degree at college entry were included in this analysis.

Undergraduate major in education. An undergraduate major in education includes elementary and secondary education and physical education and recreation. Only students who aspired to at least a bachelor's degree at college entry were included in this analysis.

Undergraduate major in allied health. An undergraduate major in allied health includes home economics, pharmacy, physical, speech, and occupational therapy, and health technology. Only students who aspired to at least a bachelor's degree at college entry were included in this analysis.

Undergraduate major in arts and humanities. An undergraduate major in arts and humanities includes English (literature), fine arts, journalism (writing), modern and other languages, music, philosophy, speech and drama, and other arts and humanities. Only students who aspired to at least a bachelor's degree at college entry were included in this analysis.

Undergraduate major in social sciences. An undergraduate major in the social sciences includes anthropology, economics, history, political science, psychology, social work, sociology, and other social sciences. Only students who aspired to at least a bachelor's degree at college entry were included in this analysis.

Undergraduate major in engineering. An undergraduate major in engineering includes aeronautical, civil, chemical, electrical, industrial, mechanical, and other engineering. Only students who aspired to at least a bachelor's degree at college entry were included in this analysis.

Undergraduate major in business. An undergraduate major in business includes accounting, business administration, and other business. Only students who aspired to at least a bachelor's degree at college entry were included in this analysis.

⅍ References ⅍

Abramowitz, A. E. (Ed.). *Proceedings for the National Invitational Conference on Racial and Ethnic Data.* Washington, D.C.: Institute for the Study of Educational Policy, Howard University, 1976.

Advisory Council of Development Institutions. "Strengthening Developing Institutions: Title III of the Higher Education Act of 1965." Annual Report, U.S. Office of Education, Washington, D.C., 1978.

American Bar Association. *A Review of Legal Education in the United States—Fall 1977.* Chicago: American Bar Association Section of Legal Education and Admission to the Bar, 1978.

Arce, C. H. "Chicano Participation in Academe: A Case of Academic Colonialism." *Grito del Sol: A Chicano Quarterly,* January-March 1978, *3* (1), 75–104.

Arce, C. H. "Chicanos in Higher Education." *Integrated Education,* May-June 1976, *14* (3), 14–18.

Association of American Medical Colleges. *Medical School Admission*

237

Requirements 1980–81. Washington, D.C.: Association of American Medical Colleges, 1979.

Astin, A. W. " 'Productivity' of Undergraduate Institutions." *Science*, 1962, *136,* 129–135.

Astin, A. W. "Undergraduate Achievement and Institutional 'Excellence.' " *Science*, 1968, *161,* 661–668.

Astin, A. W. *Predicting Academic Performance in College.* New York: Free Press, 1971.

Astin, A. W. *Preventing Students from Dropping Out.* San Francisco: Jossey-Bass, 1975.

Astin, A. W. *Four Critical Years.* San Francisco: Jossey-Bass, 1977a.

Astin, A. W. "Equal Access in Public Higher Education: Myth or Reality?" *UCLA Educator,* 1977b, *19,* 8–17.

Astin, A. W. "Measuring the Quality of Undergraduate Education: Are Traditional Approaches Adequate?" *Proceedings of the Quality of Baccalaureate Education: Expectations and Measures.* Austin: Institute of Higher Education Management, University of Texas, 1981.

Astin, A. W., Christian, C. E., and Henson, J. W. *The Impact of Student Financial Aid Programs on Student Choice.* Los Angeles: Higher Education Research Institute, 1975.

Astin, A. W., Fuller, B., and Green, K. C. *New Directions for Higher Education: Admitting and Assisting Students After Bakke,* no. 23. San Francisco: Jossey-Bass, 1978.

Astin, A. W., and Henson, J. W. "New Measures of College Selectivity." *Research in Higher Education,* September 1977, *7,* 1–9.

Astin, A. W., King, M. R., and Richardson, G. T. *The American Freshman: National Norms for Fall 1980.* Los Angeles: University of California, Los Angeles, 1980.

Astin, A. W., and Lee, C. B. T. *The Invisible Colleges.* Washington, D.C.: American Council on Education, 1971.

Astin, A. W., and Solmon, L. C. "Measuring Academic Quality: An Interim Report." *Change Magazine,* September 1979, 48–51.

Astin, H. S., and Burciaga, C. P. *Chicanos in American Higher Education: A Summary of Findings and Recommendations.* Los Angeles: Higher Education Research Institute, 1982.

Astin, H. S., and Cross, P. H. *Student Financial Aid and Persistence in College.* Los Angeles: Higher Education Research Institute, 1979.

Atelsek, F. J., and Gomberg, I. L. *Bachelor's Degrees Awarded to Minority Students: 1973–74.* Washington, D.C.: American Council on Education, 1977a.

Atelsek, F. J., and Gomberg, I. L. *Estimated Number of Financial Aid Recipients, 1976–77.* Washington, D.C.: American Council on Education, 1977b.

Bayer, A. E. *Teaching Faculty in Academe: 1972–73.* ACE Research Reports. Vol. 8, no. 2. Washington, D.C.: American Council on Education, 1973.

Berg, I. *Education and Jobs: The Great Training Robbery.* Boston: Beacon Press, 1971.

Blake, E. "Federal Policy and the Goal of Equal Opportunity." *Beyond Desegregation.* New York: College Entrance Examination Board, 1978.

Blake, E. *Target Date, 2000 A.D.: Goals for Achieving Higher Education Equity for Black Americans.* Vol. 1. National Advisory Committee on Black Higher Education. Washington, D.C.: U.S. Government Printing Office, 1980.

Bonilla, F., and Campos, R. "A Wealth of Poor: Puerto Ricans in the New Economic Order." *Daedalus,* Spring 1981, pp. 133–192.

Bowen, H. R. *Investment in Learning.* San Francisco: Jossey-Bass, 1977.

Breneman, D. W., and Nelson, S. "Education and Training." In J. Pechman (Ed.), *Setting National Priorities: Agenda for the 1980s.* Washington, D.C.: Brookings Institution, 1980.

Brown, G. H., and others. *The Condition of Education for Hispanic Americans.* Washington, D.C.: National Center for Education Statistics, 1980.

Brown, F., and Stent, M. D. *Minorities in U.S. Higher Education.* New York: Praeger, 1977.

Bundy, M. "The Issue Before the Court: Who Gets Ahead in America?" *Atlantic,* November 1977, pp. 43–54.

Burkheimer, G. J., and others. *Evaluation Study of Upward Bound*

Program: A Second Follow-up. Research Triangle Park, N.C.: Research Triangle Institute, 1980.

California State Department of Education. *A Master Plan for Higher Education in California, 1960–1975.* Sacramento: California State Department of Education, 1960.

Callan, P. M. "The State Role After Bakke." In A. W. Astin, B. Fuller, and K. C. Green (Eds.), *New Directions for Higher Education: Admitting and Assisting Students After Bakke,* no. 23. San Francisco: Jossey-Bass, 1978.

Carlson, D. E. *Student Access to Postsecondary Education: Comparative Analysis of Federal and State Student Aid Programs.* Los Angeles: Higher Education Research Institute, 1978.

Carnegie Commission on Higher Education. *Institutional Aid: Federal Support to Colleges and Universities.* New York: McGraw-Hill, 1972.

Carnegie Commission on Higher Education. *A Classification of Institutions of Higher Education.* Berkeley, Calif.: Carnegie Commission on Higher Education, 1973.

Carnegie Council on Policy Studies in Higher Education. *Three Thousand Futures.* San Francisco: Jossey-Bass, 1980.

Carter, T. P., and Segura, R. D. *Mexican Americans in School: A Decade of Change.* New York: College Entrance Examination Board, 1979.

Casera, Y. A. *Minorities in Higher Education: Chicanos and Others.* Nirvot, Colo.: Sierra Publications, 1978.

Chavers, D. *The Feasibility of an Indian University at Bacone College.* Muskogee, Okla.: Bacone College, 1979.

Chickering, A. W. *Commuting Versus Resident Students: Overcoming Educational Inequities of Living Off Campus.* San Francisco: Jossey-Bass, 1974.

Cooperative Institutional Research Program. *The American Freshman: National Norms for Fall.* Los Angeles: Graduate School of Education, University of California, 1966–1980 (annual).

Cross, K. P. *Beyond the Open Door.* San Francisco: Jossey-Bass, 1971.

Crossland, F. E. *Minority Access to College.* New York: Schocken Books, 1971.

de los Santos, A. G. *Hispanics and Community Colleges.* Topical Paper no 18. Tucson: University of Arizona, Center for Study of Higher Education, College of Education, 1980.

de los Santos, A. G., and others. *Chicano Students in Higher Education: Access, Attrition, Achievement.* Research Report Series, *1* (1). Austin: University of Texas at Austin, College of Education, 1980.

Dearman, N. B., and Plisko, V. W. *The Condition of Education, 1979 Edition.* Washington, D.C.: National Center for Education Statistics, 1979.

Dearman, N. B., and Plisko, V. W. *The Condition of Education, 1980 Edition.* Washington, D.C.: National Center for Education Statistics, 1980.

Dearman, N. B., and Plisko, V. W. *The Condition of Education, 1981 Edition.* Washington, D.C.: National Center for Education Statistics, 1981.

Dorris, M. A. "The Grass Still Grows, the Rivers Still Flow: Contemporary Native Americans." *Daedalus*, Spring 1981, pp. 43–70.

Dvorak, E. J. "A Longitudinal Study of Nonmedical Drug Use Among University Students—A Brief Summary." Paper presented to American College Health Association, San Francisco, April 1971.

Educational Testing Service. *Test Use and Validity: A Response to Charges in the Nader/Nairn Report on ETS.* Princeton, N.J.: Educational Testing Service, 1980.

Estada, L. F., Garcia, F. C., Macias, R. F., and Maldonado, L. "Chicanos in the United States: A History of Exploitation and Resistance." *Daedalus*, Spring 1981, pp. 103–132.

Executive Office of the President. *The Budget of the United States Government, Fiscal Year 1980.* Washington, D.C.: Office of Management and Budget, 1979.

Feldman, K. A., and Newcomb, T. M. *The Impact of College on Students.* San Francisco: Jossey-Bass, 1969.

Flores, J., Attinasi, J., and Pedraza, Jr., P. "La Carreta Made a U-Turn: Puerto Rican Language and Culture in the United States." *Daedalus*, Spring 1981, pp. 193–218.

Frances, C. "Influence of Federal Programs." In P. Jedamus, M. W. Peterson, and Associates, *Improving Academic Management*. San Francisco: Jossey-Bass, 1980.

Freeman, R. *The Overeducated American.* New York: Academic Press, 1976.

Gill, G. R. *Meanness Mania*. Washington, D. C.: Howard University Press, 1980.

Glover, R., and Gross, B. *Report of the National Forum on Learning in the American Future: Future Needs and Goals for Adult Learning, 1980-2000*. New York: Future Directions for a Learning Society, The College Board, 1979.

Golladay, M. A. *The Condition of Education, 1976*. Washington, D.C.: National Center for Education Statistics, 1976.

Gordon, E. W. *Opportunity Programs for the Disadvantaged in Higher Eduction*. AAHE/ERIC Research Report. Washington, D.C.: American Association for Higher Education, 1975.

Grant, V. W., and Lind, C. G. *Digest of Education Statistics, 1974 Edition*. Washington, D.C.: National Center for Education Statistics, 1975.

Grant, V. W., and Lind, C. G. *Digest of Education Statistics, 1979 Edition*. Washington, D.C.: National Center for Education Statistics, 1980.

Green, K. C. "Program Review and the State Responsibility for Higher Education." *Journal of Higher Education,* 1981a, *52,* 67–80.

Green, K. C. "Government Support for Minority Participation in Higher Education." Report to the Commission on the Higher Education of Minorities, Higher Education Research Institute, Los Angeles, June 1981b.

Green, K. C. "Compendium of Government Programs Supporting Minority Participation in Higher Education." Los Angeles: Higher Education Research Institute, 1981c.

Green, K. C. "Integration and Attainment: Some Preliminary Analyses." Paper presented at the annual meeting of the American Educational Research Association, Los Angeles, April 1981d.

Green, K. C. "Government Responsibility for Quality and Equality in Higher Education." In T. M. Stauffer (Ed.),

Political Controversies on Campus: The Making of Higher Education Policy. Lexington, Mass.: Lexington Books, forthcoming.

Green, K. C. *Government Support for Minority Participation in Higher Education.* ERIC/AAHE Research Report. Washington, D.C.: American Association for Higher Education, forthcoming.

Guerra, M. H. "The Retention of Mexican American Students in Higher Education with Special Reference to Bicultural and Bilingual Problems." In H. S. Johnson and W. J. Hernandez, *Educating the Mexican American.* Valley Forge, Penn.: Judson Press, 1970.

Gurin, P., and Epps, E. G. *Black Consciousness, Identity, and Achievement.* New York: Wiley, 1975.

Harris, J. "Gain Scores on the CLEP-General Examinations and an Overview of Research." Paper presented at the annual meeting of the American Educational Research Association, Minneapolis, March 1970.

Haynes, L. L. *A Critical Examination of the Adams Case: A Source Book.* Washington, D.C.: Institute for Services to Education, 1978.

Haynes, L. L. (Ed.). *An Analysis of the Arkansas-Georgia Statewide Desegregation Plans.* Washington, D.C.: Institute for Services to Education, 1979a.

Haynes, L. L. *The Adams Mandate: Is It a Blueprint for Realizing Equal Educational Opportunity?* (ED 143 496). Washington, D.C.: Institute for Services to Education, 1979b.

Hodgkinson, H., and Schenkel, W. W. *A Study of Title III of the Higher Education Act: The Developing Institutions Program.* Berkeley, Calif.: Center for Research and Development in Higher Education, 1974.

Holmes, D. O. *The Evolution of the Negro College.* New York: Teachers College Press, 1934.

Husen, T. (Ed.). *International Study of Achievement in Mathematics.* New York: Wiley, 1967.

Institute for the Study of Educational Policy. *Equal Educational Opportunity for Blacks in U.S. Higher Education: An Assessment.* Washington, D.C.: Howard University, 1976.

Jones, F. C. *The Changing Mood in America.* Washington, D.C.: Howard University Press, 1977.

Jones, F. C. "External Crosscurrents and Internal Diversity: An

Assessment of Black Progress, 1960–1980." *Daedalus*, Spring 1981, pp. 71–102.

Karabel, J., and Astin, A. W. "Social Class, Academic Ability, and College 'Quality.' " *Social Forces*, March 1975, *53* (3), 381–398.

Kent, L. *Puerto Ricans in American Higher Education: A Summary of Findings and Recommendations.* Los Angeles: Higher Education Research Institute, 1982.

Keppel, F. "Education in the Eighties." *Harvard Education Review*, 1980, *50*, 149–153.

Kerr, C. *The Use of the University.* Cambridge, Mass.: Harvard University Press, 1963.

Kluger, R. *Simple Justice.* New York: Vintage Books, 1975.

Ladd, F. C. "Getting Minority-Group Members into Top College Jobs." *Chronicle of Higher Education*, May 18, 1981, 21.

Lehner, Jr., J. C. *A Losing Battle: The Decline of Black Participation in Graduation and Professional Education.* A report prepared for the National Advisory Committee on Black Higher Education and Black Colleges and Universities. Washington, D.C.: Department of Education, 1980.

Leon, D. J. "Chicano College Dropouts and the Educational Opportunity Program: Failure After High School." *High School Behavioral Science,* Fall 1975, *3* (1), 6–11.

Leslie, L. A. *Higher Education Opportunity: A Decade of Progress.* Washington, D.C.: American Association for Higher Education, 1977.

Levitan, S. A., Johnston, W. B., and Taggart, R. *Still a Dream—The Changing Status of Blacks Since 1960.* Cambridge, Mass.: Harvard University Press, 1975.

Lopez, R. W., and Enos, D. D. *Chicanos and Public Higher Education in California.* Sacramento, Calif.: Joint Committee on the Master Plan for Higher Education, 1972.

Macias, R. F. "Choice of Language as a Human Right—Public Policy Implications in the United States." In *Ethnoperspectives in Bilingual Education Research: Bilingual Education and Public Policy in the United States.* Vol. 1. East Lansing: Bilingual Bicultural Education Programs, Eastern Michigan University, 1979.

Manning, W. H. "The Pursuit of Fairness in Admisions." In the Carnegie Council on Policy Studies in Higher Education

(Eds.), *Selective Admissions in Higher Education.* San Francisco: Jossey-Bass, 1977.

McNamara, P. P. *Data Sources for Tracking the Educational Progress of Minorities.* Los Angeles: Higher Education Research Institute, 1979.

McNamara, P. P. *American Indians in American Higher Education: A Summary of Findings and Recommendations.* Los Angeles: Higher Education Research Institute, 1982.

Maxfield, B. D. *Science, Engineering, and Humanities Doctorates in the United States: 1979 Profile.* Washington, D.C.: National Research Council–National Academy of Sciences, 1980.

Medicine, B. "Bilingual Education and Public Policy: The Cases of the American Indians." In *Ethnoperspectives in Bilingual Education Research: Bilingual Education and Public Policy in the United States.* Vol. 1. East Lansing: Bilingual Bicultural Education Programs, Eastern Michigan University, 1979.

Mingle, J. R. *Black Enrollment in Higher Education: Trends in the Nation and the South.* Atlanta, Ga.: Southern Regional Education Board, 1978.

Myrdal, G. *An American Dilemma: The Negro Problem and Modern Democracy.* New York: Harper & Row, 1944.

National Advisory Committee on Black Higher Education and Black Colleges and Universities. *Higher Education Equity: The Crisis of Appearance Versus Reality.* Washington, D.C.: Department of Education, 1978.

National Advisory Committee on Black Higher Education and Black Colleges and Universities. *Access of Black Americans to Higher Education: How Open Is the Door?* Washington, D.C.: Department of Education. 1979a.

National Advisory Committee on Black Higher Education and Black Colleges and Universities. *Black Colleges and Universities: An Essential Component of a Diverse System of Higher Education.* Washington, D.C.: Department of Education, 1979b.

National Advisory Committee on Black Higher Education and Black Colleges and Universities. *Still a Lifeline: The Status of Historically Black Colleges and Universities.* Washington, D.C.: Department of Education, 1980.

National Advisory Committee on Black Higher Education and

Black Colleges and Universities. *Black Higher Education Fact Sheet, #4*. Washington, D.C.: Department of Education, February 1981a.

National Advisory Committee on Black Higher Education and Black Colleges and Universities, *Black Higher Education Fact Sheet, #5*. Washington, D.C.: Department of Education, March 1981b.

National Center for Education Statistics. *National Longitudinal Study of the Class of 1972*. Washington, D.C.: U.S. Government Printing Office, 1973.

National Center for Education Statistics. *The American High School: A Statistical Overview*. Washington, D.C.: Department of Education, 1980.

National Commission on the Financing of Postsecondary Education. *Financing Postsecondary Education in the United States*. Washington, D.C.: U.S. Government Printing Office, 1973.

National Research Council. *Summary Reports 1967-1979* (separate volumes): *Doctorate Recipients from United States Universities*. Washington, D.C.: National Academy of Sciences, 1968–1980.

National Science Foundation. *Characteristics of Doctoral Scientists and Engineers in the United States: 1973, 1977* (separate volumes). Washington, D.C.: National Science Foundation, 1973, 1977.

Nichols, R. "Effects of Various College Characteristics on Student Aptitude Test Scores." *Journal of Educational Psychology*, 1964, *55*, 45–54.

Ochsner, N. L., and Solmon, L. C. *College Education and Employment—The Recent Graduates*. Bethlehem, Penn.: The College Placement Council Foundation, 1979.

Olivas, M. A. "Hispanics in Higher Education: Status and Legal Issues." A paper presented to the National Association of College Admissions Counselors, Bal Harbour, Fla., October 1978.

Olivas, M. A. *The Dilemma of Access: Minorities in Two Year Colleges*. Washington, D.C.: Institute for the Study of Educational Policy, Howard University Press, 1979.

O'Neil, R. M. *Discriminating Against Discrimination: Preferential*

Admissions and the DeFunis Case. Bloomington: Indiana University Press, 1975.

O'Toole, J. *Work, Learning, and the American Future.* San Francisco: Jossey-Bass, 1977.

Pace, C. R. *Measuring Outcomes of College.* San Francisco: Jossey-Bass, 1979.

Pasqueira, R. E. "Mexican American Student Staying Power in College." *College Board Review,* Winter 1973–1974, *90,* 6–28.

Pepin, A. J. *Fall Enrollment in Higher Education, 1978.* Washington, D.C.: National Center for Education Statistics, 1979.

Preer, J. "Lawyers v. Educators." Paper presented at the North Carolina Desegregation Conference, Raleigh, July 1979.

Preer, J. *Minority Access to Higher Education.* ERIC/AAHE Research Report. Washington, D.C.: American Association for Higher Education, 1981.

Pumroy, D. K. "Cigarette Smoking and Academic Achievement." *The Journal of General Psychology,* 1967, *77,* 31–34.

Rock, D. A., Centra, J. S., and Linn, R. L. "Relationships Between College Characteristics and Student Achievement." *American Educational Research Journal,* 1970, *7,* 109–122.

Rossmann, J. E., and others. *Open Admissions at the City University of New York: An Analysis of the First Year.* New York: Prentice-Hall, 1975.

Roueche, J. W., and Snow, J. J. *Overcoming Learning Problems.* San Francisco: Jossey-Bass, 1977.

Rumberger, R. W. *Why Kids Drop Out of High School.* Stanford, Calif.: IFG Publications, School of Education, 1981.

Sedlacek, W. E., and Pelham, J. C. "Minority Admissions to Large Universities: A National Survey." *Journal of Non-White Concerns in Personnel and Guidance,* 1976, *4* (2), 53–63.

Sloan Commission on Government and Higher Education. *A Program for Renewed Partnership.* Cambridge, Mass.: Ballinger, 1980.

Smartt, S. H. *Fact Book on Higher Education in the South: 1979 and 1980.* Atlanta, Ga.: Southern Regional Education Board, 1980.

Thomas, G. E. (Ed.), *Black Students in Higher Education.* Westport, Conn.: Greenwood Press, 1981.

Tollett, K. S. "What Led to *Bakke.*" *The Center Magazine,* Jan.//Feb. 1978, pp. 2–10.

Turner, W. H. and Michael, J. A. *Traditionally Black Institutions of Higher Education: Their Identification and Selected Characteristics.* Washington, D.C.: National Center for Education Statistics, 1978.

"Undergraduate Enrollment, by Race, in U.S. Colleges and Universities." *Chronicle of Higher Education,* February 2, 1981, p. 6.

U.S. Bureau of the Census. *American Indians.* Subject report series. Washington, D.C.: U.S. Government Printing Office, 1973.

U.S. Bureau of the Census, *1970 Census of the Population,* PC(1)-D1; *Current Population Reports*, Series P-20, nos. 110, 222, and 321; Series, P-23, No. 80. Washington, D.C.: U.S. Government Printing Office, 1970.

U.S. Bureau of the Census. *Population Characteristics. Current Population Reports,* Series P-20, nos. 283, 290, 295. Washington, D.C.: U.S. Government Printing Office, 1975.

U.S. Bureau of the Census. *Population Characteristics. Current Population Reports,* Series P-20, nos. 328, 356, 1978.

U.S. Bureau of the Census. *The Social and Economic Status of the Black Population in the United States, 1790–1978.* Current Population Reports: Special Studies, Series P-23, no. 80. Washington, D.C.: U.S. Government Printing Office, 1978.

U.S. Commission on Civil Rights. *Social Indicators of Equality for Minorities and Women.* Washington, D.C.: U.S. Government Printing Office, 1978.

U.S. Department of Health, Education and Welfare. *Data on Earned Degrees Conferred from Institutions of Higher Education by Race, Ethnicity, and Sex, Academic Year 1975–76.* Washington, D.C.: Office for Civil Rights, 1978a.

U.S. Department of Health, Education and Welfare. *Racial, Ethnic and Sex Enrollment Data from Institutions of Higher Education, Fall 1976.* Washington, D.C.: Office for Civil Rights, 1978b.

U.S. General Accounting Office. *Problems of the Upward Bound Program in Preparing Disadvantaged Students for Postsecondary Education.* Washington, D.C.: U.S. Government Printing Office, 1974.

U.S. General Accounting Office. *The Federal Program to Strengthen Developing Institutions Lacks Direction.* Report HRD-78-179. Washington, D.C.: U.S. Government Printing Office, 1979.

U.S. Office of Education, Department of Health, Education and Welfare. *Annual Report on Programs Administered by USOE, Fiscal Year 1978.* Washington, D.C.: U.S. Office of Education, 1979.

Weathersby, G. B., and others. *The Development of Institutions of Higher Education: Theory and Assessment of the Impact of Four Possible Areas of Federal Intervention.* Cambridge, Mass.: Graduate School of Education, Harvard University, 1977.

Willingham, W. W. "Free Access Colleges: Where They Are and Whom They Serve." *College Board Review,* 1970, *76*, 6–14.

Young, M. *The Rise of the Meritocracy, 1870–2033.* London: Thames & Hudson, 1958.

Index

A

Abramowitz, A. E., 22, 237

Academic preparation: fields of study related to, 69–74; and institutional types, 139; and persistence, 91–93; summary of, 180

Access and attainment: analysis of, 25–51, 129–153; and college completion, 40–43, 51; and college entry, 32–40, 51; defining, 129–130; developments in, 77–88; and excellence, conflict between, 122; by field, 177–179; government programs for, 114, 117, 119, 120–122, 125–126; and graduate and professional degrees, 45–50, 51; and graduate and professional enrollments, 43–45, 51; and high school graduation, 26–32, 51; issues of, 12; by level, 174–177, 185; minority educators' views on, 183–186; and persistence, federal programs for, 117, 119, 125–126; recommendations on, 194–196; trends in, 78–83, 179–180

Adams case, 121, 123, 124

Administrators, minority, recommendations on, 204–206

Admissions, standardized testing for, 157–158, 162–163

Advisory Council on Developing Institutions, 237

Age: and college entry, 35; and graduate and professional enrollments, 45; of high school dropouts, 27; and high school graduation, 30; and persistence, 41, 94

Alabama, flagship institution in, 135

Alaska, University of (Fairbanks), American Indians at, 137–138

Allied health fields: and academic preparation, 70, 72; as field of study, 53; and minority prefer-

ences, 66, 68; minority representation in, 57, 58, 60, 64, 74, 75; persistence in, 106
American Bar Association, 48, 50, 85, 237
American College Testing Program (ACT), 15, 55, 69, 92
American Council on Education (ACE), 15, 17, 69, 229
American Indians: academic preparation of, 70, 72, 92–93; access of, 131, 132, 133–134, 136–138, 153, 185; in allied health, 57, 60; in arts and humanities, 60, 66; in biological sciences, 67; in business majors, 62, 67; and college completion, 40, 42, 43, 82, 83, 87, 175, 176; and college entry, 36–39, 56, 80, 81, 174, 175; data limitations on, 26, 173; and demographic characteristics, 93, 95; in education, 60, 66, 76, 178; employment of, 69, 85–86, 87, 88; in engineering, 62, 67, 68; in fields of study, 58–59, 64–65, 68, 70, 72, 74, 75; and financial aid, 108; at flagship institutions, 136–138; government programs for, 117, 119, 127; and graduate and professional degrees, 46–48, 50, 83, 88, 175, 177; and graduate and professional enrollments, 43, 44, 175; and high school graduation, 31–32, 174, 175; and institutional characteristics, 98, 99, 100, 101, 102, 103, 104, 105, 182; in law, 62, 85, 88, 180; in medicine, 63, 83–84; persistence of, 51, 90, 92–93, 95, 98–105, 107, 108, 110, 111, 179; and place of residence, 110; racial definition of, 23–24, 39, 59, 184–185; report on, xii; and sample size, 23, 90; selection of, for study, 21; in social sciences, 61, 67, 76, 178
American Medical Association, 48
Aptitude tests, scores on, and persistence, 92
Arce, C. H., 25, 237

Arizona, University of: American Indians at, 138; Hispanics at, 137
Arkansas, University of: American Indians at, 138; Blacks at, 135
Arts and humanities: and academic preparation, 70, 72, 73; as field of study, 53; and minority preferences, 66, 68, 69; minority representation in, 58, 60, 63, 64, 65, 75; persistence in, 106
Asians, educational attainments of, 21
Association of American Medical Colleges, 48, 50, 84, 237–238
Astin, A. W., xi, 7, 8, 10, 16, 19, 40, 70, 92, 94, 97, 99, 101, 103, 107, 109, 121, 130, 139, 140n, 145, 146, 147, 156, 162, 176, 183, 218, 219, 226, 238, 244
Astin, H. S., xii, xv, 16, 107, 196, 238–239
Atelsek, F. J., 118, 239
Attainment. See Access and attainment
Attinasi, J., 241
Attitudes, and persistence, 97
Auburn University, Blacks at, 135

B

Baccalaureates, trends in, 82
Bakke case, 5
Ballesteros, E., xv
Basic Educational Opportunity Grant (BEOG). See Pell Grants
Bayer, A. E., 239
Berg, I., 6, 239
Bilingual Education Act of 1967, 200
Bilingual Education Programs, 117
Bilingualism, recommendations on, 197–201
Biological sciences: and academic preparation, 70, 71, 72, 73; as field of study, 54; and minority preferences, 67, 68, 69; minority representation in, 59, 61, 63, 64, 65, 75, 76; persistence in, 106
Black institutions: access to, 132; and

government programs, 121, 127; and persistence, 98, 101

Blacks: academic preparation of, 70, 72, 92–93, 180; access of, 130–131, 132, 133–136, 153, 185; in allied health, 57, 60, 66, 74, 178; in arts and humanities, 60, 66; in biological sciences, 61, 67; in business majors, 62, 67, 178; and college completion, 40–43, 81, 82, 83, 87, 175, 176; and college entry, 33–40, 56, 79, 80, 174, 175; and demographic characteristics, 93, 94, 95; in education, 60, 66, 76, 178; educational gains of, 149; employment of, 69, 85–86, 87, 88, 184; in engineering, 62, 67; enrollment trends for, 77, 78–79, 87, 88, 125; in fields of study, 58–59, 63, 65, 68, 70, 72, 75; and financial aid, 108; at flagship institutions, 134–136; and graduate and professional degrees, 45–48, 50, 83, 88, 175, 177; and graduate and professional enrollments, 43–45, 175; and high school graduation, 27–30, 32, 174, 175; and institutional characteristics, 98, 100, 101, 102, 103, 104, 105; in law, 62, 84–85, 88, 107, 180; in medicine, 63, 83–84; as part-time students, 37; persistence of, 51, 90, 92–95, 97–105, 107, 108, 110, 111, 179; in physical sciences and mathematics, 61, 67; and place of residence, 110, 183; reasons for college attendance by, 7; report on, xii; sample size of, 90; selection of, for study, 21; and smoking, 97; in social sciences, 61, 67, 76, 178; and standardized tests, 136, 163, 181; starting salaries for, 10–11

Blake, E., 78, 239
Bonilla, F., xi, xiii–xiv, 239
Bowen, H. R., 8, 22, 239
Breneman, D. W., 123, 127, 239
Brown, F., 22, 25, 78, 229, 239
Brown, G. H., 239

Brown case, 77, 114
Bundy, M., 21, 239
Burciaga, C. P., xi, xii, xiv, 238
Burke, Y. B., xi, xiv
Burkheimer, G. J., 126, 239–240
Business: and academic preparation, 70, 72, 73; as field of study, 54; and minority preferences, 67, 68; minority representation in, 59, 62, 64, 65, 74, 75; persistence in, 106

C

California: access and opportunity in, 120; administrative internships in, 205; affirmative action in, 124; flagship institutions in, 133; hierarchy of institutions in, 130, 151, 192
California, University of (Berkeley): American Indians at, 138; Blacks at, 135; Hispanics at, 137
California, University of (Davis): Blacks at, 135; Hispanics at, 137
California, University of (Los Angeles), 15; American Indians at, 138; Hispanics at, 137. See also Cooperative Insitutional Research Program
California, University of (San Diego): American Indians at, 138; Hispanics at, 137
California State Department of Education, 129, 130, 151, 240
Callan, P. M., 120–121, 122, 240
Campos, R., 239
Career plans, and persistence, 96
Carlson, D. E., 115, 240
Carnegie Commission on Higher Education, 17, 115, 132, 240
Carnegie Council on Policy Studies in Higher Education, 115, 120, 123, 240
Carter, T. P., 78, 240
Casera, Y. A., 240
Centra, J. S., 147, 247
Chavers, D., xv, 22, 39, 240
Chicanos: academic preparation of, 70, 72, 92–93; in allied health, 57,

60; in arts and humanities, 60; in biological sciences, 61; and college completion, 43, 82, 83, 175, 176; and college entry, 33–34, 36–40, 56, 80–81, 174, 175; and demographic characteristics, 93–94, 95, 181; in education, 66; employment of, 69; in fields of study, 55, 58–59, 63–64, 65, 68, 70, 72, 107; and financial aid, 108, 184; and graduate and professional degrees, 45–48, 50, 83, 88, 175, 177; and graduate and professional enrollments, 44, 175; and high school graduation, 27–32, 174, 175; and institutional characteristics, 98, 99, 100, 102, 103, 104, 105; in law, 62, 85, 88, 107, 180; in medicine, 63, 83–84; persistence of, 51, 90, 92–96, 98–105, 107, 108, 110, 111, 179; in physical sciences and mathematics, 61; and place of residence, 110, 183; report on, xii; and sample size, 26, 90, 173; selection of, for study, 21; and self-concept, 96; and standardized testing, 163. *See also* Hispanics

Chickering, A. W., 8, 109, 139, 145, 183, 240

Christian, C. E., 70, 107, 238

City University of New York, open admissions at, 34, 149, 174

Civil Rights Act of 1964, 179; Title VI of, 227

Clemson University, Blacks at, 135

College Assistance Migrant Program, 117, 119

College completion: for age cohort, 41; analysis of, 40–43, 51; by community college students, 40–41, 43, 98, 99, 100, 101, 102, 103, 176, 181–182; by racial or ethnic group, 40; trends in, 81–83, 175, 176. *See also* Persistence

College Entrance Examination Board (CEEB), xv, 15, 19, 55, 160

College entry: by age cohorts, 35; analysis of, 32–40, 51; and ethnic composition of freshman class, 36–39; and part-time students, 37; by racial or ethnic group, 33; trends in, 78–81, 174, 175

College Level Examination Program (CLEP), 149, 158–159, 160

College Work-Study Program, 117, 118

Colleges, four-year: access to, 131, 138–139, 140, 141, 142–143, 144, 145, 151–152; and financial aid, 108; and persistence, 98, 99, 100, 102, 103; selectivity of, 146

Colorado, University of, Hispanics at, 137

Colorado State University, Hispanics at, 137

Commission on the Higher Education of Minorities: function and meetings of, 19–20; recommendations of, 187–212; tasks of, 2; value premises of, 2–3

Community colleges: access to, 131, 132, 138–139, 140, 141, 142–143, 144; and financial aid, 108; and persistence, 40–41, 43, 98, 99, 100, 101, 102, 103, 176, 181–182; recommendations on, 191–192

Competency: assessment of, 167–168; issue of, 166–167

Cooperative Institutional Research Program (CIRP): access and attainment data from, 37, 38, 39, 79–80, 82; and data collection, 23, 214, 216, 217–226, 240; federal aid data from, 118; fields of study data from, 55, 56, 57, 64–65

Counseling, and standardized testing, 163

Crain, R., xv

Cross, K. P., 144, 240

Cross, P. H., 16, 107, 196, 239

Crossland, F. E., xiv, 36, 77, 240

Current Population Surveys (CPS): access and attainment data from, 26, 27, 30, 31, 33, 34, 41, 43, 44, 45; and data collection, 15, 23, 215, 216, 229

D

Data: assessment of quality of, 213–230; collection of, 15–19; limitations of, 22–24; and racial definition, 23–24; recommendations on, 208–209; and response rates, 23; sample size limitations of, 22–23; sampling errors in, 23; sources of, and quality, 217–230
Dearman, N. B., 9, 37, 46, 50, 53, 131n, 132, 241
De Funis case, 5
Delaware, University of, Blacks at, 135
de los Santos, A. G., 25, 132, 241
Demographic characteristics, and persistence, 93–96
Dentistry. See Medicine
Disadvantaged students, state programs for, 122–124
Doctorate: attainment of, trends in, 83; unemployment rate low for, 9. See also Graduate and professional degrees
Dorris, M. A., 241
Dropout, defined, 26
Dvorak, E. J., 97, 241

E

East Los Angeles College, Chicanos at, 223
Education: and academic preparation, 70, 71, 72, 73; as field of study, 53; and minority preferences, 66, 68; minority representation in, 58, 60, 63, 64, 72, 74, 75, 76; persistence in, 106–107
Education Amendments of 1972, 115
Educational Opportunity Centers, 117, 119, 126
Educational pipeline: developments in, 77–88; findings on, summarized, 173–180; longitudinal analyses of factors affecting, 89–112; for minorities, 25–51

Educational Testing Service, 15, 55, 157, 241
Engineering: and academic preparation, 70, 71, 72, 73; as field of study, 54; and minority preferences, 67–68, 69; minority representation in, 59, 62, 63, 65, 75, 76; persistence in , 106
Enos, D. D., 244
Environmental factors, and persistence, 97–110, 181–183
Epps, E. G., 243
Estada, L. F., 241
Evaluation: recommended, for minority-oriented programs, 209–211; role of, 14–15
Executive Office of the President, 129, 241

F

Faculty: data on, 17–18; minority, recommendations on, 204–206; quality of, 145
Federal Interagency Committee on Education (FICE), Ad Hoc Committee on Racial and Ethnic Definitions of, 215–216
Feldman, K. A., 8, 121, 241
Fields of study: academic preparation related to, 69–74; and admission test scores, by racial or ethnic group, 70; analysis of minorities in, 52–76; critical, 52–55; data sources for, 55–57; enrollment in, by racial or ethnic group, 64–65; high school preferences for, by racial or ethnic group, 72; minority preferences for, 64–69; minority representation in, 57–65; overrepresentation or underrepresentation in, 74–76; and persistence, 105–107, 112; racial and ethnic group distribution in, 58–59; trends in, 83–87, 182–183
Financial aid: federal government programs for, 117, 118–119; impact of federal programs for, 125;

and persistence, 107–109; recom-
mendations on, 196; state pro-
grams for, 123; summarized, 183
Flores, J., 241
Florida, University of: Blacks at, 135;
Hispanics at, 137
Ford Foundation, x, xiv, xv, 19, 21,
172; fellowships from, 16–17, 23,
202, 203
Four-year colleges. *See* Colleges,
four-year
Frances, C., 114, 123, 242
Freeman, R., 6, 7, 242
Freshman enrollments: ethnic com-
position of, 36–39; trends in, 80
Fuller, B., 162, 238

G

Garcia, F. C., 241
Georgia, University of, Blacks at, 135
Gill, G. R., 4, 242
Glover, R., 4, 242
Golladay, M. A., 242
Gomberg, I. L., 118, 239
Gordon, E. W., 119, 126, 242
Government programs: for access and
equality of opportunity, 114, 117,
119, 120–122, 125–126; analysis
of, 113–128; for disadvantaged, by
states, 122–124; federal, 116–119,
124–127; history of, 114–116; recommendations on, 206–207; state
role in, 119–124
Grade point average, factors in, 111
Grading, and standardized testing,
158–163
Graduate and professional degrees:
analysis of attainment of, 45–50,
51; in law, 48, 49, 50; in medicine,
47–48, 49, 50; by racial and ethnic
groups, 46; summary of findings
on, 175, 177
Graduate and professional education,
recommendations on, 201–204
Graduate and professional enrollments: for age cohort, 45; analysis
of, 43–45, 51; and institutional
quality, 104; and persistence, 104,

107, 112; by racial or ethnic group,
44, 50; summary of findings on,
175, 176–177
Graduate and Professional Oppor-
tunities Program, 117
Graduate Record Examination, 151,
160
Grant, V. W., 242
Green, K. C., xv, 117n, 122, 162, 238,
242–243
Gross, B., 4, 242
Guaranteed Student Loan Program,
117, 118
Guerra, M. H., 42, 243
Gurin, P., 243

H

Harris, J., 149, 158–159, 243
Hastorf, A. H., xi, xiv
Hawaii, University of (Manoa), His-
panics at, 137
Haynes, L. L., 124, 243
Health Professions Preparatory Scholarship Program for Indians, 117
Health Professions Recruitment Program for Indians, 117
Health Professions Scholarships for
Indians, 117
Henson, J. W., 19, 70, 107, 146, 238
Hierarchy of institutions: economic
reasons for, 151–152; educational
reasons for, 147–151; flagship institutions in, 132–138; in higher
education, 130; reasons for, 146–
152; resource distribution in, 141–
146
High school: curriculum of, and persistence, 93, 181; dropouts from,
by age and racial or ethnic group,
27; grades in, and persistence, 92;
racial composition of, and persistence, 95–96; recommendations
on, 189–191
High school graduation: by age cohort,
30; analysis of, 26–32, 51; trends
in, 78, 79, 174, 175
Higher education: economic value of,
6–9; hierarchy in, 130–153; limits

of, for study, 21–22, 172–173; persistence in, by racial or ethnic group, 51; reasons for seeking, 7; role of, in society, ix, 1; student benefits from, 8–9; as value added, 148, 157, 162; value-added model, implementation of, 188–189; value of, questioned, 5–11
Higher Education Act of 1965, 114, 125, 128; Title III of, 118, 126–127
Higher Education General Information Survey (HEGIS), 18, 133, 136, 143n, 228
Higher education of minorities: access and attainment issues for, 12, 25–51, 129–153; analysis of study of, 1–24; context of study of, 3–5; data collection for study of, 15–19; design of study of, 11–14; factors affecting, 12, 89–112; faculty data on, 17–18; government programs for, 113–128; institutional data on, 18–19; issues in, 12–13; limitations of study of, 21–24; recommendations on, 187–212; resistance to, 4–5; selection of minority groups for study of, 21; student data on, 16–17
Higher Education Research Institute (HERI) x, xv, 91n; and access and attainment data, 26, 42, 43; data collection by, 15, 16–17, 19, 20, 23, 213–230; simulation survey by, 162–163
Hispanics: access of, 130–131, 132, 133–134, 136–137, 153, 185; in arts and humanities, 66; in biological sciences, 67; in business majors, 62; category of, 173; and college completion, 40–42, 83, 87, 176; and college entry, 34–36, 79; in education, 60; in engineering, 62, 68; enrollment trends for, 125; in fields of study, 75; at flagship institutions, 136–137; government programs for, 127; and graduate and professional degrees, 47; and graduate and professional enrollments, 43, 45; high school and college attendance by, 31; and high

school graduation, 30–31; as part-time students, 37; in social sciences, 61. See also Chicanos; Puerto Ricans
Hodgkinson, H., 127, 243
Holmes, D. O., 243
Human resource development, government programs for, 117, 119
Humanities. See Arts and humanities
Husen, T., 160, 243

I

Illinois, affirmative action in, 124
Illinois, University of, Blacks at, 135
Indian Education—Fellowships for Indian Students, 117
Indian Health Service Office, 119
Indians. See American Indians
Institute for the Study of Educational Policy, 25, 243
Institutions: aid to, by federal programs, 116–118, 126–127; black, 98, 101, 121, 127, 132; characteristics of, and persistence, 98–105, 181–182; data on, 18–19; environmental factors of, 97–110, 181–183; flagship, and minority enrollment, 132–138; and geographical measures, 105; hierarchy of, 130, 146–152; quality of, 101–105, 182; selecting and sorting function of, 150–151, 168; tracking students into, and standardized testing, 163–164; types of, 98–101; types of, and educational resources, 141–145; types of, and minority enrollment, 131, 138–141, 143; types of, and student characteristics, 138–141. See also Colleges, four-year; Community colleges; Private institutions; Public institutions; Universities

J

Johns Hopkins University, Center for Social Organization of the School at, xv

Johnson, L. B., 114
Johnston, W. B., 244
Jones, F. C., 4, 243–244

K

Kansas, University of, American
    Indians at, 138
Kansas State University, American
    Indians at, 138
Kappner, C., xv
Karabel, J., 146, 244
Kent, L., xii, xv, 244
Keppel, F., 116, 244
Kerr, C., 122, 244
King, M. R., xv, 7, 40, 140n, 146,
    176, 218, 219, 238
Kluger, R., 114, 244

L

Ladd, F. C., 206, 244
Lambert, L. J., xv
Land-Grant College Appropriations,
    117, 118
Law: as field of study, 55; minority
    representation in, 59, 62–63, 64,
    75, 76; persistence in, 107; trends
    in, 84–85, 180
Lee, C. B. T., xi, xiv, 101, 130, 238
Legal Training for the Disadvantaged,
    117
Lehner, J. C., Jr., 4, 244
Leon, D. J., 42, 244
Leslie, L. A., 125, 244
Levitan, S. A., 244
Lind, C. G., 242
Linn, R. L., 147, 247
Lopez, R. W., 244
Louisiana State University, Blacks at,
    135

M

Macias, R. F., 199, 241, 244
McNamara, P. P., xii, xv, 39, 56, 244–
    245
McPartland, J., xv
Maine, University of (Orono), Ameri-
    can Indians at, 138

Maldonado, L., 241
Manning, W. H., 158, 245
Maryland, University of, Blacks at,
    135
Mathematics. See Physical sciences and
    mathematics
Maxfield, B. D., 9, 69, 245
Medicine, B., 200, 245
Medicine: as field of study, 55; mi-
    nority representation in, 59, 63,
    64, 75, 76; persistence in, 106, 107;
    trends in, 83–84, 180
Meritocracy: alternative to, 166–168;
    and competency, 166–167; devel-
    opment of, 155–157; and intel-
    ligence testing, 155–156; as obstacle
    to education, 154–155; shortcom-
    ings of, 164–166; standardized
    testing and, 154–169
Michael, J. A., 248
Michigan State University, Blacks at,
    135
Mingle, J. R., 78, 245
Minimal-competency testing, uses of,
    159–160
Minnesota, University of, Blacks at,
    136
Minorities: access and opportunity of,
    129–153; educational pipeline for,
    25–51, 77–112, 173–180; educators
    among, views of, 183–186; employ-
    ment of, 69; in fields of study, 52–
    76; findings on, summarized, 170–
    186; institutional distribution of,
    130–141; overeducation argument
    and, 10–11; research on, recom-
    mended, 211–212; and standard-
    ized testing, 154–169; as under-
    represented in higher education,
    1–2. See also American Indians;
    Blacks; Chicanos; Higher education
    of minorities; Hispanics; Puerto
    Ricans
Minority Access to Research Careers,
    117
Minority Biomedical Support, 117
Minority-oriented programs, evalua-
    tion of, recommendations on,
    209–211
Minority talent, distribution of, 13

Mississippi State University, Blacks at, 135

Missouri, University of, Blacks at, 135

Montana, University of, American Indians at, 137

Montana State University, American Indians at, 138

Morrill Land-Grant College Act of 1862, 116

Myrdal, G., xiv, 245

N

National Academy of Sciences, 15, 83

National Advisory Committee on Black Higher Education and Black Colleges and Universities, xv, 4, 245–246

National Center for Education Statistics (NCES): access and attainment data from, 40, 47, 49, 81, 82; data collection by, 15, 18, 23, 228, 246; faculty data from, 206; and fields of study, 53, 54, 55, 56, 60, 61; government programs data from, 120. *See also* Higher Education General Information Survey; National Longitudinal Study

National Commission on the Financing of Postsecondary Education, 129, 246

National Defense Education Act of 1958, 114, 123, 156

National Direct Student Loan Program, 117, 118

National Forum on Learning in the American Future, 4

National Longitudinal Study (NLS): access and attainment data from, 35–36, 37, 38, 39, 40–41, 43, 176; and data collection, 15, 23, 229–230

National Merit Scholarship Corporation, 156

National Research Council, 15, 69, 83, 214, 230, 246

National Science Foundation, 15, 85, 86, 246

Nelson, S., 123, 127, 239

New Jersey, affirmative action in, 124

New Mexico, University of: American Indians at, 137, 138; Hispanics at, 136

New York: affirmative action in, 124; State Regents Scholarships in, 123

Newcomb, T. M., 8, 121, 241

Nichols, R., 147, 246

North Carolina, University of Blacks at, 135

North Carolina State University, Blacks at, 135

North Dakota, University of, American Indians at, 138

O

Ochsner, N. L., 10, 246

Office for Civil Rights (OCR): access and attainment data from, 31–32, 36–37, 38, 39, 43, 44, 47, 176; and data collection, 15, 221, 222–223, 227–229

Oklahoma, University of, American Indians at, 137, 138

Oklahoma State University, American Indians at, 138

Olivas, M. A., 22, 25, 78, 132, 246

O'Neil, R. M., 5, 246–247

Opportunity. *See* Access and attainment

Oregon State University, American Indians at, 138

Ortiz, A. A., xi, xiv

O'Toole, J., 6, 247

Outcome variables: descriptions of, 231–236; minority talent pool related to, 13–14

Overeducation: issue of, 5–11; and minorities, 10–11; shortcomings of argument on, 7–9; and unemployment and underemployment argument, 9–10

P

Pace, C. R., 8, 22, 247

Parents: demographic characteristics of, and persistence, 94–95, 181; and institutional types, 138–139

Pasqueira, R. E., 42, 247

Pedraza, P., Jr., 241
Pelham, J. C., 80, 247
Pell Grants, 107, 114, 117, 118, 125
Pennsylvania State University, Blacks at, 135
Pepin, A. J., 247
Persistence: and academic preparation, 91–93; and access, federal programs for, 117, 119, 125–126; analysis of factors affecting, 89–112; and attitudes, 97; and career plans, 96; and demographic characteristics, 93–96; and environmental factors, 97–110, 181–183; by ethnicity and institution type, 98, 100; factors influencing, 180–186; and fields of study, 105–107, 112; and financial aid, 107–109; in higher education, by racial or ethnic group, 51, 98, 100; and institutional characteristics, 98–105, 181–182; and place of residence, 109–110; sample sizes for study of, 90; and self-concept, 96–97, 181; and smoking, 97; undergraduate, 110
Petrovich, J., xv, 19
Physical sciences and mathematics: and academic preparation, 70, 71, 72, 73; as field of study, 53–54; and minority preferences, 67, 68; minority representation in, 58, 61, 63, 64, 75, 76
Pittsburgh, University of, Blacks at, 136
Plisko, V. W., 9, 37, 46, 50, 53, 131n, 132, 241
Precollegiate education, recommendations on, 189–191
Preer, J., 78, 114, 116, 247
Prefreshman and Cooperative Education for Minorities and Indians, 117
President's Commission on Higher Education, 114
Private institutions: access to, 131, 132, 139, 140, 141, 142–143, 144; and persistence, 99, 100, 101
Professional education: government programs for, 117, 119; selective

admissions for, 148–149. See also Graduate and professional degrees; Graduate and professional enrollments
Programs, effects of, on outcomes, 13
Public institutions: access to, 131; 132, 139, 140, 141, 142–143, 144; and disadvantaged students, 126; and persistence, 99, 100, 101
Puerto Ricans: academic preparation of, 70, 71, 72, 73, 92; in allied health, 57, 60; in arts and humanities, 60; in biological sciences, 61; in business majors, 67; and college completion, 43, 82, 175, 176; and college entry, 33–34, 36–40, 56, 80, 81, 174, 175; and demographic characteristics, 94, 95; educational gains of, 149; employment of, 69; in fields of study, 55, 58–59, 64, 65, 68, 70, 71, 72, 73; and financial aid, 108, 184; and graduate and professional degrees, 45–48, 50, 83, 88, 175, 177; and graduate and professional enrollments, 44, 175; and high school graduation, 27–32, 174, 175; and institutional characteristics, 98, 99, 100, 102, 104, 105; on island and mainland, 19; in law, 62, 85, 88, 180; in medicine, 63, 83–84; persistence of, 51, 90, 92, 94, 95, 98–100, 102, 104, 105, 108, 110, 111, 179; in physical sciences and mathematics, 61; and place of residence, 110; report on, xii; and sample size, 23, 26, 90, 173; selection of, for study, 21; and social sciences, 67. See also Hispanics
Puerto Rico, University of, and social-class stratification, 19
Pumroy, D. K., 97, 247

Q

Quality: and access, conflict between, 122; of data, 213–230

R

Racial or ethnic group: college completion by, 40; college entry by, 33; data quality for, 213–217; enrollments in fields of study by, 64–65; fields of study and admission test scores by, 70; fields of study distribution of, 58–59; graduate and professional degrees by, 46; graduate and professional enrollments by, 44, 50; and high school dropouts, 27; and high school preferences for fields of study, 72; and persistence, 51, 98, 100
Reagan administration, 4
Residence, place of: and institutional type, 139–141; and persistence, 109–110; summarized, 183
Resources: distribution of, and hierarchy of institutions, 141–146; educational, distribution of, 122; financial, 141–145; other, 145–146
Richardson, G. T., xv, 7, 40, 140*n*, 146, 176, 218, 219, 238
Rock, D. A., 147, 247
Rossman, J. E., 149, 247
Roueche, J. W., 126, 247
Rumberger, R. W., 247

S

Satisfaction, and persistence, 111
Schenkel, W. W., 127, 243
Scherrei, R. A., xv
Scholastic Aptitude Test (SAT), xv, 19, 69, 70, 71, 72, 73, 92
Scientists and engineers, minorities employed as, 69, 85–86
Second Morrill Act of 1890, 116, 118
Sedlacek, W. E., 80, 247
Segura, R. D., 78, 240
Self-concept, and persistence, 96–97, 181
Sex, and persistence, 93–94
Sloan Commission on Government and Higher Education, 120, 247
Smartt, S. H., 78, 132, 247
Smith, C. J., xv

Smoking, and persistence, 97
Snow, J. J., 126, 247
Social sciences: and academic preparation, 70, 72, 73; as field of study, 54; and minority preferences, 67, 68; minority representation in, 58, 61, 63, 64, 74, 75, 76; persistence in, 106
Solmon, L. C., xv, 10, 156, 238, 246
South Carolina, flagship institution in, 135
South Carolina, University of, Blacks at, 135
South Dakota State University, American Indians at, 138
Special Services for Disadvantaged Students (SSDS), 117, 119, 126
Staff of the Office of Research, 222
Staff Training for Special Programs Staff and Leadership Personnel, 117
Standardized testing: for admissions, 157–158, 162–163; and Blacks, 136, 163, 181; construct validity in, 157; and counseling, 163; disadvantage of, to minorities, 162–163; and grading, 158–163; and institutional tracking, 163–164; of intelligence, 155–156; issues of, 157–164; and meritocracy, 154–169; as normative measures, 161–162; as predictors, 149, 158; and student's absolute level of performance, 160–161
State Student Incentive Grants (SSIG), 117, 118–119, 123
State University of New York (Buffalo), Hispanics at, 137
State University of New York (Stony Brook): Blacks at, 135; Hispanics at, 137
Stent, M. D., 22, 25, 78, 229, 239
Stockard, R., xv
Strengthening Developing Institutions, 117, 118, 123
Students: characteristics of, summary of, 180–181; data on, 16–17
Study habits, and persistence, 92–93, 181

Supplemental Educational Opportunity Grants, 117, 118
Support services, academic and personal, recommendations on, 192–194

T

Taggart, R., 244
Talent Search, 117, 119, 126
Tennesse, University of, Blacks at, 135
Testing. *See* Standardized testing
Texas, community colleges in, hierarchy in, 192
Texas A&M University: Blacks at, 135; Hispanics at, 136, 137
Texas, University of (Austin): Blacks at, 135; Hispanics at, 137
Texas, University of (El Paso), Chicanos at, 221
Thomas, G. E., xv, 247
Tollett, K. S., 5, 248
Tribally Controlled Community Colleges, 117, 118
Turner, W. H., 248
Tutoring, perceived need for, and persistence, 93
Two-year colleges. *See* Community colleges

U

Unemployment and underemployment, and college attendance, 9–10
U.S. Bureau of Indian Affairs, 118, 119
U.S. Bureau of the Census, 32, 36, 52, 56, 79, 209, 229, 248. *See also* Current Population Surveys
U.S. Commission on Civil Rights, 21, 32, 248
U.S. Congress, 4
U.S. Department of Education: access and attainment data from, 47–48; programs administered by, 117, 118–119

U.S. Department of Energy, 119
U.S. Department of Health, Education, and Welfare, 248; access and attainment data from, 44, 46, 50, 82; fields of study data from, 55, 64–65
U.S. General Accounting Office, 127, 248–249
U.S. Office of Civil Rights. *See* Office of Civil Rights
U.S. Office of Education, 123, 126, 249
U.S. Supreme Court, 5, 77
Universities: access to, 131, 132, 138–139, 140, 141, 142–143, 144; and financial aid, 108; and persistence, 98, 99, 100, 102, 103
Upward Bound, 117, 119, 126

V

Value-added model of higher education, 148, 157, 162, 188–189
Veterinary medicine. *See* Medicine
Virginia, University of, Blacks at, 135
Virginia Polytechnic Institute and State University, Blacks at, 135

W

Washington, University of, Blacks at, 136
Weathersby, G. B., 127, 249
Weinberger, C., 215
Whites: academic preparation of, 70, 71, 72, 92–93; access of, 130–131, 132; in allied health, 60; in biological sciences, 67; and college completion, 40–43, 175, 176; and college entry, 33–35, 38–40, 174, 175; and demographic characteristics, 94, 95; in education, 66; employment of, 69; enrollment trends for, 78–79, 87; in fields of study, 58–59, 65, 70, 71, 72, 106, 107; and financial aid, 108; and graduate and professional degrees, 46–48, 50, 175, 177; and graduate

and professional enrollments, 43–45, 175; and high school graduation, 27–30, 32, 174, 175; and institutional characteristics, 98, 99, 100, 102, 103, 104, 105; in law, 63, 107; in medicine, 63; and parental background, 181; as part-time students, 37; persistence of, 51, 90, 92–95, 97–100, 102–105, 106, 107, 108, 110, 111, 179; in physical sciences and mathematics, 67; and place of residence, 110; sample size of, 90; and smoking, 97; and standardized testing, 163; starting salaries for, 10–11

Williams, M. R., xii, xv
Willingham, W. W., 129, 249
Wilson, O. M., x–xi, xiii
Wisconsin, affirmative action in, 124
Women, minority, recommendations on, 207–208
Wright, S. J., xi, xiv

Y

Young, M., 155, 249